PSYCHOLOGICAL PREPARATION AND ATHLETIC EXCELLENCE

BY

Bryant J. Cratty, Ed.D.
University of California
Los Angeles

PSYCHOLOGICAL PREPARATION AND ATHLETIC EXCELLENCE

BY

Bryant J. Cratty, Ed.D.
University of California
Los Angeles

MOUVEMENT PUBLICATIONS INC.

109 East State Street
Ithaca, New York, U.S.A. 14850

Woodstock
19 Oaks Way, Gayton
Heswall, Wirral
L60 3SP United Kingdom

Woorkarrim
Lot #7 Strathmore Drive
Torquay, 3228
Australia

Production by Sandy Sharpe
Typesetting by Strehle's Computerized Typesetting, Ithaca, N.Y.
Printed by McNaughton & Gun Co. Inc., Ann Arbor, MI

ISBN 0-932392-17-2

TABLE OF CONTENTS

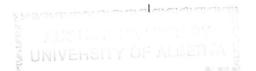

CHAPTER 12 SELF-PREPARATION, GUIDELINES FOR ATHLETES 169

THE FOCUS

Several motives prompted the writing of this book. A major impetus was the desire to share with others some of the remarkable information gleaned from athletes during several years of research-interviews conducted by me and my staff. The useful and creative ways they reported dealing with the demands of sport and with their emotions while competing, form the bases of many of the recommendations found in the following chapters.

Previous psychological "self-help" books written for athletes and coaches have presented a number of potentially helpful approaches to the problems athletes encounter in athletic competition. However, the philosophies which seem to underlie these previous efforts are often in marked contrast, when one views the structure and operations they advocate. For example, some writers have achieved popularity by recommending that an athlete should not become overly structured, and not try to analyze performance or emotions too much or too closely. This "go-with-the-flow" methodologist often explains that one may paralyze one's best efforts by over-analysis, and that too much intellization about performance and emotions in sport leads to performance blocks which impede the achievement of the athlete's maximum potential.

In contrast, other writers have outlined carefully structured programs for athletes to use when preparing themselves for competition. These special methods may include useful "catch-words" or phrases which should be faithfully recited prior to, or during competition. Often the method includes ways of achieving muscular relaxation, involving special positions to sit or lie in, together with recommendations of how one should retire to one's own preparation place prior to competition. These latter authors often prescribe structured types of visual imagery which may accompany other finely honored psychological tools they recommend.

Despite these main differences in the approaches advocated, the authors writing on the subject of psychological preparation have one thing in common, they are rather dogmatic: They are emphatic about two things: (1) Virtually all athletes may be aided to perform better if they will follow certain psychological strategies and interventions; and (2) The unique strategies offered within the pages of each book are presented as the "only-way-to-go." One school-of-thought thus, is rigid and dogmatic in so far as they advocate that all athletes should simply feel their way through their sport; while the second group of writers also present faces of granite, as they argue convincingly for highly structured operations and methods.

The dogmatism displayed in these "self-help" books, however, contrasted strikingly with many of the things athletes told to us in our interviews with them. For example, it was usual to find that the successful competitors we contacted engaged in a rich and varied group of psychological strategies when confronted with the stresses of competition. The competitors we queried were thus often extremely flexible, and were able to adopt various methods as conditions might change in successive contests and practices. Many of the creative "head-games" played by the athletes we talked to could not be found in contemporary sport psychology books. Additionally, the athletes often informed us that the rigidly applied "methods" eminating from various sport psychologists who had briefly contacted them (or their teams) had proved less than successful. For the most part, these methods, they told us, had been quickly discarded, after the supervision of the psychologist ended, to be replaced by their own methods fashioned by the athletes as they took into account their unique psychological needs, coupled with the demands of the sports situations which confronted them. Often they reported dogmatic methods imposed upon them by others had interfered with the main business that they perceived as most important: conditioning themselves and acquiring the skills necessary to the successful execution of their report.

The interviews we carried out thus revealed that the psychologists approaching the teams and athletes had usually applied what might be termed a "systems-first" approach. These often well-meaning emotional health professionals had apparently decided in advance that their "system" was superior to what the athlete might have already been doing mentally and emotionally to deal with the demands inherent in high level competition. Seldom did athletes report that the sport psychologist contacting them had asked about what problems they had encountered, and then attempted to deal with them in ways which allotted for the vast individual differences inherent in the psychological make-ups of all of us.

The contents of this book reflects a back-lash to this kind of "systems-first" approach to the application of psychological methodologies within an athletic environment. An effort has been made to present in the chapters which follow what might be termed an "athlete-centered" strategy. It is believed that in order to aid someone psychologically in the stressful environment represented by competitive athletics, one should start with the client-athlete. Initially, care should be taken to determine what kinds of coping and self-teaching, as well as motivating mechanisms the athlete is already using, prior to imposing some special form of "psychic-medicine!" Often the athletes we interviewed displayed coping strategies which illustrated a high level of emotional health. This superior psychological functioning coupled with superior athletic performance should be signs to the psychologist-helper that the athlete should be left alone! The imposition of useless psychological methods takes time from the important job of training confronting the athlete, and thus, the operations imposed by an inept psychologist may prove to be a primarily source of psychological stress in themselves. The contents of this book are thus not based upon the premise that all athletes may be improved if each were only exposed to sport psychology.

An "athlete-centered" approach, however, does not mean that the psychologist, or other helper, should always adopt a passive role in the quest for better psychological functioning in athletes. Rather an "athlete-centered" approach implies flexibility and accommodation to individual differences and needs. An "athlete-centered approach" involves several steps: (a) Begin by learning about the unique mental content and psychological coping strategies reported by the athlete; (b) Combine this information with observations made by others in a position to observe the athlete, as well as with current research findings bearing upon the unique situation in which the athlete finds himself/herself; and finally (c) Proceed to engage in any one of several "roads" which include:

1. The athlete may be left alone, if it is ascertained that the coping strategies evaluated are serving the competitor well.

2. If minor problems are present, the athlete may be aided to help himself/herself. One way to carry this out is to acquaint the athlete with useful strategies which may be self-applied together with research findings which may bear upon the problem(s) at hand. Often the coach or a friend, may be enlisted as a "psychological helper" at this point. The coach and athlete, or a teammate together with the athlete, may learn to work in tandem in an effort to optimize the psychological dimensions of athletic performance.

3. Finally, the athlete may need, and seek the help of a trained professional. The psychiatrist or psychologist should not only possess the proper experience and credentials, but also should have experience dealing with athletes, and a knowledge of current research on the problems of athletes. It is thus not assumed, by this author that all problems may be corrected if one is only given the "right" way to think, "catch words" to elicit the "correct type" of visual imagery, or perhaps tools to elicit a "relaxation response." Sometimes the help of professionally trained others *is* needed and essential.

The competitive athletic environment has exerted an attraction for me, as it has for many behavioral scientists, for many years. Athletics are highly charged with "psychological electricity," energy which rarely permits either spectator or athlete to stand idly by and not become emotionally involved. The highly visible nature of sport, together with the exact ways apparent success and failure are measured, are ingredients which invariably create stresses in those who participate. The physical power together with the emotional strength needed to perform well inevitably changes the hearts and minds of coaches and athletes alike. I have been concerned, as have many over the years, with the directions of that change. It is hoped that the information contained in this book will channel those changes in positive directions.

I am grateful to many colleagues who have molded my ideas and clarified by thoughts on this subject over the years. Miroslav Vanek, a co-author in a previous endeavor, provided me with great insights into what a sensitive and useful sport psychologist should and should not do when working with an athletic team. Dr. Vanek, long-time President of the International Society of Sport Psychology, is a most revered colleague, not only of mine but of all who have been fortunate enough to have been associated with him in his native country of Czechoslovakia. Dr. Yuri Hanin has also helped me to understand how a social psychologist works within a team setting. Our book written together in his apartment in Leningrad in 1978, represents a collaboration of which I am proud. Graduate students Phillip Davis and Karen Kadish have aided me in my research, as did Paul Carpinter during his leave from his work in New Zealand during the summer of 1982. Finally, I am grateful to the athletes, teams, and coaches who aided us in our research by permitting us to interview them over the past several years. The sections in the following chapters, headed by "What Athletes Say," represent the results of these interviews. These athletes' experiences provided reality, warmth, and validity to the following discussions.

B.J.C.

CHAPTER 1

INTRODUCTION: THEMES, DIRECTIONS AND GUIDELINES

Sociologists who have studied the role of sport in society tell us that athletic competition began as the members of ancient cultures became efficient in the skills necessary to provide the basis of life, food, and shelter. In the 1980s it could be argued that sport *is* a basic of life. Player strikes, or threatened strikes, send social shock waves through the members of the neighborhood bar more pronounced than might a nuclear explosion. Many pre-schoolers are indoctrinated early into the rituals of baseball, football, and other sports within the United States as well as abroad. While many so-called mature adults devote the primary parts of their lives to various coaching and administrative roles in athletics.

Competitive athletics are a vital part of most cultures of the world. Through sport, people are often able to forget their troubles, bask in the prowess of the physically powerful, enrich sometimes dull existences, and perhaps release aggressions that might be otherwise directed toward governments, wives, husbands, friends, as well as dogs and cats! Sport fans throughout the planet incorporate sport as an important and often essential avocation. Sporting pastimes produce zealous on-lookers who place more importance upon athletics than they do upon their loved ones, or upon their "real occupations."

It is the athlete, however, whose total being and emotions are most profoundly caught upon the thorns of sport. Many have reported to us that the majority of their waking hours are spent ruminating about the rewards, seductions, tragedies, and elations of sport in their lives. A primary thrust of this book is to survey the complex mental machinations in which athletes engage. It is hoped that in this way a second purpose will be served, to understand the athlete better. Clearly illumination of the athlete's thoughts, fears, and emotions, it is believed, will help athlete and coach alike to achieve superior performances, efforts which in turn rest upon solid platforms of good mental-emotional health.

Thoughts, however, are difficult to "get one's hands on." Many behavioral scientists have instead focused their energies on the more observable measures of physical performance, or dwell upon the markings of those taking tests of intelligence, perception, or maybe of giftedness or creativity. For those who have persisted in searching the minds of others, however, there are often exciting rewards. They are treated to displays of brief impressions, of quick mental pictures that flash through the brain at a speed of about eight a second. Others probing mental activity have been audience to the rich fantasies making up the day-dreams of their subjects. Some scientists have discovered that while some thoughts exist in isolation, flicking briefly like barely glimpsed shooting stars, other thoughts persist. The athlete, as

1

well as others in highly visible achievement situations often report of the hammer-like impressions that incessantly pound upon the consciousness, exerting marked influences upon mind and emotions.

The content of this book reflects upon the mental activity of athletes, and how that activity may modify performance, by first altering emotions. Moreover, the chapters which follow also focus upon how thinking in more direct ways modifies skill, activation, and concentration. Thus, despite the treacherous journey one takes when entering the often murky and subtle nuances of the mind, I have had two main goals in the writing of this book. The first of these is to present information to both coaches and athletes that will lead toward a better understanding of the mental lives of athletes. A second goal is to illustrate how altering mental states and changing how the performer thinks, will in turn change emotions and thus performance.

In order to accomplish these two ambitious ends, two sources of information have been consulted. The first well which has been tapped consists of studies in psychology and in sports psychology. This emerging branch of applied psychology, although enjoying expansion since the 1960s, extends back in the literature before the turn of the century. Sources have been consulted, and summarized which describe contacts between a psychologist-therapist, as well as, materials which involve well-controlled experimental studies of how emotion and mental activity mold athletic behaviors.

A second source of information was athletes themselves! My staff and I talked to athletes, using structured interview forms during the past several years. We simply asked them to describe the thoughts they had about their sport, as well as the dreams reflecting athletic competition which found them at night. Their usually candid responses opened new doors of understanding to what seems to make the athlete "tick." Additionally, their answers often suggested useful startegies for changing the mental lives of athletes in positive ways. They often told us of intelligent ways they had discovered for cushioning the sometimes severe emotional shocks encountered before, during, or after a contest. This kind of probing of athletes in many sports and on several continents, led us toward discovering useful ways to alter the closely linked chains of emotional feelings, physical expressions of performance, as well as, the content of athletes' consciousness.

The way in which most of the chapters are organized reflects the kinds of information upon which the book is based. Each chapter contains a first part discussing "What The Research Says" about a given topic. A second part of the chapter generally covers what athletes told us in interviews. The final section contains implications for improving performance through modifications of what athletes think and feel.

Some of the chapters deal with various components of the athlete's emotional life. These include parts of the book devoted to aggression, anxiety, fear, as well as motivation. Other chapters deal with more specific operations, including the acquisition of skill, improving concentration, and the like. Still other chapters are concerned with various aspects of the manner in which the athlete interacts with others.

A final chapter contains numerous "score-cards" which may be applied by an athlete to his or her own situation, feelings, and performance. It is hoped that through the use of this kind of self-assessment the lessons in the initial parts of the book will become practical and useful to the reader.

In some ways this book is similar to others dealing with optimizing athletic performance through various psychological adjustments. It contains sections dealing with calming down, "getting-up" and the like. However, the book contains ideas which stamp it as quite different from most of its predecessors. An "athlete-centered" approach is advanced on these pages, one which reflects a concern about and a respect for differences in both the emotional needs and psychological make-up of athletes. The approach here is labeled "athletic-centered," in so far as it is advocated that an athlete has the right to be left alone, or to engage in various self-help when appropriate and useful.

In contrast, it has not been difficult in recent years to obtain literature, which espouses a "system-centered" approach. At times the system advocated is quite restricting, containing exact guidelines for how to and what to think, where to think it, and even what to say to yourself if you are an athlete in various situations. At other times the system contained in texts like this one, has advocated a "laissez-faire attitude," that the athlete should "hang-loose" and to "go-with-the-flow," when attempting to acquire skill and to otherwise manage emotions. Often these systems are useful to at least some of those who contemplate the operations suggested. However, at the same time the rigidity and dogmatism ingrained in such an approach may be at best confusing, or at the worst actually impede athletic performance.

Those searching for my "system" within the following pages will likely be disappointed. Rather a non-system approach is advocated. My system is no-system! Indeed, I have attempted to present a selection of strategies which should be carefully applied. The methods include those which permit the athlete to express his or her needs, including the need to be left to his or her own devices!

This book, thus, advocates that the athlete or the athlete-counselor combination should first look inward, and assess the individual make-up of the athlete. Having done so, the next step is to determine what methods or combination of methods are likely to work best, or at least are worth trying. Upon arriving at a conclusion about the strategies or strategies which may be useful, and applying them, the final effort should focus upon assessing whether or not positive changes in the emotions and performance of the athlete have taken place. Thus, this book reverts back to what sometimes has apparently been lost, when some contemporary behavioral scientists write about, and practice sport psychology; the application of old-fashioned client-centered clinical interventions.

At times the athlete, with the help of another, may work backward, when assessing the needs of psychological interventions. That is they may first assess performance, and if performance is already superior, it may be best not to tamper with subtle internal mental and/or emotional states. However, if help is needed to either optimize the performance of an otherwise emotionally healthy athlete, or to drastically change the mental health of a disturbed performer, help should be obtained.

The athlete-centered, individualistic psychology written about in this book, is not a throw-back to the strict client-centered therapy of the 1930s and 1940s involving a counselor who might sit back and periodically mutter "un-huh," while the patient struggled with his or her own redemption. It is not suggested on these pages that athletes are somehow immune from moderate to severe emotional trauma needing the help of emotional health professionals. However, it is believed that many athletes who are emotionally sound may benefit from the self-administration of some of the methods outlined in the chapters which follow. Some of the methods may need a helper consisting of the coach, a parent, or perhaps a trusted friend. The methods which follow are based upon several principles. These include:

Principle 1

Understanding athletes thoughts, and the content of their mental lives are keys to helping the performers adjust their emotions in positive ways, and thus to improve their physical efforts. Acceptance of this principle includes giving credence to the assumption that to change how a person behaves, one should not focus only on behavior, but upon the thoughts which underlie that behavior. The formulation of this principle has been molded by the contemporary ground swell of interest in what has been termed "cognitive-behavioral modification." Throughout the history of psychology some have shown interest in human thought, and since the first German "gestalt" psychologists performed their experiments with primates within the first decade of this century. Until recently, however, few organized and coherent theoretical models have been formulated which combine what was formally simple simulus-response psychology, and what is termed "cognitive psychology."

One cannot help but be impressed with the research literature based upon the principles within this "new wave," holistic psychology. This work is based upon the idea that thoughts are like behavior, they may be modified and learned. Additionally, as one changes how he or she thinks, subsequent changes in behavior are likely to occur. Writers and researchers in this subject-area, thus, contend that previous attempts to simply change behavior without first changing the sub-structure to behavior thinking, are either doomed to failure or are at least superficial.

It is with this principle in mind, that at several points in the text the reader-athlete is encouraged to perceive how thoughts and visual images connect with, and often change both emotions, and the skilled performance based upon these thoughts and emotions. A useful and close cousin of this general cognitive-management approach has been the strategies advocated by Albert Ellis, and labeled "cognitive emotive therapy." Within this sub-branch of cognitive therapy special efforts are made to reduce harmful habits such as drug addition, as well as to reduce negative feelings of aggression and anxiety. The strategies used by Ellis include "self-talk." That is, the athlete in this context, tried to think, using specific phrases that signal a positive mental attitude. The self-talk, sometimes spoken aloud, consists of phrases which are intended to correct what Ellis believes are erroneous impressions about achievement, the opinions of others. The applications of this method are used in education, psychotherapy, sport, love, and in achieving better social relationships. Particular attention is paid to the alteration of negative thoughts (statements made internally) about the apparent need some have for perfection, and for the absolute approval of others at all times. Reference to this work, with regard to athletic performance, is found in chapters dealing with aggression and anxiety adjustment and management (Chapters 5 and 6). More detailed explanations of the rationale underlying this method as well as examples of specific strategies and applications are found in these and in other sections of the text.

Principle 2

Athletes evidence a diversity of psychological differences. Numerous studies in the beginnings of sport psychology consisted of efforts to identify an "ideal" personality type for various sports. As more sophisticated thinking and model building occurred, it was decided by most that even within a given sport, event, or position, a variety of personality "types" were often found functioning quite well. The acceptance of this principle makes invalid a simple "system centered" approach to assisting all athletes. Numerous examples of this principle are found throughout the following chapters. For example, it is found that some athletes may perform best when

4

at a high level of activation, while some perform better when calmer. The vast variety of responses we have obtained to similar questions, when obtaining samples of the mental life of athletes, also suggests the truth of this principle.

Attempts to classify mental operations have resulted in lists of from eight or ten, to over one-hundred in number. Lists of personality traits also number into the scores. These numerous qualities coupled with the complexities of the performance situations faced by athletes, suggest thousands of combinations of abilities, traits, and performance contexts might be theoretically constructed. The athlete, for example, contends with various "layers" of social forces when engaged in athletic competition. These include forces involved when the athlete interacts with those within his or her immediate social context, consisting of family members, friends, as well as team members. Spectators and fans consist of still a second "layer" of people who potentially influence the athlete, while the nature of the country and the broad culture in which the team performs constitutes still another group of social factors. These social variables, coupled with the variety of mental operations, visual imagery variations, as well as physical ability traits all of which interact make a simple "system centered" approach to the psychological "management" of an athlete an extremely tenuous undertaking. In diagram form, the interaction of these groups of variables may be depicted as followed.

CHART 1

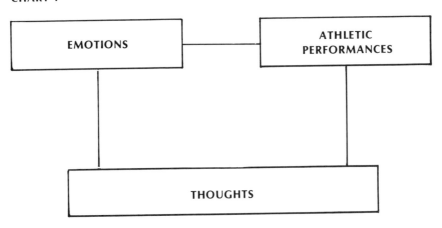

Principle 3

High striving, achievement oriented people want to do it themselves. Numerous findings attest to the fact that superior athletes prefer to exert control over themselves, their performance, and use physical performance to exert mastery over their environment. Furthermore, even when losing, those highly motivated toward achievement and success seem too try harder, rather than to become discouraged. They do not make excuses that involve others, or conditions not under their control when they do not win. Rather they believe that in future contests, they are going to be successful, simply by exerting more effort. Furthermore, these achievement oriented individuals will set difficult but achievable goals when they estimate changes of future success rather than setting goals which permit them an easy excuse if not reached. Goals which are either easily attained, or virtually impossible to achieve, are not likely to be voiced prior to competing by these striving individuals.

Moreover, highly achievement-oriented athletes are likely to prove irritable when others including the coach seem to be trying to be taking more of the credit than is fair, following a win. This type of athlete prefers to incur both the risks and rewards of athletic competition. Thus, the athlete is likely to become impatient with the coach who suggests that it is he/she who actually engineered the win; or with the coach who is too expressive when exhibiting various "coaching behaviors" during the time of the contest. The achievement-oriented athlete appreciates a coach who keeps a low profile at press conference, and suggests that a win was achieved through the efforts and talents of the players, rather than being due to the excellence of the coaching available.

Some of the excellent psychologists with whom I have worked in the Eastern European countries, have been well aware of these kinds of qualities among superior athletes. My colleagues in Russia and Czechoslovakia have informed me, for example, that:

1. Most superior athletes prefer to know all they can about themselves. They are vitally interested in the data obtained about their personality traits, and the like. At the same time many do not wish to be dealt with directly by a sport psychologist. One woman Olympic performer was quoted as saying that "If I am in need of you (the sport psychologist) I am not strong enough to win." Her subsequent efforts, and gold medals won, seemed to justify this strong view of herself and of her physical and emotional strength.

2. Many superior athletes are particularly opposed to undergoing hypnosis. They do not apparently wish to have others know that their performance success might have been due to some kind of post-hypnotic suggestion, rather than due to their own emotional strengths and physical talents. They wish to take full responsibility for their successes and possible failures, rather than "laying it off" to another, in this case a hypnotist.

If one accepts the validity of this third principle, it is not difficult to understand why many athletes have problems with not only the "credit-taking" engaged in by a coach, but also may resist further intrusions into their needs to display their own efforts and ability that may be made by a psychologist. Often a sport psychologist poses a pronounced threat, as he or she seems to have the capabilities of delving rather deeply into the most inner recesses of mind and emotion. It is for this reason that a book like this one may prove to be a psychologically "safe" tool for a superior athlete to use. Many performers may prefer to read, and then to apply psychology to themselves for several reasons. These include: (a) the "book psychologist" is not likely to later seek publicity, or attempt to gain credit for efforts and successes put forth by the athlete, (b) the reading and application of principle from a book, may signify to the athlete, that he/she posseses personal strengths and virtues in addition to those displayed in competition, (c) only the athlete may best know himself/herself, as well as the situations confronting him/her. Thus, the transfer of principles from a book such as this one to the athlete's own needs, may be best accomplished by the athlete. Thus, in part, this book has been written to help athletes become better "lay-psychologists" as they seek to understand and to help themselves. Furthermore, it is hoped that the material on these pages will aid both coaches, as well as psychologists to better deal with athletes.

THREE HANDLES FOR CHANGE

The principles stated in the previous section may help little when the reader seeks to discover a focus for the book. These three principles, however, point to operations of a rather specific nature. Most important to athletes and psychologists alike, is how to elicit change. Thus, in this section it is intended to provide a flexible and general model for change. At the same time this model provides rather concrete ways in which an athlete, either alone or with the help of others, may in some ways improve various components of their psychological "self;" improvement which in turn is likely to aid their physical performance.

The formation of a model for change is not an easy undertaking. The task is made difficult by the tendency, over the years, for psychologists to give the same type of behavior several different names and labels. This tendency has also been apparent as sport psychologists have attempted to present their case over the past several decades. For example, a myriad of labels have been attached to similar forms of visual imagery, arousal adjustment, as well as, relaxation training.

However, when people attempt to somehow prepare others, or themselves, to perform better intellectually, emotionally, and physically there are a limited type of ways in which these changes may be elicited. These strategies are rather straight forward, despite the numerous and purportedly different methods which may be found in the various self-help guides dealing with sport psychology, as well in books intending to improve "wellness" in general. Broadly conceived these three main strategies are as follows:

1. *Methods intended to modify some qualities of the human body itself.* These include adjustments to breathing, muscular tension, and perhaps heart-rate. Muscular relaxation and various modifications appear with regularity in various publications.

2. *Methods which encourage the individual to engage in various kinds of internal visual imagery.* The imagery may be of a general or specific nature, involving performance situations or broader life experiences.

3. *Efforts directed toward helping the athlete modify and re-adjust thoughts in*

CHART 2

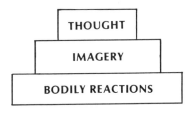

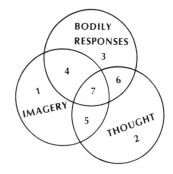

various ways. Recently these methods have often employed encouraging the athlete to engage in useful "self-talk" either internally, or voiced speech which others might hear.

These strategies are at times offered singularly or in various combinations. For example, muscular relaxation is frequently combined with various kinds of imagery. Some of these strategies may be best combined, it will be learned, with specific kinds of changes desired. Additionally, it is sometimes desirable to think of the concept of "direction" when applying these strategies. When eliciting certain changes, the reduction of excess aggression to give one example, one may best start with some kind of muscular relaxation, then proceed to useful imagery, and finally to the re-adjustment of how the athlete thinks about aggression and its outcomes. In other cases it may be best to approach the problem of change, using only one of the three levels, perhaps only the adjustment of thoughts.

Finally, an intensity dimension should be considered when selecting one, or more of these levels of strategies for change. Many athletes may need help not only in selecting, which of the methods is best and how it may be applied, but also may re-quire assistance with how intensely he or she should pursue a given method or methods. The athlete, thus needs to both properly pair a given method, or methods, with the type of change that is desired, but will also have to consider how long each day should be devoted to the practice of a strategy. Further, "intensity" decisions may involve the location in time and space a given strategy is practiced and how "hard" the athlete works when engaged in the strategy selected. Often a strategy, or method, needs to be carefully placed within various times of the practice week, or perhaps at critical moments during the days of the competitions. Specifically the athlete, perhaps with the help of another, needs to arrive at answers to such questions as . . .

1. What is best to use, when trying to calm myself before a critical game . . . relaxation training, visual imagery, or attempting to adjust how I think about the outcome of the game?

2. If I become too relaxed, will visual imagery become difficult for me? What should be the content of the imagery I engage in?

3. During what periods of the game day, should I try to remove myself mentally from the stresses of competition? Might attempts to think about other things impede me in the game?

4. What kinds of things should I be thinking about during the game, during the intermissions, and at the end of the game?

5. When will I be able to terminate some of the mental practice of the skills in the game, and perhaps devote my energies to improving my physical condition, or with other dimensions of my emotional make-up?

In chapters which follow the answers to these and other questions may be found. Within each chapter there is a section describing: (a) how one may pair each of the three types of strategies outlined with specific qualities one is attempting to change, (b) how one may select one, or a combination of strategies with which to deal, and finally, (c) examples of how a given strategy may be applied.

OVERVIEW

The contents of this book are based upon the premise that the effective application of sport psychology starts with an in-depth study of the mental life of the athlete with whom one is dealing. This "athlete centered" approach contrasts with many contemporary self-help books which seem to rest upon the idea that a unique method or approach represents the only starting point from which to adjust the emotions and thus the performance of athletes.

The book, thus, reflects a broad approach, one based upon individual difference in the psychological makeup of athletes in various sports and from various orientations. This emphasis on individual differences stems from interviews my staff and I have held with athletes over the past several years, resulting in research which suggests that three types of strategies may be used individually or collectively, in various ways to improve such qualities as attention-concentration, fear reduction, aggression, and skill improvement. These three types of methods include: (1) those involving physical changes including muscular relaxation and visual imagery of various kinds, (2) efforts to readjust the thoughts of athletes, (3) the use of coping strategies employing "self-talk" procedures, practicing the principles of cognitive-behavioral therapy, and its close cousin, rational-emotive therapy.

In the chapters which follow are guidelines, as well as specific methods, which the athlete alone, or with help, may apply to his or her unique needs and situations. The chapters contain several sections, including those discussing "What The Research Says" as well as those involving what our athlete-subjects have told us in research-interviews about the content of their thoughts about sport. Each chapter concludes with implications which point to ways of changing psychological processes, qualities which may then modify athletic performance in positive ways.

REFERENCES

Cratty, B.J., *Psychology in Contemporary Sport,* Prentice-Hall Inc., Englewood Cliffs, N.J., 1983.

Cratty, B.J., *Social Psychology in Athletics,* Prentice-Hall Inc., Englewood Cliffs, N.J., 1981.

Cratty, B.J., and Y. Hanin, *The Athlete in the Sport Team,* Love Publications, Denver, Colorado, 1980.

Ellis, A. and R.A. Harper, *A New Guide to Rational Living,* Prentice-Hall Inc., Englewood Cliffs, N.Y., 1975.

Gallway, W.T., *Inner Tennis,* Random House, New York, 1978.

Kaus D., *Peak Peformance,* Prentice-Hall Inc., Englewood Cliffs, 1978.

Kendall Philip C., and S.D. Hollon, (Eds.), *Cognitive-Behavioral Interventions,* Academic Press, New York, 1979.

Vanek, M., and B.J. Cratty, *The Psychology of the Superior Athlete,* MacMillan, New York, 1970.

Weiner, B., *Theories Of Motivation, From Mechanism To Cognition,* Rand McNally, Skokie Ill., 1972.

CHAPTER 2

INSIDE ATHLETES' HEADS

Neurosurgeons have become able to trigger vivid and exact memories in some of their patients if just the right portions of the brain are stimulated. However, for most of us it is difficult to determine exactly what another person may be thinking or feeling. It would be useful to researchers studying the mental activity of others, if they could somehow view on an internal video-screen just what images others are experiencing. Useful also would be the ability to plug into another's internal thoughts, by inserting an audio-jack into the brain of someone else. These possibilities for research at this time, however, are found only in science fiction stories.

Our talks with athletes did, however, enable us to view with reasonable detail some of the kinds of mental activities they experienced as a result of their association with athletic competition. They told us of the visual pictures that seem to flash on their "internal television screens," as well as of the words and phrases which go through their minds before, during, and following important contests. Although their reports were highly diverse, what they told us did enable us to make generalizations and to form categories depicting how various of our subjects seemed to deal with the complexities and stresses of sport.

Their report, overall were classified in the following ways:

1. The reports indicated that one should consider the *times and places* of the mental activity in which athletes engage. The places might include athletic arenas, or practice fields specific to athletics; or general "life spaces" which we all might inhabit, including the home and school. Very few told us of the use of a "special preparation space," to which they retired to prepare themselves mentally for athletic competition. The times they experience thoughts about athletics at various times during their careers, before, during, or after a season, or at various times relative to an important contest.

2. *The content* of their thoughts, suggested still another category. This content might include general thoughts about the fears of competition, tactics of the forthcoming game, or perhaps the potential success they might experience. More specific thoughts might also be reported, thoughts about individuals and situations that would likely be experienced in a forthcoming contest.

3. A *"person dimension"* seemed also important within the mental activity of the athletes we interviewed. Their thoughts might include ideas imposed or suggested by another, or thoughts they seemed to have formulated on their own.

4. The athletes also reported that their thoughts often occurred while they were in various *"states."* Some images and phrases came to them while the athlete was in what might be a "natural" state, perhaps while competing, or while day-dreaming in general. Interesting "altered states" in which mental activity might be distorted in various ways included times during which the athlete was highly elated, under hypnosis, under stress, or perhaps while engaged in relaxation training of various kinds.

5. Finally, the *"type" of intellectual-imaginal process* seemed to be important to consider. Some frequently reported experiencing visual imagery, while some said

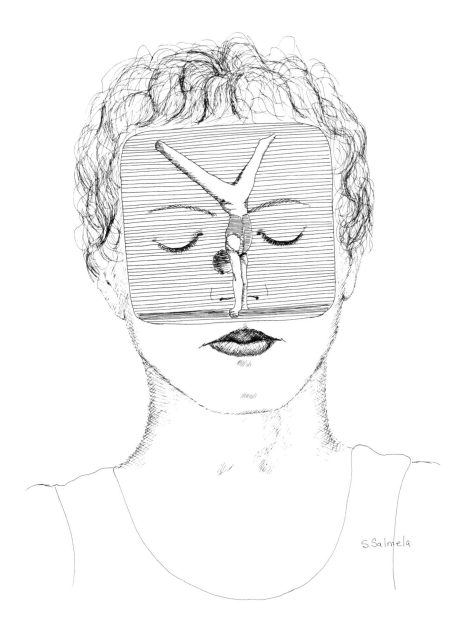

Figure 1   Athletes often go around with a "television screen" in their heads, imagining themselves performing . . .

that they often heard the words of others while competing or working out. The thoughts of some included more penetrating attempts at thinking through the complexities of their sport, while others seemed to simply let thoughts come to them, thoughts which were focused upon more superficial aspects of competition. Technical thoughts involving skill and tactics were experienced by some athletes, while others told us that thoughts involving their emotional frame of mind more frequently passed through their minds. The chart on the following page contains a full list of these dimensions and sub-categories.

It is believed, at this point, useful to spend some time describing some of these dimensions of an athlete's mental life using a hypothetical gymnast as an example. Following this discussion, a final section of this chapter deals with a typology, or classification system, into which most athletes may be placed. This classification system deals with three primary dimensions of the mental lives of athletes: (a) the intensity with which the athlete seems to deal with internal thoughts and images, (b) the duration of time "athletic thoughts" seem to occupy daytime hours, and (c) whether or not the athlete consciously plans mental activity connected with sport, or whether the thoughts "just come" in random ways into his or her consciousness.

Paul's Thoughts

First we shall spend some time during a spring day inside the head of Paul, a third-year university-level performer in gymnastics. He has competed internationally, representing the United States. Paul competes in six events in the all-round competition. This requires him to execute twelve routines, two on each of the events.

We are assuming that we are miniaturized, residing within a portion of Paul's brain which permits us to view images which our young subject visualizes, as he thinks in this way. Also our location permits us to hear various sentences, and fragments of phrases which represents the thoughts that Paul verbalizes. In other words, we can also hear Paul's internal speech or "self-talk."

Paul is intense and serious about his sport. His ability places him within the top ten men performers in the United States. He has a chance to make the Olympic team with additional improvement. His mental life is largely devoted to thoughts about his sport. Thoughts about the twelve routines and more numerous tricks within each, do not occur at only brief periods throughout the day, but persist for over half of his waking hours. He thinks in general terms about his sport, as well as in specific ways. Some of these thoughts dwell upon future competitors, as well as upon the locations in which he will later compete. His mental life also contains thoughts which involve new and risky tricks he is attempting to master. Some of these thoughts are laden with fear, as he incurred a serious injury only two years before.

As Paul gains consciousness in the morning, while struggling to remember a dream, his noisy roommate awakens him as usual, while Paul tries to make the dream last long enough to see if the girl it contained was his current girl friend, or someone else. He turns to see what time it is, as the struggle to remain in the dream is lost. His internal "television screen" is a blur, and then his mind begins to turn to "self-talk" which informs him that he has a bio test the next day, and a class that morning at 8 o'clock. The mechanics of getting ready, dressing, and eating are accomplished almost automatically, as he begins to think by feeling the movements to be used in his workout that afternoon . . . movements on the side horse with which he has been having difficulty. He feels the handles of the horse pressing into his palms, as he imagines the movements of his trunk and legs during the difficult part

I. WHO, AND WITH WHOM?

Solitary

1. Performer self-talk randomly occurring
2. Performer "programmed" by another to engage in helpful mental work, and/or "self-talk"
3. Self-initiated "program" of "mental improvement"

With Another

1. Therapist-assisted mental status, self-talk and the like
2. General suggestions by another
3. Random thoughts triggered by the sight and/or association of another
4. Hypnotic suggestion
5. Specific contest-skill-related mental practice guided by another

II. WHAT INTELLECTUAL PROCESSES?

1. Observational imagery, verbal imagery
2. Memory
3. Classification, categorization
4. Analysis-synthesis
5. Divergent production
   Convergent production
6. Other problem-solving processes, behaviors, evaluation

III. IN WHAT STATE?

"Free," Natural States

(a) Performer initiates
(b) Comes to performer without effort

Altered States, due to

(a) Drugs
(b) Suggestions
(c) Hypnosis
(d) Biofeedback
(e) Exhilaration, due to effort winning, and the like
(f) Induced relaxation
(g) Depression, due to losing, negative thoughts, eliciting

IV. ABOUT WHAT? CONTENT

General Focus

(a) Fear of competition
(b) About self-efficiency
(c) Attempts to regulate physiological processes
(d) About reasons for winning, losing
(e) Inner seeing—i.e., focusing on body organs, cells
(f) General dissociation
(g) About meaning of rewards
(h) General tactics

Specific Focus

(a) A fear of a contest
(b) Reasons for losing or winning a contest
(c) Meaning of a specific reward
    Outcome of specific contest
(d) Tactics and skills in specific game or sport
(e) Of situational variable—i.e., referee, gym
(f) Of opponent efficiency
(g) Of own, others' efforts
(h) Of too little or too much fear prior to a contest

V. TIMES AND PLACES

Places

(a) Athletic arena, practice place
(b) Life's "general" spaces
(c) A special place for thought preparation

Time

(a) Before, during, after contest
(b) Early, middle, late season
(c) Prior, during, and after season
(d) Early, during, late career, post-career
(e) Childhood thoughts

B.J. Cratty, *Psychology in Contemporary Sport,* 2nd Edition, Prentice Hall, Englewood Cliffs, New Jersey, 1983, with permission of the publishers.

of the routine. Breakfast is finished without him aware of having eaten.

During the walk across the campus, his internal television screen lights up. Vivid pictures appear. He now seems to be watching himself from a short distance. His dismounts from the rings are repeated with increasing efficiency and height. He scores himself 9.8's and 9.9's on the routines, as he smiles to himself. Halfway to his class a new picture appears on the screen. He watches himself performing the new change into and out of a one-arm giant swing on the hi-bar. He will work this out later in the gym. His self-talk reports . . . "There I made it, but sloppy."

His muscles tense briefly, as the trick is performed again on the "internal screen" inside his head. He tightens again, as he imagines the fall, feels the pain, and thinks about his accident two years before. The door to his class appears, and he finds his seat.

The voice of the instructor begins, and his hand automatically takes notes. Biology thoughts and notes fill his mind for thirty minutes, and then are replaced for brief intense and sweet intervals of visions of his girl friend. "I wonder if she is up yet?" he asks himself and imagines her arising, the imagery is pleasant.

Toward the end of the 50 minute period his internal screen lights up brightly. "I can get them from Don," he tells himself of the notes he is missing. Impulses come from the movement planning centers in his brain now, at a rapid pace. He begins to mentally practice his optional free-exercise routine. He feels muscles tighten, as he feels the springy mat pound against his feet. He feels the tumbling mount, the scratching that is required during the middle of the routine, the effort needed to press a handstand, and the blur and whirling sensations as he twists and tumbles to his final dismount. The screen switches off, as the lecture ends and he gathers up his books to leave.

Paul strides across the campus greeting friends. He is well liked and outgoing. Members of the gymnastic team who say hi, trigger gymnastic thoughts. The next meet is thought about, and the visual screen again lights up with the opponent's gymnasium in which he has competed before. The gymnasium seemed cold to him the last time he was there, emotionally and physically forbiding. He self-talks. "Next time I am there I will touch each piece of apparatus, making them my friends and take away some of the threat of the place. I'll walk around each one, and make their apparatus and that gymnasium like me, make them mine!" Thoughts of his routines mesh with general images of the forthcoming competition, the trip by air, the mountains surrounding the campus in Utah. Thoughts come and go as he enters his next class.

While he eats lunch, the images on the internal television screen come faster and more vividly. The blue gymnasium mat flashes by as he mentally performs, and re-performs his free-exercise routine. The pull and tensions on the high-bar are felt, while the springy parallel bars bounce him from trick to trick. Watching himself on the victory stand in the opponent's gymnasium gives him the most pleasure.

Paul feels increasing tension in his muscles as the two o'clock practice nears. The stroll to the gymnasium brings him in contact with more members of the team. Sensory impressions increase as he warms up. Familiar touches of the mat to his stomach as he stretches, and someone else pounds his back to help loosen him up. Coaches voices come, on a calm voice. The team lines up formally, hands slap at his sides signaling the end of a brief team meeting. The workout begins.

A teammate yells a German's first name at him. "Heinrich is working out hard today," he is reminded. His teammate knows the German beat him in a recent meet abroad. Paul becomes irritated and works harder, concentrates more. His practice begins physically.

The visual screen inside his head contains brief flashes, rather than the long sustained routines possible in the biology class. Demonstrations by others and voices of others intermingle. Most important are short commands, self-talk he gives himself as the practice continues. "Tighten that left hand, you dummy," he chides himself.

14

The two coaches are low key as usual. His commands to himself are not! His self-talk begins to reflect irritation. "Damn you, you missed it again . . . try harder," he admonishes himself. Elation is also expressed. "I did it, it felt good!" he rewards himself.

Tension, and then fatigue is felt. The practice draws to a close. All of the events are reviewed, and polished today. He files out, dresses, and eats, after a walk across the campus.

After-dinner study comes more easily tonight than it will later in the week, just before the teams leaves for Utah. On the night before competition it is nearly impossible to study, to think of anything but the meet. Routines block out chemistry and biology, while physics is obliterated on his internal television screen on these critical evenings. Taking work to study on these trips is often futile. Tonight is different, study continues. Images of his girl friend intrude as they always do. A phone call is made, and a late date for pizza arranged.

Tiredness. A last review of the change from the one-handed giant swings, before sleep. The dismount from the side-horse, and the dismount from the hi-bar are done three times each, through imagery. Sleep comes before a fourth dismount can be seen on his internal screen.

A Brief Analysis

In this "case study" of the mental life of Paul several categories of thought were revealed which are typical of those in his sport, and of those competing at his level. Even among gymnasts, however, we found that a rather diverse pattern of thought was carried out. Most of those we interviewed in this sport, however, believed that *their* own way of thinking *was* typical of others!

Paul's visual imagery was reasonably vivid, and constant. However, these images seemed to come and go, with little attempt made by Paul to control or mold the visual impressions of his competitions. Other athletes in gymnastics, and in other sports, often reported that they rather carefully programmed this part of their mental life.

Paul's thoughts about the specific skills of this sport for the most part involved remaining inside his own body, feeling the movement, and "seeing it" as though he were performing. Less time was spent by Paul, "outside his body" observing his efforts from a distance. The larger proportion of time spent "inside himself" in this respect is typical of most athletes to whom skill acquisition is important.

Like many athletes Paul made little attempt to structure, control, or otherwise mold his mental life. Thoughts seemed to come and go at random, particularly during the times of day he was not practicing or competing. The sight of, and contact with other athletes in his sport, however, did seem to trigger images of competition. Thoughts about sport came to him when he was bored, in classes or at other times when he was not occupied. Due to the fact that he had many routines (twelve . . . each containing from six to twelve movements) he did not seem to engage in skill imagery with a great deal of intensity, as he went about his daily chores.

Like most athletes, his thought patterns and imagery changed when he was confronted with practice conditions, and the people important there, his coaches and teammates. Casual low-key visual images and statements were replaced with stronger feelings, impressions, and commands which were self-administered, when he began to practice. The "self-talk" during practice was punctuated with statements meant to alert him, focus concentration, and otherwise obtain a high level of effort. Congratulatory "self-talk also occurred during practices, at levels not "heard" during other parts of the day.

Paul's thoughts, as is often true among gymnasts, flashed from specific to general components of his sport in ways which were often rapid. Images of specific skills, and skill difficulties often quickly alternated with broader feelings about competition in general, or with mental "pictures" of environments in which he was to compete.

Due to a previous injury Paul's thoughts were uniquely his own in many ways. Fears of new tricks, routines, and performance environments were perhaps greater than would be true of an individual not previously injured in the sport. Thus, Paul's background molded his thoughts in ways which were not "typical" of others.

Moreover, like many of us, Paul used his day dreams to portray success situations in which he was receiving awards. Additionally, his thoughts permitted him to move imaginally from place to place as he "practiced in advance" competing in a "foreign" gymnasium which was to be the site of his next competition.

This case study approach to an athlete's mental life is a useful undertaking, and one which should preceed attempts at trying to change the images and thoughts the performer possesses. However, what we may learn from one person's reports of his or her mental activities can be rather limited. Predicting what various types of mental activities and imagery relate to successful or unsuccessful performance is an almost impossible undertaking when only viewing a single athlete. It was for these reasons that my staff and I conducted numerous research-interviews with athletes in a number of sports over the past years. One of the more obvious kinds of reports we obtained as the results of these contacts involved the *time* they reported spent thinking about their sport. The athletes seemed to differ, also, about how *intensely* they thought about the various aspects of their sport when not competing or practicing. Finally, the athletes rather neatly divided themselves into a third, two-part-category. This final category reflected whether the athlete reported that he or she tried to somehow manage and control their mental life relative to sport, or whether their thoughts about competition seemed to come to them in a random fashion. In the following section, a classification system is discussed based upon three dimensions; duration of time, intensity, and planning.

TIME, INTENSITY, AND PLANNING

Our research interviews with athletes covered many topics. Many of the sections of this interview are covered rather thoroughly in the chapters which follow. However, during the course of these interviews it was relatively easy for an athlete to place an exact number (a percentage) upon how much of the time during his or her waking hours was devoted to thoughts about their sport. We asked for the percentage of time devoted to "athletic thoughts" at three points in the season; during the off-season, during the season when they were not practicing, and during the day of competition.

When surveying university-level athletes, we were struck by the consistent finding that they characteristically reported devoting between 90-100% of their waking hours thinking about their sport during the day of a competition. Even during the off-season (and some reported that they experienced no off-season) they said that they thought about competition about 50% of the time. These same athletes told us that even during the days of the season that only involved practices they thought about the sport from 40-60% of the time.

16

CHART 3

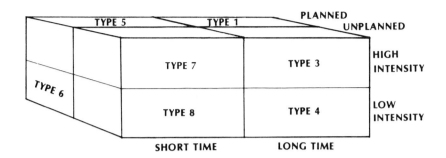

TIME—INTENSITY—PLANNING

Although it was of course more difficult to score the "intensity" with which an athlete seemed to be thinking about his or her sport, it was relatively easy to determine whether an athlete was a high-intensity or low-intensity "type." Some athletes, for example, said that they believed thinking about their sport involved real work, and if they thought about their sport too much they would incur fatigue. These athletes were often able to limit the duration and intensity of the thoughts they devoted to their sport in order to devote energy to the actual physical practices in which they engaged. A performer specializing in the ring event in gymnastics, for example, recognizing that he was a "high-intensity" type, said that he consciously devoted only brief, but intense periods of time to thinking about his routine. He tried to match the brief duration and intense effort expended when actually performing with the brevity and intensity of his mental efforts. In this way, he explained, he tried to "save up" his effort for the actual physical execution of his event which lasted only a few seconds.

In other data we obtained in a team sport (Carpinter and Cratty 1984), the validity of the gymnast's statements were confirmed. Comparisons we made in an investigation of waterpolo players between the player's estimates of the duration of the time they thought about their sport, and their coach's ratings of "intensity and motivation" while practicing and playing, revealed a negative correlation. That is, the players who seemed to spend the least time ruminating about the sport when not practicing were seen by their coach as devoting the greatest amount of psychological energy while actually practicing. Just as better athletes seem to become able to conserve their *physical energies* well, these same athletes may also be those who can best harbor the energy they devote to *thinking* about their efforts in athletic competition.

In all of our studies we asked athletes whether they consciously "managed" their mental lives, controlling the content and intensity, or whether thoughts about sport "just came to them in a random fashion?" The responses we obtained to this type of question were often somewhat difficult to interpret. While over half consistently stated that they did not try to somehow control their thoughts, a considerably greater percent in a later question posed about what they tried to do to overcome fear, proceeded to tell us of their intricate solutions to anxiety reduction. The nature of these anxiety reduction plans are discussed fully in Chapter 7. What is important, however, is that when athletes are asked general questions about "thought management" they are likely to answer in the negative. However, when they are actually confronted with the fears connected with competition most are somehow forced into some kind of "management strategy."

Despite the difficulty of interpreting the answers to questions about intensity, duration, and the planning of athletes' mental lives, the following "types" emerged from the data we obtained. Each of these eight "types" are discussed together with implications for other aspects of their emotional make-up, and their athletic performance.

Type 1

A careful planner of mental activity, who engages in it for prolonged periods of time and in an intense manner. These athletes are very meticulous in the ways they plan their rather extensive mental life, devoted to sport. They will usually report that over 50% of the time when they are just "walking around" during their sports season, they devote to various mental aspects of their competition. Much of the time this athlete is devoting too much energy to the mental aspects of the sport, and may find it difficult to activate himself or herself for practice sessions. At times, this athlete may be described as over-anxious. The athlete may be "paralyzing" performance with too much analysis, and may experience a kind of "burn out," common to high-intensity executives or coaches, mid-way during the season, or mid-way during a career. This type of athlete may pass through this high-intensity period as they pass from one level of competition to another; from high school to college competition, or perhaps from the university level to professional competition. Often such an athlete needs "outside help" in order to place the importance of competition into perspective. This kind of help may be needed to assist the athlete to manage his or her anxieties about competition. Often help acquired to permit the athlete to begin to block off, or redirect thoughts about sport, is translated into more productive performance.

Type 2

This athlete plans carefully, and in a relaxed way engages in prolonged periods of time thinking about various aspects of sport. This athlete, unlike Type 1 described above, engages in an extreme amount of mental activity devoted to sport, but does so in a manner which is less intense and not as compulsive as was the athlete previously described. This athlete also carefully attempts to control the time during which this activity takes place, as well as the content of thoughts devoted to sport. A superior athlete of this type is sometimes found among archers and shooters, but is more likely an athlete whose sport requires a great many intricate skills. A gymnast who has eight to twelve routines to master might engage in this quantity of relaxed skill rehearsal, for example.

This type of athlete is seemingly careful not to expend too much energy in the mental component of sport, and thus is able to activate himself or herself well for competitions, and practices. At times, however, this type of athlete, if the nature of their performance is for brief intense periods, may be aided to match the nature of their mental practice with the physical demands of their sport by reducing the time they devote to sports thoughts. Heightening the intensity of their thoughts may also be of some help.

Type 3

An athlete who thinks about sport intensely and for long periods, but who does not plan or try to control the thoughts that randomly enter his/her consciousness.

This random planner finds sports thoughts constantly entering his or her head, and also requires moderate to great effort when dealing with these impressions. This athlete generally may need help from others, or may benefit from self-help, to reduce the time devoted to thoughts about the sport in which he or she is competing. These competitors need help in both excluding sports thoughts, in order not to invite "mental fatigue" and also to focus the nature of the thoughts which do arrive inside their heads. They may appear to their coach as somewhat erratic as they try to expend their energies in practices and competitions. An effort should be made by someone trying to help such an athlete to determine what kinds of random, high-intensity thoughts course through his or her mind. Often this high level of intense, uncontrolled mental activity is laden with high levels of anxiety that may also need the attention of a psychologist or psychiatrist.

Type 4

An athlete who does not plan thoughts, which arise for prolonged periods of time, and are "low intensity" in nature. This non-planner finds himself or herself thinking about sport "a lot" in a relaxed manner. There is no self-initiated plan applied to their mental life, and the thoughts do not seem to consume too much of this athlete's energy. Care should be taken in the case of this athlete not to quickly try to change the manner in which they think. He or she may be a "natural" who cannot exactly describe why or how they perform, or the mental underpinnings of his or her performance.

At other times this athlete's "laid back" attitude may reflect problems with motivation, and thus he or she may need to be aided to think more intensely and for briefer periods of time about his or her sport. Sport may have a low priority in their lives, and thus there may be relatively low levels of anxiety attached to possible failure, a frame of mind which may aid performance. These athletes if they have talent, may need some guidance to discover why they might continue in sport, as they often contemplate dropping athletes from their lives. More often, however, a poorly motivated athlete involves another category in which lack of planning, and thoughts of low intensity are engaged in for brief periods of time.

Types 1-4, An Overview

Generally, the four previous types discussed reflect the fact that many athletes report spending a great deal of time thinking about their sporting endeavors. However, the intensity and planning of these thoughts differs from one to another, as indicated. In the following four categories, 5-8, are found athletes who report that sport occupies relative little of their mental lives. Again, however, they differ as to the intensity of their thoughts, as well as whether they engage in conscious planning of their mental lives.

Type 5

This individual plans mental activity which takes place for brief, intense periods of time. This athlete reports carefully planning the brief and intense periods of time in which "sport thoughts" enter his or her mind. They may devote certain periods of the day to mentally practicing a specific skill, or imagining themselves in competition. Often they select ideal locations for this type of mental activity. They may vary, however, about how they think about their skills. For example, an ice-skater within this category may decide to "mentally practice" her or his routine first by imaginally walking through it. A next mental practice session, might involve imagining more rapid movement, while perhaps a third session might involve the athlete mentally "standing back" and viewing himself or herself from a distance and judging the routine as might occur in competition.

They may seek a distraction free place in which to engage in this kind of mental practice, a need which should be provided for by their coach. Often just prior to a competition is the time they may see this type of activity. Before falling asleep at night is another favorite time in which they like to engage in this type of mental preparation.

Often this athlete is highly efficient, and a strongly focused performer. The matching of this short-intense mental practice with such sports as weight lifting, shot-putting, and the like, is often desirable. Other "short-spurt" performances such as those found in sprinting, may benefit from this brief intense practice carried out imaginally. Thus, these athletes may limit and match the length and intensity of their thoughts with the brief intense requirements of the sport.

Although this type is more often found among individual sport performers, at times team sport athletes report this "style" of thinking. The team sport athlete, however, does not expend short intense mental efforts to general team tactics, but usually imagines brief skills occurring within the sport; shooting in waterpolo or perhaps rebounding in basketball are commonly engaged in mentally. This type of athlete, in either team or individual sports is more often found among more experienced athletes, than among novices.

Type 6

This careful plannner does short periods of low intensity thought to sport. This athlete regularly devotes short periods of time to thoughts about sport, and does so in a relaxed manner. This type, may be an experienced competitor in such sports as archery, pistol shooting, and the like in which aiming and steadiness are requisite. Events which require force, endurance, and/or power, may not benefit from this short low-key kind of mental effort.

At the same time this "type" of athlete, similar to other types devoting short periods of time to mental practice, may have other components of his/her life which are more important than athletic participation. They, thus, may compartmentalize the mental aspects of their sporting experience, just as they limit the time and energy given to the actual physical practice. However, this type of mental life may be less than useful to the athlete if the demands of the sport require relatively intense efforts of either a long or short duration, such as are found in many running events, swimming, cross-country skiing, or perhaps weight lifting, discus throwing, or shot-putting.

Some endurance athletes may be of this type. Often athletes in distance running, to give one example, appear extremely "laid-back" between rigorous practices. They seem reluctant to spend mental energy, when not physically taxing themselves, in an effort to harbor their strength and to apply it to the difficult practices and competitions in which they engage.

Type 7

This non-planner experiences short, intense "spurts" of mental activity about sport. Athletes experiencing this type of mental life, may be those whose sports demand short spurts of activity. Perhaps, unconsciously such an athlete does not tire himself or herself too much by prolonged and intense mental activity. Thus, this athlete while reportedly not a "planner" may actually be productively combining the demands of the sport, with the nature of the mental life in which he or she conjures up.

Trying to encourage this type of athlete to change, and to better plan his or her mental "life" may be disruptive of performance. This disruption may be more likely to occur in the case of superior athletes, than if the athlete is just beginning. At times the content of this type of mental life, includes short images that may depict besting an opponent in a game, or competitive situation. Success imagery also appears in this type of mental life, with some frequency.

Type 8

This athlete does not plan mental activity, and their thoughts occur in short "bursts" that are of low intensity. This type may be a "natural" whose mental efforts reflect a relaxed approach, who may be participating in a sport which requires a great deal of stress and strain. This athlete may, however, be helped to improve performance by becoming better able to adjust the intensity of their thoughts upward, in an effort to match the intensity of the sport. If performance is poor, and this type of mental life is reported, that athlete may be trying to tell others that he or she does not care about competition. Often this mental type is seen among substitutes in a team sport, individuals who may be planning to drop out of the sport soon. A younger competitor, of this type, may be trying to let others know that he or she would like to engage in another type of sport.

IMPLICATIONS

Making decisions about where a given athlete may reside, within the previous classification, may prove fruitful. However, it may be found that an athlete's apparent "thinking style" may change at various times in the season, or during different periods in his or her career. Coaches or psychologists who try to "type" an athlete, or a group of athletes in the ways described, should also combine their efforts with data obtained in other ways. Among the other fruitful sources of information about athletes in this context include: (a) the results of a sports autobiography, (b) data from mood and personality tests, (c) interview data, and also (d) observations made of the athlete's emotional state and performance during contests and practices.

The classification discussed in this chapter reflects various "mental thinking styles." In the chapters which follow, attention is paid to the *content* of athletes' mental lives, and how that content may either facilitate or impede performance. The overall content of an athlete's mental life may reflect more attention in a relaxed way to skill rehearsal, than time and attention given to negative mood states, and fearful thoughts. Thus, some of the ways the mental lives of athletes may be adjusted, which are explained in the following chapters may facilitate performance for two primary reasons: (a) adjustments permit an athlete to devote sustained periods of time to skill rehearsal, and (b) the athlete may learn to remove negative emotional blocks, thought content which takes time away from useful skill rehearsal.

The previous discussion was based upon the idea that optimum thinking style is one which best combines the nature of the mental activity with the demands of the sport facing the athlete. Thus, adjustments in an athlete's mental "style" might be considered if the following situations occur.

1. If an athlete devotes a great deal of low-intensity thought to a sport whose demands require high levels of effort over a short period, the performer may be encouraged to reduce the time and raise the attention of his or her thoughts about sport.

2. An athlete who is experiencing skill problems may be aided to better plan his

or her mental life, and to optimize the techniques needed when rehearsing skilled actions.

3. An endurance athlete whose sport requires relaxed and prolonged effort may be aided to reduce the length and intensity of their thoughts about the sport. In this way the athlete may become less wasteful of the emotional energy he or she is spending, and thus should have more physical energy available to devote to the endurance competition confronted.

4. If skill demands require precision in the sport, but at low levels of intensity as in shooting, the athlete may be encouraged to devote a less intense burst of mental activity to rehearsing the sports skill, if he or she is one of the several "high intensity" types described.

OVERVIEW

Two approaches were taken in this chapter to try to get a "handle" upon just how athletes may think about sport. The case-study approach was used to typify how an athlete might engage in internal thought and self-talk, as well as in visual imagery throughout a "typical" day during the season. Additionally, a three-way system was proposed consisting of eight "types" of thinking "styles." These styles involved varying amounts of planning on the part of the athlete, as well as thoughts which differed in duration and in intensity.

Using this system, implications were discussed as to how various athletes competing in different sport might think in optimum ways, and in ways which might impede performance. For example, it was proposed that the mental activity of the athlete to "work" best should match in intensity and duration the nature of the effort confronting him or her in the sport. It was also suggested that changes in how the athlete thinks should be made only when performance seems less than optimum, and that changes in the thinking "style" reported by a performer should not be made capriciously.

The classification system presented in this chapter thus, represents a beginning and not an end. Most important is not only to consider the general thinking "style" of the athlete, but also to consider carefully the content of the athlete's thoughts, and how that content may be either positively or negative influencing performance. In the chapters that follow two kinds of mental content are looked at in some depth. One type of content reveals and influences the athlete's mood and general emotional state. A second type of content reflects how the athlete may be dealing with specific operations in a sport. Examples of this second kind might include thoughts about concentration, team tactics, and about the specific skills needed.

REFERENCES

Carpinter P., and B.J. Cratty, "Mental activity, dreams and performance in team sport athletes, *Intl J. of Sport Psychology,* publication pending.

Cratty, B.J., "Mental states" in *Psychology in Contemporary Sport.* Prentice-Hall, Englewood Cliffs, New Jersey, 1983.

Cratty, B.J., and P. Carpinter, "Mental activity in team sport athletes," *Sportwissenschaft,* publication pending, 1983.

Cratty, B.J., and Philip E. Davis, "The content of athletes' mental lives," in *Cognitive Sport Psychology,* Straub, W., and J. Williams, (Eds.), Sport Science Associates, Lansing, New York, 1984.

Cratty, B.J., C. Lange and M.R. O'Neil, "Mental activity in individual sport athletes," *Sportwissenschaft,* publication pending.

Cratty, B.J., C. Lange, and P.A. Whipple, "Aggressive feelings reported by male and female karate participants," *International Journal of Physical Education,* submitted.

Singer, J.L., *Mind-Play: The Creative Uses of Fantasy,* Englewood Cliffs, New Jersey, 1980.

CHAPTER 3

THINKING ABOUT SKILLS: MENTAL PRACTICE

Conceivably the Greek athletes of old spent time thinking about the skills they were to exhibit, just before entering the arena for the first Olympics. It was not, however, until this century that organized research efforts were made to find out in exact ways how rehearsing skills mentally might really aid performance. Many of the studies that were carried out were confined to the laboratory, rather than taking place on the athletic field. Seldom can one find a continuing program of research on this fascinating topic, one which involves a thorough effort in several studies to determine how mental practice effects skill acquisition.

As more and more of these studies appeared, it became possible to say that indeed thought about a skill often aids that skill. However, it is even more useful to consider such questions as: (a) What kind of thoughts improve what skills? and also, (b) What are the best combinations of physical and mental practice?

In all of the studies we conducted involving the interviews of athletes, we asked questions concerning how they mentally practiced skill. After first ascertaining whether or not the athlete consciously engaged in some planned rehearsal of skills. We then proceeded to find out the type of imagery, or "self-talk" the performer habitually employed, and where this kind of mental practice usually took place.

As has been true in past studies of mental practice, when we asked athletes about how, where, why, and when they mentally practiced we were dependent upon their descriptions of processes which we could not measure directly. We hoped, however, that the words we used when questioning them, accurately portrayed various types of imagery and the like in which they were actually engaged. Additionally, the information extended to us aided us to formulate ideas about the ideal ways in which mental practice should be carried out.

Previous findings about mental effects will be discussed in the following section. Next, I will relate what we found out about the thought processes of the athletes we polled, during the past several years. The final section contains guidelines reflecting what we believe represents the current "state of the art," relative to the use of mental practice to improve athletic skills.

WHAT THE RESEARCH SAYS

Researchers exploring mental practice effects have used many words to describe this kind of mental activity. These terms have included "mental rehearsal," "skill imagery," and the like. Additionally, a number of theories have been proposed to explain just how thought may "work" to improve physical skills. For example, some have suggested that "pure" thought will not really enhance physical performance. Rather, they explain, thinking triggers muscular responses which in turn form patterns of physical actions, thus enhancing the skill of the thinker. An individual, when thinking about hammering a nail, often evidences muscular twitchings in the arm involved.

More recent studies have shown that the problem of translating thoughts to minute muscular responses involves several complicated questions. For example, one investigation using both experienced and inexperienced skiers found that thinking about a complicated maneuver, triggered appropriate muscular and breathing rhythms in the experienced performers only. The inexperienced skiers, on the other hand, paired mental practice with visual imagery (measured by monitoring eye movements) without any involvement of the appropriate muscular patterns.

Three sets of variables were generally focused upon in both recent and earlier studies of mental practice. These included: (a) The nature of the imagery used. (b) The characteristics of the one practicing the skill mentally. (c) The nature of the skill rehearsed.

Other investigations compared mental practice which was presented in a organized manner, to more casual opportunities of a performer who merely observe another perform a skill. Various combinations of physical and mental practice were used to determine how one might optimize mental practice effects. Overall, the research both in the United States and abroad has produced the following principles and guidelines which suggest ways to optimize "mental practice effects."

1. The more a task requires "pure" skill, in contrast to elements of power, endurance, and the like, the more likely it will be that mental practice will be useful. Thus, mental practice should be moderately helpful in skills which combine physical accuracy with power/strength and/or endurance. However in such "pure" skills as pistol shooting, mental practice is likely to be more productive. In few athletic skills, however, is mental practice alone, likely to be more useful than physical practice.

2. When incidental learning, observation, and various combinations of mental and physical practice have been contrasted the order of their effectiveness seems to be as follows.

(a) Least effective is incidental learning, performing a skill after merely having been in the presence of another performing the skill.

(b) If the learner carefully observes another performing, as would be the case of boys watching experienced basketball players dribble behind their backs, moderate to minimal skill improvement occurs. If this observation is directed by another, by asking the observers to watch for specific components of the skill, skill is enhanced to a greater degree. This positive effect of "directed observational learning" makes it important, for example, for effective verbal instructions to accompany the showing of a film.

(c) Mental practice of a skill, in an organized manner, is more effective than merely observing a skill. This instruction should be geared to the level of the learner. Some studies have indicated that individuals who have the best visual memories are likely to benefit more from mental practice of physical skill. Athletes usually report "feeling a skill," thinking about it while remaining "inside their own head." Visualizing themselves from a distance is less often reported; while infrequently do athletes report verbalizing the nature of the skill. Usually, instructed mental practice which lasts longer than from two to five minutes is not likely to prove more effective than shorter practice periods. Perhaps after five minutes athletes and others are not able to concentrate well upon skills in which they are not engaged physically.

(d) Physical practice of most athletic skills is usually more effective than only the mental practice of the skills. While I am unaware of any studies which indicate that "pure" mental practice is superior to physical practice, there have been findings which indicate that often during the initial stages of learning a highly complex skill, physical practice effects and mental practice effects may be equal in "strength."

(e) Finally, it has been found that most effective are optimum combinations of mental and physical practice. Structured and organized attempts to aid athletes to think abut skills, paired with effective physical conditioning and practice will usually elicit better learning and performance, than *only* mental *or* physical practice.

3. Most important when applying mental practice, is to consider the type of practice or mental rehearsal in which to engage. Several different variations of ways to get people to think about physical skill may be attempted. There does not seem to be any best way, and the most positive improvement will likely be dependent upon how well matched the type of mental practice is to the preference of the athlete or athletes involved. Often the specific strategy which is employed will be preceeded by, or accompanied by, other kinds of psychological strategies. Thus, mental practice might be engaged in after moderate relaxation is achieved via muscular tension techniques. Various kinds of general imagery promoting calmness are often used before, or are placed between, attempts to encourage the athlete to think about the specifics of a skill or skills. Sometimes the mental practice includes attempts to help the athlete recall vividly the nature of a skill error, for which remediation is needed. At other times the practice session only includes positive rehearsal of the skill(s) components.

Typically, another individual, coach, or psychologist, "talks" an athlete, or a team through the skill in a rather structured way. An example of some "scripts" for this kind of practice follows.

(a) If the desire is to encourage an athlete to "think in words," his or her way through a skill, the "script" might be read to the performer as follows.

Say to yourself . . . "I am stepping up to the free throw line." Now say, "I am holding the ball lightly with both hands, evenly placed on the ball." Now repeat . . . "I am slowly bending my knees while lowering the ball between my knees with both hands." Now say, "I am beginning to extend my knees, while bringing the ball up in a smooth movement." Now say to yourself, "I will continue by releasing the ball as my knees extend." Now repeat, "I will follow through with my hands ending up high above my head." Now as you repeat the words again, imagine yourself watching a spot just behind the front-middle part of the rim toward which you are shooting.

This kind of "talking through" mental practice, encourages the athlete to verbalize, and to engage in useful internal speech or "self-talk." Care must be taken, however, when encouraging this type of mental practice that the internal speech does not impair rapid, ballistic type movements, actions which may occur too rapidly to be effectively paired with speech. Structured attempts to help the athlete verbalize the skill, in the way described, may not be as helpful as other methods which encourage various kinds of visualization. These alternative methods are described in part (c).

(b) Sometimes mental practice guidance may encourage the athlete to "feel the skill," to depend upon various sensory impressions involving touch, sight, and movement cues. Sometimes, sound cues are also added to the mental practice session, when appropriate. An example, involving a gymnastic skill follows.

"Imagine yourself suspended between the parallel bars. Feel the pressure of the

26

bars in each hand, as you bear your weight on them. Now begin to swing, stretching so that your hips move in front of your hands. Now swing twice, higher each time, keep your eyes forward and on a point between the bars, as you feel the stretch in your shoulders during the back swing. Now feel yourself moving to a handstand position. Tighten your hands on the bars to stop your momentum. Imagine your feet stopping over your head. Stretch! Maintain your position.''

This kind of imagery practice may be accompanied by requests to tighten the musculature involved. The athlete also may be asked to imagine the feelings without tightening the muscles in a conscious manner. For the most part, these feelings are reported often when athletes say that skill imagery just comes to them, in a random fashion.

(c) The most reported type of skill imagery, when athletes are questioned, involves either of two types of visual imagery. In one type the athlete "remains in his or her own head," and watches the surroundings during the trick. In a second type the athlete imagines himself or herself performing from a distance. It is almost as though the athlete's eyes are removed from his or her head, and the form of the skill is being looked at, as a spectator might during the actual competition. Examples of these two types of imagery, encouraged through formal mental practice sessions, might occur as follows.

"In head" imagery might be elicited by the following directions, given to a baseball player.

"You are stepping up to the plate. Imagine seeing the pitcher looking past you at the catcher. Concentrate on the ball in his hand, not on him. Relax, look at the outfield, and now back to the pitcher. Watch his wind-up, looking for cues as to what kind of pitch is coming. Get set at the plate, dig your feet into the ground. Be sure your hands are tight on the bat, and that you are in a comfortable, relaxed stance. Now watch the delivery, trying to guess how the ball is coming in. Swing your bat, and feel it hit squarely on the ball. Hear the noise of a solid hit, and watch the ball as it sails to the outfield, farther and farther over the wall!!''

Imagery in which the athlete is visually removed from his or her own body might be encouraged as follows in a scenario involving an ice-skater.

"You are starting your spin. Watch yourself from this sidelines. See your hands wrap around your body, and see how your speed accelerates. Your legs tighten as your speed picks up. Watch the line of your body as you spin faster. Next, your elbows are coming against your body as your speed increases. Your arms are now over your head, tightening, your body becomes a blur, and you seem to have acquired several heads! Now you stop suddenly, as your eyes find a spotting point, and your foot goes out to act as a brake. Your eyes appear clear, as you smile and take a bow.''

Blanket application of one of these methods to a group of athletes, or to a team may have less than positive results. More than one athlete reported to us that psychologists who had been briefly associated with their team engendered both anger and frustration among their teammates. The psychologists exposed them to excessive amounts of skill imagery, often imagery which was not needed nor suited to the individual athletes involved. The athletes reported that both they and their teammates were anxious and mad because the excessive amount of time devoted to mental practice prevented them from adequately preparing themselves physically. Thus, not only should excessive time, over 5 minutes or so, not be given to mental practice in groups but the type of mental practice should be suited to the needs and tendencies of individuals. Conceivably two principles should apply:

(a) If an athlete already performs in a superior manner, the type of mental practice encouraged should aid in the refinement of skill.

(b) If the athlete is experiencing some kinds of skill problems, he or she should be encouraged to experiment with the kinds of mental rehearsal techniques which may be innovative and new to him or her.

Experienced athletes may need to rehearse subtle refinements of skills, whereas less experienced athletes may need to be led through entire skills and skill sequences in a more formal manner. In any case the type, duration, and conditions of mental practice imposed should be suited to the athlete involved, and should not be the result of some pre-conceived "best" method formulated by the person applying these techniques.

4. The available findings indicate what appears best for groups of subjects, but guidelines for the application of just what kinds of mental practice techniques for an individual are not always as clear. Some have contended that visualizing skill, while remaining in one's own head, is superior to viewing oneself from a distance. However, whether this is true, or not, is not clear at this point.

5. For the most part, skills which are classified as "closed" seem more amenable to mental practice effects, than do so-called "open skills." A "closed skill" is one which is able to be pre-programmed somewhat in advance of the competition, and whose execution is not dependent upon the actions of one's opponents. Thus, a "closed skill" might be a gymnastic routine, or perhaps, a discus throw, or a clean-and-jerk in weight lifting. For the most part, these are not dependent upon outside and unpredictable other people. Although competitive environments which often change even slightly from place to place may make even these somewhat "open" in nature. "Open skills," on the other hand are those requiring numerous reactions which one may have to make while working in a defensive role in a basketball game, or ice-hockey competition. Returns in tennis are open skills, as one's opponent dictates how each should be accomplished. On the other hand, a tennis serve is generally a closed skill, one whose execution may be pre-planned, and thus mentally practiced in advance.

It could be argued, on the other hand, that mental practice which is flexible and accommodates to too many changing conditions could well aid a person to perform better in "open skill situations." The coach who aids his or her players to learn all the possible reactions on defense to all the possible actions of opponents, will likely do the players a favor when actually in a game. Mental practice which similarly is flexible, and diverse in nature, could improve performance of athletes within "open skill" situations.

In the section which follows are some of the findings obtained when we asked about the type of mental practice engaged in by athletes in a number of sports.

WHAT ATHLETES SAY

In our questionnaire-interviews we asked questions which directly dealt with mental practice techniques, as well as queries which related to mental practice in indirect ways. For example, we were concerned with the type of imagery involving skill in which each athlete habitually engaged. At the same time we were interested in whether that imagery was carefully planned by the athlete, or whether it just "came randomly" into their thoughts. Responses the athletes gave to questions about special preparation places also related indirectly to the amount and kind of mental practice in which they engaged.

We additionally attempted, when possible, to determine possible relationships between mental practice and such variables as the type of skill the athlete engaged in, whether or not the athlete played in a team or individual sport, and at what level of competition the athlete was currently involved. The duration of time and experience of the athlete was also looked at in relation to the type and intensity of the mental practice reported.

We were particularly interested in the athletes' reports of whether they planned their mental practice or not. This question and the responses they gave us, were important, in so far as we wanted to shed light upon whether planning, or non-planning seemed to elicit the best performances. This argument, as has been pointed out, is one which current "self-help" books do little to settle.

In the vast number of findings and relationships we obtained, one thing started to become clear. For the most part the athletes who engaged in relatively brief performances while in competition, profited best from brief intense periods of mental practice of their skill. Whereas, those whose competitive efforts consumed a prolonged period of time, profited best from prolonged periods of time devoted to the practice of their skill.

The degree to which an athlete structured and planned their mental practice efforts seemed to differ from skill to skill. For the most part, athletes in individual sports that required a great deal of pre-programming, and which were essentially "closed skills," most often told us that they carefully tried to regulate their mental practice efforts. Team sport athletes, generally those whose competitive responses were more diverse in nature, and composed of more "open skill" situations were not as likely to engage in carefully planned and structured mental practice efforts. In at least one of our studies of these latter athletes, it was found that those who were perceived as most intense and able in practices, were those who devoted the least amount of their day-dreams (outside of practice) to their sport.

Another important division was apparent in the reports we obtained from athletes about their mental practice efforts. Some reported mentally practicing their sport's skills in relatively unemotional ways; while others seemed to engage themselves emotionally as they thought about their skills, placing themselves into the social situation and the stresses which accompanied their actual physical performance in competition.

Frequently an athlete would report he or she would vary the amount of physical practice which accompanied mental efforts, from session to session. For example, a gymnast said that he would first practice the skilled routine without any observable muscular actions, but relying totally upon thought. Next, he would insert arm movements of his ring routine, while standing and thinking about the routine. Similar reports were obtained from other athletes, including figure-skaters. They might "move" in either direction using mental-physical combinations. They might first combine rudimentary movements with mental planning, and then gradually phase out the movements, and rely solely upon thoughts about their skills. On the other hand, they might start with "pure" thought, and gradually accompany their thoughts with more and more movements resembling their skill. This kind of combined pre-programming was also reported by gymnasts and divers. In both sports, competitors reported this type of mental practice, joining muscular and mental activity. However, whatever kinds of rudimentary physical and mental practice combinations were described to us, it was obvious that many athletes had a well-planned routine of these "practice bouts" in which they participated at various times throughout the day. In the evenings, during practices and between parts of their competition, were the times mentioned most often.

We were also interested in relationships between types of imagery reported, and the apparent success of the athletes we interviewed. We, thus, asked the athletes whether, when they thought about their skills, they habitually and characteristically seemed to "view" the skill as thought, i.e, "looking out of their own eyes," and feeling the movement, or whether they somehow stood back and viewed themselves performing, as though their eyes were not in their heads. This latter type of imagery is sometimes called "spectating."

Previous studies have indicated that "staying inside one's own head" is superior to "spectating." However, our own findings do not confirm this superiority of "inhead viewing." We did however find that: (a) by far the most common way of "seeing" one's self performing while mentally practicing skill, is from "within" the head, and (b) most athletes, while spending more time, inside their heads, tend to alternate "spectating" with "inhead" imagery. "Spectating" seems to help them check their form, and to relax. "Inhead" visualizing, on the other hand, helps them correct minute skill problems, and to integrate their entire routines. Distance runners, gymnasts and ice-skaters all reported this kind of alternating imagery. At times the "spectating" also took the form of "success imagery." For example, a runner while watching his or her form might also imagine crossing a finish line victorious!

Another interesting finding when polling both coaches and athletes as to what was the best mental imagery, was that members of both groups are by-in-large highly egocentric. Virtually all of them thought that the way they habitually imagined their skill, was true of others. Thus, coaches often came forth with "exact" formulae as to what to do imaginally, formulas that were at marked odds with the reports of what their athletes actually did! Marked divergencies were found when polling coaches of alpine skiers, who said that skiers should "feel the gate they are in, visualize the gate ahead, and think two gates ahead," when going through a slalom course. On the other hand, the young skiers whom they were coaching, reported a diversity of methods used when thinking their way through the difficult courses; methods which for the most part did not resemble the "exact" formula taught by their coaches!

Although we were interested in possible relationships between the type of skill imagery reported and success of the athelete(s) we queried, exact correlations were often difficult to pin-point. More useful was the indication that the quality and nature of the visual imagery, rather than its exact type, were most important. By far the vast majority of the reports, about 70% reported staying "inside their heads" while thinking about their skills. Less often did they report "spectating" using visual imagery. However, it soon became apparent, that among athletes who said they planned their mental lives, highly individualistic "programs" of mental practice had been formulated. Among the "mental practice types" we identified were as follows.

(a) Some planned carefully, and included in their plans the exact time(s) of the day they engaged in mental imagery, as well as the type of imagery they used. The places they used, as well as the degree to which they incorporated rudimentary muscular responses were also carefully thought about. These individuals adopted their methods because of being introduced to them by others, or reading about them in various books. They virtually all reported that such measures helped them perform better.

(b) Although some reported not planning the skills of their sport, many of these non-planners reported: (1) making special plans to fend off anxiety, and (2) spending time before contests in an attempt to "get it together" including time spent on skill rehearsal. They often reported that this important time for their own thoughts before contests, was not always attainable due to pressures from their coaches.

(c) Some non-planners, mostly those of high skill levels in team sports, were also able to perform well. They were often high level performers, whose skills were relatively engrained. They often reported that too much time spent thinking about their skills at higher levels of competition, might conceivably cause them to either tighten up and perform poorly, or would heighten their anxiety about forthcoming contests.

(d) Frequently reported were types of imagery which varied from in-head images, to "spectating." Those who alternated in this manner, devoted more time to "in-head" mental practice than to "spectating!" Very few athletes reported spending inordinate amounts of time thinking through their skills using words.

(e) Many athletes found that when engaging in mental practice, unwanted skill deficiencies or errors would "crop up" in their thoughts. At times these intrusions would cause an athlete to "give up" in attempts to positively rehearse skills. However, some more sophisticated performers would "use" these intrusions in positive ways by: (1) Over-practicing the error consciously, until it became silly and could be eliminated mentally, and later physically. (2) Spending time alternating the mental practice of an error, with its correction, time and time again, until the error was somehow overcome by the correct response. Earlier literature has shown that often it is useful to over-practice an error until its exact nature is well known, and felt by the performer, before trying to overcome it physically. Although this would seem to "fly in the face" of common sense, some superior coaches, including John Wooden, have been found to use this technique on occasion, when trying to eliminate errors. This same over-practice of an error mentally could have the same positive effects, when one later tries to eliminate it.

(f) Some athletes reported practicing the skill within a social context which might include fans and coaches as well as teammates. Others said that they rehearsed skills in a distraction-free environment, often imagining a cocoon-like cover placed over them and their opponent or apparatus. Some gradually phased in social stresses, as they rehearsed skills under increasing social pressures.

Thus, in the main, the athletes revealed highly original and individualistic ways of trying to help skill through imagery. Their reports enabled us to draw useful implications as to how skill imagery and mental practice may be best used by athletes to enhance performance. These guidelines are explained in the section which follows.

IMPLICATIONS FOR COACHES AND ATHLETES

Our interviews with athletes did not reveal "best ways" of imagining skills, which are optimum for large groups of athletes. Rather, it was shown that athletes reveal marked individual differences. Moreover, the reports from athletes revealed variations in skill imagery which may be applied in useful ways if an athlete's efforts at producing optimum skill seems blocked in various ways.

Mental practice effects upon physical skill are well documented. Unfortunately, most of the data has come from well-controlled laboratory experiments in which the tasks may have little resemblance to "the real world" of athletics. However, when reviewing the reports of athletes, and how they engage in mental rehearsal of skills it is possible to formulate various modifications of skill rehearsal, which are potentially useful for competition and practice.

In general, it appears that mental practice is engaged in with more precision when an athlete is faced with "closed" skills in competition. It is likely also that mental rehearsal of a specific nature has greater effects on the case of this kind of "pre-programmable" type of activity. More variable kinds of mental rehearsal, rehearsal which includes social stresses and the like, is used by athletes who engage in competition that requires more "open skills." It also appears that the mental practice effects in these latter skills, in which responses are dependent upon the transitory reactions of one's opponents, are dependent upon how closely the variations in the mental rehearsal "bouts" resemble the divergent responses which may be required in the actual competition. In summary, specific kinds of rehearsable skills are most amendable to specific kinds of mental rehearsal; whereas performances which require a divergence of responses as in the case of defense reactions in ice-hockey and soccer, may be benefited most by mental rehearsal which includes thinking about numerous possible responses.

Therefore, it becomes apparent that recommendations for precise imagery or rehearsal of a skill or skills may at times consist of focusing upon specific sub-skills within some sports. Free-throwing might be benefitted in basketball, for example, by specific kinds of mental practice, while defensive skills would not.

Care should be taken, however, even by "closed skill" athletes (gymnasts) not to mentally rehearse their routines or movements in ways which are too restrictive. For example, a gymnast may confront slightly different competitive environments or apparatus which may differ from place to place. These differences, as well as variations in routines which may occur because of "breaks" or mistakes, should be included in the mental preparation engaged in.

Athletes who are evidencing performance-skill problems should be encouraged to engage in short sessions of mental practice each day. These sessions should occupy from 5-10 minutes, and be composed of several short periods within each of those sessions. At times two sessions a day is useful, with one of the sessions best placed in the evening before retiring.

Our interview data tells us that it is probable that visual imagery which includes both "in-head" imagining, as well as "spectating" may be best. The majority of the time, depending upon the skill, should be devoted to feeling the movements and visualizing them (or it) while the athlete imagines "looking out" of his or her own eyes. Overall impressions of form may best be gained, however, if at least occasionally the athlete imaginally "backs off" and watches himself or herself from a distance, as might a judge or a coach.

Athletes indicated that from time to time it is sometimes helpful to combine the rehearsal of a specific skill, with imagery that may deal with other problems they face. For example, an athlete who has problems concentrating in competition might begin mental practice "bouts" within an "empty gymnasium." Later, this same athlete may attempt to mentally perform routines with the addition of more and more imaginary spectators. In this way the athlete may aid himself or herself to program future performances which include the real stress of others present. In a similar way the athlete may aid concentration in competition through mental practice which may be used later in competition. Mental rehearsal, for example, which includes imaginary "cocoons" placed over the performer, might be useful. Further ways to combine mental practice of skill with other useful objectives will become more evident as the material in the following chapters is reviewed. However, some further examples of these ways to combine skill rehearsal with other objectives are as follows.

Success imagery may be combined with specific skill rehearsal, and frequently *is* according to the reports we obtained. Research by others has pointed out that engaging in what has been termed "self-efficacy"[1] statements, is likely to enhance not only self-confidence but also performance. Thus, a distance runner, for example, may insert "internal speech" as well as internal imagery depicting success, into thoughts which also dwell upon running form and skill. The athlete may interject mental pictures of winning, as well as "self-talk," which reflects self-administered rewards (I am really improving this time), into mental imagery focusing also upon skill refinements.

Mental practice may also be used to reduce, or eliminate skill deficiencies.

This reduction of error(s) may be carried out in at least two ways: (a) The correct skill, or series of skills, may be over-learned mentally; practiced to the point of boredom. A difficult portion of a skill may likewise be "over-practiced" mentally in the ways described. (b) A second way to eliminate a performance flaw involves first "bringing-out" and making more vivid the nature of the flaw itself. Some coaches require an athlete to moderately re-perform a performance error, so that it may be brought vividly to mind, and thus may be more easily eliminated. This kind of mental rehearsal of an error, before its "mental elimination," may also be practiced. At times the error may be practiced, either physically or mentally to the point of absurdity. At this point the athlete should be encouraged to "switch," either physically or mentally, to the proper execution of the skill.

The athlete and coach may give attention to what might be termed "variable skill" mental rehearsal. This type of practice may be useful for skilled athletes wishing to improve "open skills." These performers, requiring a variety of responses that must be quickly "called up" as they are confronted with unpredictable responses from opponents, may benefit from skill rehearsal which also contains a variety of situations, opponent actions, as well as, many skilled reactions of their own. This type of athlete may, thus, be encouraged to mentally rehearse the variety of moves which may be required of them. Indeed it was found in some of our research that often defensive players, needing this variability of response, reported frequently "trancing out" before games in an effort to mentally remove themselves from others. They often used this "quiet time" to imagine in their minds the variety of skills which were to be required of them in a forthcoming competition.

This type of "variable" mental rehearsal should attempt to incorporate both what the athlete is likely to see and perceive when performing as well as the nature of the responses required. Thus, a goalie in ice-hockey for example, might spend useful time imagining a variety of shots coming at him, the ways in which other players may screen out the impressions of incoming shots, as well as imagining the actual blocking movements needed in this difficult position. Many goals in this sport occur when a "mess" occurs in front of the goal, thus, the goalie should imagine these visual difficulties when rehearsing the skills needed. Defensive backfield players in football

---

[1]"Efficacy" is defined as the power or capacity to produce a desired outcome.

Figure 2 Distance runners report thinking about three things during races: they imagine themselves winning, success imagery; they think about and carefully monitor their bodies and its processes, including heart-rate, respiration and how their muscles feel; and finally, they "watch" their form, from a distance, as though they are riding a bicycle beside themselves!

should also try to imagine the various kinds of "pass routes" run at them by offensive players, as well as the unusual bounces and "tips" that the ball may take when they are required to deal with it in actual competition. They might even benefit from mentally "watching themselves" intercept a pass and running it back!

These ways of combining mental practice of skill with other useful imagery are made clearer in the following examples.

1. Combining "in-head" and "spectating" imagery.

A gymnast mentally practicing a free-exercise routine might be asked to visualize his or her routine as follows. "Now imagine yourself beginning the routine. Run vigorously for your mount, your first trick. Hit a solid landing after your beginning. Now stretch and leap high in the dance movement. Stay with the music as it is played. Now feel the second run, feel the floor on your feet as you approach your front moves. Your walk-overs should feel good, stretch! Your leaps are high and strong, relax the expression on your face. Keep your eyes straight ahead as you run for your dismount. Your full twist should feel tight, and now feel your feet hit the mat with a single movement, a solid landing."

Now let's do your routine a second time; let's watch it together, from the positions of two judges. "Watch yourself during the first run, are you relaxed, are your arms precise, and your head up? Are you high and tight as you spin in your first movement, your mount? Are you now relaxed as you start your rhythmics? Are your leaps high and strong, is your face pleasant, relaxed? Watch your second run, and front walk-overs, and then the "whip-overs." Are they well executed? Move fast for your dismount, do you show strain, or are you relaxed? Watch a solid and precise dismount."

2. Incorporating increasing amount of environmental stress.

A basketball player might use the following imagery when mentally rehearsing the free-throw, during successive "mental practice bouts."

Low stress situation

"You are in a quiet room, its walls are plain, and at the end is a basket with the key drawn on the floor in front of it. Bounce the ball three times, take a breath, now slowly flex your knees, as you bring the ball back toward your shoulder with one hand. Fix your eyes on an aiming point just in back of the front of the basket. Slowly extend your arm and extend your body in one fluid, relaxed movement. The ball swishes through the net, watch it fall good!"

Next level of stress

"You are now in an empty gymnasium. The seats in back of the backboard are empty. No teammates are around, nor is the coach. Again you relax, time your leg extension with the follow through of the arm. Watch your aiming point as the ball comes toward it. A clean shot. Now try it again, and think through it in the same manner."

The next level

"It is during practice, your teammates are watching you as is the coach. She is not worried about your performance, however. A deep breath, now start your free-throw movement again. Relax, follow through, a success! Now try it again, your teammates are smiling, the coach is pleased also. Now think through it again."

Another level of stress

"A game is being played, but the score is not close. No spectators from the visiting team are present, only your supporters who are noisy, but happy. Relax, it is the same free-throw movement you did in an empty gymnasium. Follow-through and watch the ball enter the basket. The fans cheer, and then quiet down a little as you make another successful attempt. Now they really let go! Nice job!''

A high level

"The gymnasium all night has been crazy. The other team's fans are close to the floor, and noisy and abusive. They have been calling you names all night, and they are waving and yelling in the seats behind the clear backboard as you look at the rim preparing to shoot your free-throws. They scream as you come to the foul line. You can hardly hear anything, you must mentally stop-up your ears, turning the volume down imaginally. You ignore everything but the aiming point just behind the front of the rim's middle. The screaming grows louder, but you are muffling it, it is quiet as you take your breathes, and relax. Bend your legs as you bring the ball back toward your shoulder, ready to release it in a fluid manner. The extension of your arm and legs occurs together, and the follow-through is effortless. The ball passes through, as the fans quiet down. You got to them, you quieted them down.''

3. Success imagery combined with skill imagery.

The long periods of time a distance runner engages in the event permits time to engage both success imagery and thoughts about form. This type of self-talk, an underpinning to both success imagery and form inspection might be encouraged. "You are loose now, running in a relaxed way. Feel your feet hit the ground rhythmically, you are now well into the first quarter of the race. You are among the leaders, reel them in as on a fishing line . . . one by one. You are now in front, crossing the finish lines to smiles all around you. Now back to your relaxed gliding lope, stretch out. Bring an imaginary bicycle up next to you, get on it. Now ride the bike a few feet away from where you are running. Move past, look back, and now get behind yourself on the bike. Look at yourself from several angles. People always say you run with good form, they are right, look at the glide. Notice how your head does not bob up and down, but remains level as you move. Now get off your bike, and merge into your body again. Pretend you are speeding past everyone, passing the front runners, and winning it again, and again, crossing the finish line. Now back to the good rhythm, breathe rhythmically, think a tune which keeps you in rhythm. Watch your posture, do not lean forward. Remember the relaxed glow, the successful feeling that you have when you win, or do well. Now work and finish hard, to make that feeling happen again. Breathe, push, flow, and relax.''

4. Thinking, and an error to be eliminaed.

A gymnast working on a high-bar might try to eliminate an error as follows. "There I missed my re-catch again. I was too high and too far from the bar. Let's do (think through) the routine again in my head. There, a miss again. There I missed again. Now I'll pretend I am a clown in a circus routine, missing the trick by more, and falling humorously in the net. Boy this is dumb! I will think of missing it once more, by a larger margin, by a foot, as a clown might. Now it is time to think with precision. Get rid of the clown costume, put back on my gymnastic clothes. There, a perfect catch, and I am able to proceed into the next trick. Now again, leading into the release trick and out of it, with precision and accuracy. Now the whole routine again, in my thoughts, as I look up at myself. Again, as I feel the routine, with my perfect release tricknow. The first swing feels good in my hands, and strong. The shoot to a hand-stand, and grip change is also perfect. A shoot to eagle-giants, and now the release trick is executed perfectly. The continuing tricks are smoothly performed, and finally the dismount, with a solid landing comes well.''

The gymnast may now be encouraged to "walk through the routine," without actually mounting the hi-bar. Finally, the physical practice of the trick and tricks leading into and out of the "problem release," may be attempted physically.

5. Variable skill practice by an athlete who must execute "open skills".
The defensive skills of a basketball player require many variations of responses, and thoughts. Many of the movements needed, are difficult to predict, just as are the offensive movements of opponents. Some of the various situations may be predicted, and practiced mentally as follows.

(a) "You are backing up well, fast short steps, arms just right as you imagine yourself on defense. Keep your eyes on his/her mid-section, not on the head or arms. He goes to the right. Your right arm should be down, left up. Get a step on him, do not let him go along the baseline. Force him toward the center."

(b) "Now he is coming down to your left. You are quickest in this direction. Get lower, left foot back, left arm down. Stop him in his trip to the baseline. Cut him off."

(c) "He is cutting across the key. Move with him. Look for the screen. Feel the screen out of the corner of your eye. Hands up!"

(d) "The dribbler is coming toward you, cutting from left to right. Move with him, get low. Do not cross your feet, make shuffle steps, don't bounce. Watch his body's mid-point. You are as fast as he/she is!"

This mental practice may be combined with various other kinds of useful imagery. Practice in concentration may also be included, as may be found in Chapter 7.

OVERVIEW

Proper mental practice of physical skills is likely to prove beneficial. Most useful is often a combination of both physical and mental practice in proper proportions. Mental practice effects are likely to improve skills most during the initial stages of learning, and if the skills are reasonably complex. Optimum time during which to practice a skill mentally is from five to ten minutes, with "bouts" within this period of a shorter duration. The most often reported method of imagining a skill involves athletes remaining inside their own heads. Less often reported is imagery involving the athlete somehow removing himself or herself from their own eyes, and "spectating." Numerous athletes, however, combine "in-head" and "spectating" in useful ways.

Mental practice of a skill or skills may be combined with imagery useful in correcting other problems, or enhancing other dimensions of performance. For example, a runner might engage both in imagined "success imagery" as well as consideration of form, as he or she proceeds in a race. Likewise, improvement in concentration, reduction of anxiety, as well as the ability to deal with stressful social conditions may be combined usefully with skill imagery.

Variable mental skill practice, of different skill combinations is most useful for athletes who must respond in varied and unpredictable ways when in competition. Defensive players in many sports must perform in this way. On the other hand, athletes whose efforts are clear and straight-forward prior to competition, as in the case of gymnasts, and the like, benefit most from simple direct efforts at skill imagery.

REFERENCES

Corbin, C.B., "Mental practice," in W.P. Morgan, (Ed.), *Ergogenic Aids And Muscular Performance,* Academic Press, New York, 1972, pp. 93-118.

Cratty, B.J., "Mental practice," in B.J. Cratty, *Physical Expressions of Intelligence,* Prentice-Hall Inc., Englewood Cliffs, N.J., 1973, pp. 118-130.

Mahoney, M.J., Chapter 13, "Cognitive skills and athletic performance," in P.C. Kendall, and S.D. Hollon, (Eds.), *Cognitive-Behavioral Interventions, Theory, Research And Procedures,* Academic Press, New York, 1979, pp. 423-445.

Suinn, R.M., "Body thinking: psychology for Olympic athletes," in R.B. Suinn (Ed.), *Psychology in Sports, Methods and Applications,* Burgess, Minneapolis, MN, 1980, pp. 306-309.

White, K.R., and L. Lewis, "Learning a complex skill: effects of mental practice, physical practice, and imagery ability," *Intl. Journal of Sport Psychology,* 1970, 10, pp. 71-78.

CHAPTER 4

ACTIVATION AND AROUSAL: "GETTING-UP" AND "CALMING DOWN"

One of the more pervasive problems encountered by athletes involves "getting up" to perform at peak emotional and physical levels when confronting an important competition. Even more problems are encountered when it is necessary to remain at some kind of optimum level for a long season, during which there may be many contests for which a "high" is needed. Athletes and coaches often use such words as "psyching-up," to describe attempts to reach this optimum level of performance; while in the psychological literature such terms as *activation* and *arousal* are employed to denote these same processes.

A great deal of time and energy is expended by sport psychologists in exploring various relationships between activation and performance. Effort is also spent by professionals in the behavioral sciences to prepare individual performers for working at their best at just the right time.

Activation is usually not an isolated "state," but a condition which interacts with other moods and thoughts discussed in other parts of this book. Aggressive feelings, fear, as well as the need to concentrate are likely to affect arousal and activation. Delineating exact relationships and performance optimums is not always an easy undertaking. Athletes differ in the "signs" they give off when they become excited. Tasks in sport also differ as to what levels of activation seem best when performing at an optimum.

Research on this topic began early in the history of experimental psychology. Psychologists at Yale, around the turn of the century, found that reaction times would improve if subjects were asked to respond to noises of various volumes, until a point was reached after which a louder noise would tend to lengthen reaction time. This initial work has been followed by a great deal more exploration of often complex inter-actions between levels of activation, physical performance, and responses.

Since these early beginnings, various techniques have been tried in order to adjust the levels of activation upward or downward in numerous groups of performers. This type of research has been conducted with astronauts, factory workers, soldiers, as well as athletes. Some of the methods attempted have bordered on the bizarre. Other techniques have been more straightforward, and have included the adjustment of muscular tensions, the use of deep breathing, as well as the employment of various kinds of visual imagery.

Several decades ago, sport psychologists in Eastern Europe began experimenting with the uses of visual displays of an athlete's heart-rate and other signs of arousal, in an effort to aid the performer to control his or her own levels of activation. These methods, now refined, are incorporated into various forms of what are termed "bio-feedback." The use of isolation chambers in order to relax athletes is now being employed by some professional football teams in the United States. While in Russia, and other "Eastern Block" nations, work is continuing on various methods to apply highly individualized techniques to the adjustment of arousal of athletes, methods which are of critical importance to their pursuit of success in international sporting competitions. The athletes whom we interviewed in our investigations, performing usually within a unversity context, had seldom been exposed to well conceived and well designed attempts by others to aid them to "get up" or "calm down," as has been true among athletes in the countries of Eastern Europe.

Among the newer trends in the literature are ways of activating athletes by employing the adjustment of thoughts. Recognizing the processes that the body uses to prepare itself for some threat seldom exist in a vacuum, but are the result of an individual's interpretation of the situation, more and more psychologists are using various forms of "cognitive-behavioral therapy" to either arouse or calm athletes prior to contests.

WHAT THE RESEARCH SAYS

Looked upon broadly, experimental psychologists dealing with human behavior are mainly concerned with two primary dimensions. One dimension involves the *choices* people make, the ways of human decision making. A second dimension concerns the *intensity* underlying how and what people do. This second area of investigation thus revolves around questions about relationships between effort and both mental and physical performance.

It was not until the 1940s that experimental psychologists began to recognize a common thread within many of their studies that pointed to the influences of an intensity component in human physical and intellectual performance. These research studies had as a common focus, the attempt to determine how and why people mobilize energy and focus effort when dealing with challenges in sport, life, and love. Various labels have been attached to this effott or intensity dimension in the psychological literature. Activation, arousal, and excitation are commonly used.

As athletic performance itself implies intensity and effort, it is inevitable that sport psychologists from around the world have focused upon understanding, molding, and channeling this "energy concept." Numerous sport psychologists have proposed methods which are often exotic, through which an athlete may raise himself or herself to a level which is optimum just prior to an important competition. Often these methods are initiated as long as one year prior to an important contest. Equally as often the more able sport psychologists in Europe continue to search for the individual indices of activation which are "given off" in highly different ways by different athletes, rather than simply assume that all people "get-up" or "calm down" in a similar manner. The labels given to these programs at times contain the names of their instigators. These techniques have been named "psychotonic training" by others.

Many of these techniques work reasonably well. If an athlete thinks a method will aid him or her, it probably will. Taking an athlete's mind off an impending contest, usually helps the athlete to relax, and these strategies usually accomplish at least that. Some of these methods may have effects in opposition to what their proponents desire. For example, if an athlete has been encouraged to engage in rather deep and prolonged muscular relaxation, and then to attempt visual imagery, "calling-up" mental pictures may prove more difficult or impossible. In this case the athlete's body and mind, may attempt to work at cross purposes, with negative effects upon performance the result.

Additionally, research indicates that there are individual differences in the manner in which various people manifest activation and arousal. Some may activate with relatively slight muscular tension change in only a specific number of muscle groups. Others habitually tense all their muscles as the body prepares itself to meet some threat. The specific patterns of muscular tension change also differs from individual to individual. Other indices of activation and arousal that are likely to differ from athlete to athlete include changes in endocrine function, palmar perspiration, as well as heart-rate and frequency and depth of respiration. Thus, a system which is applied in a blanket manner to a large number of athletes, intended to either relax or arouse all of them is likely to have mixed effects.

Sometimes athletes are somehow "roped into" trying some kind of activation-adjustment technique prior to contests, with results that are less than promising. The athlete may be underaroused, and the method may further calm him or her too much. An overly excited athlete, needs methods which are flexible, applied prior to a game. This latter performer may have his or her efforts disrupted, if he/she is further activated, rather than calmed down.

The control and management of activation, however, is important, and forms a vital background and base upon which useful visual imagery and/or cognitive adjustments may then be imposed. Adjustment of arousal at times requires only the involvement of the athlete himself or herself. At other times, the help of another is required. Often the outside help is able to prepare the athlete to later help himself or herself without the intervention of another.

Activation and thought interact in ways which may be depicted along a time-line. As the athlete is confronted with a potentially threatening situation, he or she thinks and interprets the nature of that threat, and its severity. Next, the athlete's activation system and sub-systems, prepares the individual to meet the degree of threat that has been decided upon previously, through interpretative thought. Next, the athlete, as performance takes place, may pay conscious attention to the levels of activation and the signs of this activation that are being experienced. For example, the athlete may say to himself or herself . . . "I must be really excited, just listen to how my heart pounds" . . . At times this interpretation may include labels of specific mood states. For example, "I really must be scared, my muscles are so tense," or perhaps, "I must really be angry, as I sit on the bench. How fast my breathing is!" Following the actions which have taken place, the athlete again considers the results of what has taken place, taking into account signs of activation that may still be present. This post-performance interpretation again is likely to modify successive levels of arousal-activation, which in turn influence successive performance efforts.

These interactions of thought and activation-arousal may be depicted as follows. This picture suggests that simply thinking positive thoughts, or engaging in useful "self-talk" may not be enough. At the same time simplistically applied visual imagery or muscular relaxation techniques in attempts to control activation may prove equally superficial. It is believed that it is important to pay heed to both what the individual is consciously attending to and thinking about, together with what the unconscious mechanisms of activation seem to be "thinking" about on their own. This consideration of these dual forces, it is believed, is necessary if real and useful changes are to occur in the body's activation base!

41

CHART 4

As Activation Changes — thoughts turn on: changes are interpreted!

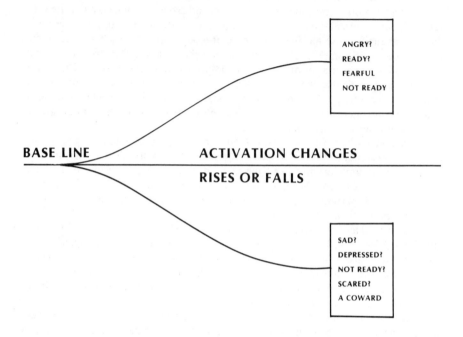

What is Activation?

Prior to discussing in some detail the research, pairing athletic performance with various methods and measures of activation, it is believed important to briefly delineate the dimensions of activation itself. These findings reflect both physiological and psychological changes and mechanisms. For example:

1. Fluctuations in signs of activation occur continually in both healthy and unhealthy people. Daily, in a normal person, the activation-arousal "curve" is in a constant state of flux, from a low during the deepest sleep, to a high, usually around the middle or late morning. It is during this latter period that superior physical performance is likely to take place.

Hourly fluctuations are likely to occur, as are changes in activation from day to day. Pathologically low and high levels are seen when an individual is in a coma, or when having an epileptic seizure. Any normal athlete, however, will evidence performance modifications in physical effort as these hourly and daily changes in activation occur.

2. People tend to try to keep their world, their experience, and their body in balance. These attempts at maintaining "balance" (sometimes called homeostasis) when a threat is encountered, may result in temporary imbalances. That is, when a person experiences a situation which is interpreted as threatening, their body and mind together may activate. In this way they are thus preparing to meet the threat,

and thus maintain their "balance" during the time the stressful situation, person, or athletic contests is being dealt with. Thus, the athlete, contemplating the big game, will tend to activate, if indeed he or she perceives the event as important. In this way the performer hopes to maintain psychological and physiological balance or integrity, as they approach a situation which may involve a threat to the need to win.

3. The physiological sub-systems, triggered by the automatic (autonomic) nervous system work in concert, in systematic "tune" with each other in normally functioning individuals. Some of these changes occur as the body prepares to meet a threat physically. These include modifications of heart-rate, increased respiration rate, and depth, as well as changes in brain wave activity, together with endocrine functions which bring energy to the blood and muscles. Other systems which are not essential to the meeting of a threat, tend to "shut-down," or at least lessen their activity. Stomach movements required in the digestion of food, for example, slow down when a threat is perceived, and the body activated.

These signs of activation may be evaluated directly by, for example, monitoring heart rate. Activation may also be studied indirectly, by gathering successive measures of performance, reaction time, accuracy of movement, as well as persistence in a task. Measures of sensory and perceptual acuity are also used to ascertain levels of activation reached. Visual acuity, for example, changes when an individual is activated, as do measures of auditory perception and tactile awareness. A properly activated athlete is likely to react faster and to see clearer, than one who is not.

4. Despite apparent consistencies in what systems and behaviors change, there are marked individual differences in: (a) How people may perceive the same objective event, and thus the levels of arousal that subsequently are seen. (b) The degree to which each of the sub-systems manifest themselves as an individual activates. Differences in patterns of muscular tension changes have already been discussed. At the same time, *a given individual* will tend to display the *same* type and pattern of "activators" during successive exposures to threat. Thus, sensitive and sophisticated sport psychologists abroad focus upon just what patterns of activation occur within single athletes. Using this kind of information, unique to a given athlete, they are then able to formulate highly useful individual "prescriptions" for patterns of activation, which enable them to best prepare each athlete for optimum performance at just the right times each year.

Some Models

Through the years, several models depicting relationships between activation and physical performance have been formulated. Generally these models have become more sophisticated during the decades, as more data was obtained, and additional thought was devoted to these relationships. A brief look at the most important of these models and theories follows.

The first studies of activtation, generally involved measures of simple reaction time. The activators used were both sounds, as well as visual stimulation. It was usually found that reaction time was likely to be faster, the louder the noise cue that was used to trigger it. Thus, at first, it was decided that simple linear relationship was present relating performance and activation. Or in terms of an athlete, "the harder you try the better you will be," was the axiom formulated.

Soon afterward, however, a wider variety of physical tasks were used, including those which resembled skills seen in athletics. Instead of simply asking subjects to perform, the experimenters tried to vary how activated they were. Some groups of subjects were asked to "relax" before performing, while others were asked to

43

"tense" their muscles before responding. These later studies, revealed that both mental and physical tasks were generally performed best under moderate amounts of activation, rather than under conditions in which the subjects were too "high" or too calm.

CHART 5

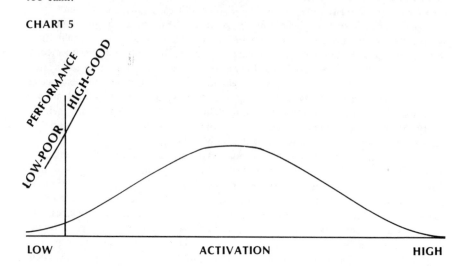

LOW   **ACTIVATION**   **HIGH**

The previous diagram depicts this more advanced thinking concerning arousal and performance relationships. This theory suggests that if an athlete is too excited or too calm, he or she is not likely to do as well, as when a moderate level of excitement is achieved.

However, not all the studies which followed confirmed this simple model. It came to be found that in simple tasks which required greater effort, high levels of activation were beneficial. Whereas, in tasks that were extremely complex, new to the learner, or that were engaged in by the inexperienced, high levels of activation were not beneficial. Rather, under these three conditions, a more relaxed performer was likely to do better. Thus, while the earlier experimenters had simply varied levels of activation, these latter researchers also modified the requirements of the task in various ways. The implications of these latter findings for athletes and athletic performance are as follows: (a) A recently learned skill in practice may be seriously disrupted when the athlete is activated to high levels during subsequent competition. and (b) Simple, direct forceful acts in sport are likely to be effected positively if an athlete "gets extremely high."

Thus, the simple U-shaped curve shown in the previous model was replaced by a more complex model-diagram. This latter theory suggests that a "narrower band" of optimum activation is desirable when performing precise complex tasks.

Although this last model was acceptable to those involved in research, practitioners of sport psychology, as well as athletes and coaches often had difficulty deciding just when a sport skill was simple or complex. Equal difficulties were encountered when trying to assess: (a) how high or calm an athlete was, (b) the levels of calmness required in a given task, as well as (c) how to adjust levels of activation in the real world of sport.

CHART 6

A broader range of optimum activation is permissible for an easy-well learned forceful task than with a difficult complex task.

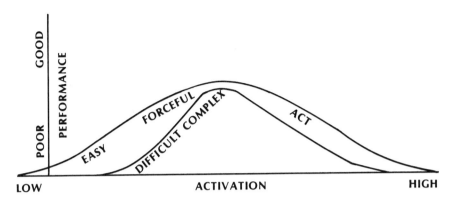

Further complicating the "picture was the observation by many, that at times, apparently *high* athletes and relatively *calm* athletes often performed equally well in the same athletic competition. It was observed, for example, that:

(a) Some athletes seemed to do best, when an observer might classify them as unexcited, or unconcerned about the athletic competition. The lackadaisical manner often angered coaches who believed that they did not care; and yet the same coach was often surprised to see a good effort in subsequent competitions.

(b) In contrast, some athletes seemed to do best when most would consider them too "hyper." These apparently over-activated performers would often surprise the team psychologist and/or the coach by consistently displaying excellent efforts.

(c) Further complicating the problem were observations about self-management of activation, as related to the experience of the athlete. The less experienced athlete was often seen to have more problems adjusting levels of activation as the competition approached. On the other hand, the more experienced performer seemed able to correctly adjust levels of activation when it was required despite signs of either over or under-activation seen well before a competition was to take place.

Taken together, these observations in the world of sport pointed to differences in the psychological make-up of athletes which rendered questionable some of the neat models which have been drawn for you in the previous paragraphs.

Recent work, both in this country and in Canada has thus served to verify the validity of the concept of "activation types." One type performs well when seemingly over-activated. Many times this same "type" is able to raise himself or herself to high levels, or to appropriate levels, just before a contest, despite well-meaning attempts by others to thwart their attempts to "get excited."

The second type also emerged. The outward signs of excitement were absent, or blunted, in this individual's personality. However, this athlete calmly goes about his or her work with a purpose and vigor that reflects high levels of performance. The presence of both "types" on athletic teams, thus poses even more complex problems for those attempting to aid athletes to prepare emotionally for competition.

45

The research thus indicates, that one must consider the interrelationships between three sets of factors when either understanding, or trying to better match, activation and performance in athletes. These factors include variables: (a) present in the task, (b) in the complexity level of the task, and (c) qualities within the personal make-up of the athlete.

A Look at Methods

For the most part, however, both coaches and many sport psychologists are not interested in the theories underlying "getting up" and "calming down." They only want to know what "works" when efforts are made to adjust activation levels of athletes. Among the more popular and effective methods which are applied by sport psychologists around the world are the following:

1. Relaxation Training.

Edmund Jacobson was one of the first writers-researchers to advocate the principles of muscular relaxation, and how muscle tension changes could elicit modifications of emotions and performance. This writer, publishing his work in the 1930s, has been widely copied. Modifications of these techniques are seen not only in contemporary writers about sport psychology, but in literally every kind of "getting-your-head together" self-improvement manual currently on the market.

Sport psychologists in Eastern Europe have seemingly been intrigued with relaxation training, during the decades. As a result, many methods have been described in the literature since the end of World War II. Often these methods involve combining muscular relaxation techniques with various kinds of visual imagery. Moreover, these techniques are used not only to "bring an athlete down" prior to a competition, but also are employed to heighten levels of activation. They believe, for example, that in order to "get someone up," one may best accomplish the task by first relaxing one's athlete client. The first uses of bio-feedback also permeated their methods. Additionally, it is sometimes suggested that the athlete relax a given limb, by imagining it growing hotter. The limb *would* often change temperature as a result of these suggestions.

2. Activation and Individuals.

The sport psychologists in the "Eastern Block" countries often administer muscular relaxation in highly individualistic ways. An individual athlete's activation indicators might be monitored for over a year, prior to a contest. As a competition approaches, these measures are brought up to the individual's optimum, if the psychologist is able to do so.

During the short-term phase the athlete is monitored even more closely. The psychologist may check self-reports of the performer, and consider them in relationship to various measures obtained just hours before competition. At times the psychologist may accompany the athlete into the arena, as final efforts are made to adjust the athlete's activation level to an optimum.

These individualized methods are often engaged in during practices. For example, a diver might be monitored during practice in order to determine what levels of activation immediately preceed a "good effort." A favorite method might consist of monitoring muscular tension in the forehead, using the frontalis muscle. Then during competition and between efforts, the same athlete is monitored, and the activation levels transmitted to him or her. In this way short-term efforts to either activate, or calm, are attempted just prior to each dive, depending upon whether the measure immediately before a competitive dive correlated with a superior effort achieved in practice.

At times the methods and measure employed are less than scientific. However, the benefits gained are often marked. The possible placebo effects engendered in these are welcomed by both athlete and psychologist, when performance improves, with little effort made to determine why the task had been changed. Entire books in the Russian language, for example, deal with these kinds of short-term efforts to change the activation of various athletes.

3. Activation Modeling.

Activation games are sometimes played with athletes. These "strategies" are employed to help the athlete to become able to quickly adjust levels of activation prior to contests. They are used in aiding the performer to quickly adjust activation, when unexpected schedule changes take place. These psychological strategies might consist of informing a performer that a given effort is to be carried out at 3 PM the following afternoon. Measures of activation indices are then taken continuously, up to the performance time indicated. However, at 3 PM the next day, the athlete might be told that "No, we will not perform at 3 PM, but will delay our all-out effort until 5 in the afternoon." The next day, the athlete may be similarly misinformed and then informed again of a schedule change relative to the performance of an all-out effort. During these shifts in scheduling the athlete is carefully watched to find out: (a) what levels of activation are being experienced, (b) what shifts occur in arousal when schedule changes are introduced, and finally (c) how rapidly an athlete's "activation system" accommodates, and in what directions, as schedule changes are introduced.

Other times of stress modeling of this type are employed in the countries in Eastern Europe. For example, changes in activation are measured as athletes perform in front of audiences.

4. Activation Predictions in Time.

At times, an athlete's future prediction of his or her activation levels are obtained, in advance of an important competition. These are sometimes coupled with predictions by the same athlete of the future "readiness" of one or more teammates. These predictions are then contrasted to: (a) actual measures of activation taken at the same time as the contest, (b) measures taken from those teammates about whom the original athlete made the prediction, and most important (c) accuracy of predictions, activation indices, and performance comparisons are made.

5. Monitoring Performance-Delay Periods.

Many sport psychologists in Eastern Europe have described how they carefully measure the amount of "wait" time between efforts in such sports as weight lifting, high-jumping and the like. It is believed that often optimum activation, and thus optimum performance will result if just the "right" time transpires between trials. Additionally, during these breaks, an athlete will be given various mental techniques with which he or she may "psych" themselves up or down. Often the psychologist is able to "get to the athlete" during these intervals to administer special activation or calming techniques. Although many times, neither the athlete nor the psychologist has control over the duration of these time periods, they are considered very important in the activation process. An athlete may be encouraged, for example, to plan special strategies which may be necessary to prolong an activation high, during a prolonged break in the competition. At the same time, if the athlete and coach do exert some control over this interval of time, they are encouraged to do so in ways which will match optimum waiting time with the athlete's best performances.

6. "Self-Psyching."

Several researchers during the 1970s and early 1980s have delved into the processes

Figure 3   Skill imagery often is useful as an athlete learns to relax.

which take place as an athlete is asked to "psyche-himself (or herself up)" (Shelton and Mahoney 1978, Gould and Jackson 1980). These general directions, as might be assumed, were interpreted in various ways by athletes. The types of "psyching up" "self-talk" reported by their subject-athletes are explored in more detail later. For example, some athletes tried to activate themselves in order to improve their attention and concentration (Chapter 7). Others imagine themselves winning and successful. Some attempted to reduce distracting thoughts, while still others tried to readjust their bodily systems in order to meet challenges. These latter athletes would report trying to speed-up their heart rates, or their depth and speed of respiration, or perhaps change their level of muscular tension.

To summarize, the efficiency of "pure" efforts to raise or lower activation is somewhat difficult. Seldom do changes in an athlete's level of arousal occur, without the performer attaching some meaning or label to the change. Often an athlete will, to give one example, begin to feel anxious and afraid of his or her indices of activation rise. On the other hand "getting-down" often signals to the the athlete that fear is being reduced. Others might attach meanings which reflect concerns about concentration, when activation changes. These latter performers might, for example, begin to fear that they are not concentrating well when they begin to feel relaxed.

One researcher crystallized the problem quite well (Lazarus 1966). It was pointed out that as an individual becomes over or under-activated, a verbal label is quickly attached to the feeling. Thus, the performer is highly likely to try to put a label on changes experienced in the body's activation system. Thus, it may be unrealistic on the part of sport psychologists, to administer "pure" methods which purport to modify activation, without helping the athlete-client in attaching realistic interpretations to changes in how aroused the body feels.

In any case, many of the athletes we interviewed reported to us highly useful and creative ways they employed when trying to calm or arouse themselves prior to competition. Although much of the time we did not directly ask the question, many athletes quickly volunteered information about how they aroused or calmed themselves.

WHAT ATHLETES SAY

The various interview-forms we employed in our research did not always contain a direct question concerning how the athlete might activate or calm himself or herself. However, the athletes often covered this topic when they were asked to supply information which might bear upon their psychological preparation. We were also interested in whether or not the athletes often retired to "special preparation places" in order to mentally deal with a forthcoming contest. This latter question was posed in so far as some writers (Kauss 1981) have suggested that this kind of "place" is important in an athlete's pre-contest plans. We also posed queries bearing upon whether or not they had received help by others (psychologists and the like) in their pre-competition readiness programs. When the athlete informed us that he or she did take special "steps" which aided in the pre-contest activation problem, we asked about the nature of the methods they used.

Virtually none of the athletes in our investigations reported that they had a "special place" to which they retired in order to somehow "get themselves" together. However, almost all of the competitors we talked to said that they usually retreated to a "special place" in their minds, prior to contests. Some described a special state of mind, sometimes a kind of "buzzing" high, which they tried to achieve before important competitions. They frequently said that they were able to tell whether or not they would have a good game, or do well, by whether or not they achieved this kind of "special state." More discussion of these "special states" is found in a chapter which follows.

The athletes we interviewed seldom told us that they had had any help in aiding them to adjust their arousal-activation prior to games and competitions. They said that they had either devised their own plans, "just let it happen," or had followed the advice in various of the "psyching-up" sport psychology books available to them.

Several athletes, however, said that at one point in their careers someone from the psychological or psychiatric community had been given permission to aid their team relative to pre-competition preparation. However, they also said that most of the time the contact they had had with this person, and the services they provided were brief. Further, they told us that the psychologist involved had not been considerate of the time they needed for training, and spent too much time in "special kinds" of relaxation training combined with imagery. As a result, the athletes told us, they had discontinued the practices extended to them, as soon as the member of the psychological community broke-off contact with their team. None of the athletes said that the psychologist, or psychiatrist dealing with their team had first approached each member in an effort to determine how each one was already dealing with skill imagery and pre-competition preparation. Rather, the athletes stated, the psychologist involved seemed intent upon applying his or her "system," with a disregard for the possible individual differences in mental activity that were the "possession" of each athlete.

Most of the athletes reported that usually "pure" efforts to get themselves up, or down, prior to a contest were accompanied by other feelings and thoughts. The most common pairing was fear with activation. They equated anxiety with being, or becoming "too high." They also combined feelings of arousal and activation with problems in concentration. They often said that when they became too activated or high, they began to worry about whether or not they were going to be able to concentrate in a forthcoming contest. This kind of worry about concentration as a function of over-activation was a frequent concern of athletes whose competition requirements involved the expression of precise skills.

The athletes interviewed seemed less concerned about being "down" or under-activated. When they did express worry about this too-calm state, they frequently equated this feeling with "not caring" and being under-motivated. Often the athlete that felt himself or herself too frequently down, cast about frantically for a reason for their apparently non-caring posture. The too-calm athletes, however, did not as frequently attach feelings and meanings to their under-activated condition as did the "too high" performers. At times the "down" athlete did not seem energetic enough to even search for reasons for their apparently laizze-faire attitude.

Virtually none of the athletes we interviewed, in a dozen studies, said that they had engaged in calming techniques involving muscular relaxation. A few had heard of these strategies, and had read about them in the numerous books on the subjects. However, few were currently using them in efforts to aid their pre-competition readiness.

The athletes who were the focus of our investigations *did* however, describe highly creative ways in which they tried to manage the tensions which beset them prior to contests. Many of these techniques are not to be found in the currently available "self-help to athletes" books. Some of the helpful techniques explained to us, are as follows:

(a) *Substitution*. Often athletes substituted meaningful or distracting activities, for the "worry time" that frequently plagues competitors prior to contests. Each athlete seemed to have a special way of filling that period of time, during which he or she might have become too activated, or too calm. Some of the activities mentioned most were recreational pursuits and music. Many athletes employed music, in almost ritualistic ways, before games and competitions. Carefully planned recreation, including competition in "light" sports, was also used. Some said that they tried to escape in movies. Most said that the type of movie they watched was important. A too-violent film, for example, was usually avoided. At other times the athlete's said that they thought about the skills and tactics of their sport, in ways that were unemotional and detached from their personal involvement. Thus, mental rehearsal of skills and tactics were used as time-filling techniques.

(b) *Unconsciousness*. We were struck by the marked importance many athletes attached to the precise nature of their sleeping time and patterns prior to games. If the competition was to take place late in the afternoon or evening, they often stayed up late the prior evening, so that they could sleep-away some of the pre-competition time during the day of the contest. In one survey we conducted, about one-fourth of the athletes interviewed said that they managed their pre-competition time with the adjustment of their sleeping habits in this way. Most knew, after awaking, just how much time they needed to become fully activated and ready to perform well. They thus tried to sleep long enough and to awaken at just the right time, prior to a contest, to permit themselves to become fully activated at levels which enabled them to perform at their best.

(c) *Selective Association*. A few of the athletes we talked to reported that they selectively associated with "key" teammates prior to games. This technique, also described in a previous book of mine (Vanek and Cratty 1970), involves attempting to adjust arousal levels by socially contacting and associating with others whose activation levels resemble the level you might be trying to attain. Thus, if you are down and wish to "get up" you associate with an energetic, enthusiastic person. If on the other hand, you are too activated, you seek the company of those who are more calm than you are. This important strategy is discussed further in another part of this chapter.

Overall, therefore, the athletes we contacted were sometimes aware of the "traditional methods" explained in sport psychology books, with which to either calm or activate performers. However, the methods they actually practiced did not often resemble the strategies written about. For the most part they carefully tailored personal methods to meet their needs and unique personalities. The methods many times involved the filling of time, and the shortening of conscious time, just prior to contests.

IMPLICATIONS FOR COACHES AND ATHLETES

Two general approaches may be adopted when trying to adjust the arousal levels of athletes. These same two overall strategies are useful to consider if the athlete is trying to engage in self-management techniques. First, the technique may "zero in" directly upon levels of activation. Using imagery and attempts at adjusting levels of residual muscular tension, the coach or psychologist may try to, in a straight-forward manner, either heighten or lower arousal-activation. Prior to attempting this, of course, assessments of several types should be undertaken. (a) The current activation level of the athlete needs to be considered. (a) The optimum level needed in a given athletic event or contest should also be ascertained. (c) The difference between the current state of an athlete and the requirements of the task should be assessed. (d) The best way to change the activation level of a specific athlete should be decided upon. And finally (e) A judgement should be made concerning whether the athlete in question is a "high" or "low" activation type; whether or not he or she performs best when apparently "too high" . . . or extremely calm.

A second approach involves probing deeper. An attempt might also be made to ascertain *why* an athlete is too high or too calm prior to a contest. This second strategy will often lead both the athlete, and perhaps the psychologist toward methods which include anxiety reduction as explained in Chapter 6. Aggressive feelings and the need for their adjustment may also need to be considered, as strategies are decided upon which purportedly will aid activation levels. These methods are explained in Chapter 5. This second general approach to the adjustment of activation and arousal is a more comprehensive one than simply applying relaxation techniques. It is likely to involve three levels of techniques discussed in Chapter 1: efforts to adjust muscular and physiological responses, visual imagery of various kinds, and finally, various kinds of cognitive-thought change. This third type of "cognitive-type adjustment" is found in several of the following chapters. Examples of some of these strategies for change are discussed below.

Muscular Relaxation Techniques

These techniques have appeared in print, within English language publications, since the 1930s (Jacobson 1938). Muscular relaxation methods are based upon two main ideas: (a) muscular tension in the larger skeletal muscles reflects internal stress, or emotional states; (b) excess, or "residual" muscular tension is often indicative of undesirable anxiety, aggression, and/or depression; (c) learning to control one's muscular tension leads to desirable changes in one's emotional state.

Although these ideas are simple and easily understood, at times muscular relaxation may not "work" with all athletes. Some athletes may not evidence a great deal of muscular tension, when in truth they may be extremely upset prior to a contest. Each athlete evidences a unique pattern of muscular tension changes under stress, which may or may not be "reached" by a given kind of muscular relaxation intervention. That is, the muscle groups which in a given athlete manifest tension changes, may not be those muscle groups which are the focus of another's efforts at muscular tension adjustment.

If a decision is made to use these techniques several general guidelines are useful. (a) These methods may have to be applied over time, as often a few administrations may have little or no discernable effect. Sometimes these techniques "work" immediately, and translate at once into positive performance changes. Other times, they make a difference over time. While in a few cases they may be of little use. (b) Sometimes the athlete may learn to take-over the administration of these methods, after being instructed by another, proficient in their use. At other times, the athlete will continue to need the help of another, when trying to relax. At times self-administration is facilitated if the athlete obtains a tape containing instructions as to how the method is applied to various muscle groups.

A quiet distraction-free place is recommended for the administration of muscular relaxation. The athlete should be in a comfortable, reclining position. A pad under the knees is helpful to relieve strain in the leg muscles. As tension many times is focused in the head-neck region, this may be a good place to start in our instructions. Let's start with the face first. "Tighten your eye brows together. Squint forcefully. Now relax the muscles between your eyes. Take a deep breath inward and exhale it slowly as you try to relax the rest of your face and body. Now let's work with your mouth. Draw the corners of your mouth back in an exaggerated smile. Tighter. Now relax your facial muscles. Now tighten your eyes together again and your mouth "smiling" muscles at the same time. Now relax them and take a deep breath. Clench your jaw muscles. Harder, make them twitch. Now relax and wobble your jaw from side to side. Tighten again, and now relax again, place your hand on your relaxed jaw and move it back and forth, checking to see if you are really relaxed. Now let's go over these muscle groups again, your eyes, mouth, and jaw muscles, only let's tighten then only one-half as hard as you did the first time. On our final round among these muscle groups, let's tighten then, then only one-fourth as hard as we can, while alternately relaxing them as I have shown you."

The neck is an important focal point for the collection of excess tension. Thus, our instructions take us there now. "Move your head back, tighten the back of your neck as you do so. Now relax it forward, slowly. Place your chin on your chest, relax and take a breath as you do so. Let the breath out slowly, and tighten the muscles in the front of your neck, make them hard and large. Touch them with your fingers to see if they are tense. Now relax them, move your head forward and backward gently, to see if the tension is gone, take another deep breath and let it out slowly. Repeat the exercise again with the muscles to the rear of your neck. Move your head down into your shoulders, and lift your shoulders as you do so. Try to tighten both the muscles to the rear, and to the front of your neck as you do so. Now place your head in a normal position, while lowering your shoulders. Relax and take a breath. Repeat these exercises using one-half your maximum tension and then one-fourth of the tension you used the first time around."

Moving down the body, the arms and chest should be dealt with next. "While lying down, rotate your arms inward at the shoulders, tightening the large muscles in the front of your chest as you do so. Now move each arm across your chest tightening these same large chest muscles, as you clench your fists. Relax completely and let your arms move outward at your sides, becoming limp. Take a breath, let it out, and relax. Again cross your chest with your arms, clenching your fists, at one-half tension. Separate each crossing with a relaxation phase, and a deep breath. Repeat these cycles several times. Now use only one-fourth tension as you tighten your arm and chest muscles in the way described. Relax between each cycle, with a breath."

The hips and legs are next, as we work down the body. "As you recline, tighten the large hip muscles as hard as you can, squeeze your hips together as you do so. Now relax them completely. Trying to think that you are now sinking into the mat upon which you are reclining. Now tighten the larger muscles in the front of your legs. Make them hard. Touch them with your hands to see if they are tense. Relax them completely, while taking a deep breath and letting it out. Now try to keep your calf muscles, and those in the rear of your legs relaxed, as you again tighten the muscles in the front of the legs as hard as you can. Now relax them, and breath in and out deeply. The next cycle of hip and leg muscle tightening should be done at one-half tension, and then finally at one-fourth tension. Each cycle should be interpolated by deep breathing as described."

It is sometimes useful to finish such a session, (or to begin it) by using the whole body in an effort to become aware of various amounts of tension.

"As you are lying here, tighten all your muscles as hard as you can. Tighten your face, arms (make your hands into fists), as well as your hips and thighs. Tighten also your chest muscles to the maximum. Hold this tension briefly and then relax. Breath in and out deeply, and try again using only half-tension. Again breath deeply in and out, and now try using only one-fourth of the maximum tension available to you. Continue gradually reducing the amount of tension you exhibit, until you are at one-tenth of your maximum. Be sure to relax between tightening, and to include a deep breath or two during these relaxation periods."

The methods, explained here, are intended to help the athlete become aware of residual or extra muscle tensions, and to vary and control these intensions well. The final objective is to become able to eliminate tensions when they are impeding performing, and contributing to a negative mood state. A program of this type may be engaged in daily for from fifteen to twenty minutes. More than one application daily may be useful also.

Relaxation Training Acompanied by Visual Imagery

Muscular relaxation is often accompanied by visual imagery which is also intended to reduce activation levels, or heighten arousal. Sometimes suggestions for visualization may take place between contractions as is illustrated below.

"Imagine yourself a large balloon. When you take a breath, blow yourself up. As you let out your air, imagine air rushing out of a balloon, and imagine yourself flying around the room as light as a feather."

Sometimes visual imagery may be placed within periods of muscular tension, found in relaxation training. An example follows.

"As you relax your muscles, think of taking all the bones out of your muscles. Pretend that your arms and legs are like just-cooked macaroni, let them flop around. Here, I will lift and drop one to the mat, to see if you are really relaxed."

Tranquility imagery, may also accompany relaxation training, as the following example suggests.

"Imagine yourself beside a still brook. The grass is soft, and smells fresh. Relax back on the grass, and let yourself sink into it." or perhaps . . . "Imagine yourself in the most desirable place you can imagine . . ."

As muscles tighten, imagery may also be employed to heighten the tension desired.

"Make your muscles like steel. A nurse is trying to give you an injection, try to keep the needle out of your arm! Nothing can even scratch the hard surface of your muscles."

Often muscular relaxation is first used, prior to trying to activate an athlete. An athlete may be gotten "higher" by first bringing him or her down in the ways described below (Vanek and Cratty 1970).

"Now you are relaxed, you can visualize the fight in which you must engage! Watch the other fighter (or team) come at you! Be ready to fight (or react) strongly. Show him (them) who is best. Defeat them!"

Or perhaps.

"Imagine your opponent (name him or her) laughing with their friends after the game in which they defeated you . . .! Get mad about their laughing. What are you going to do about the competition, so that they can't enjoy beating you! Show them! Imagine yourself trying hard in competition, never letting up, winning!"

Skill imagery may also be combined with relaxation training in the ways described in the previous chapter. Care must be taken, however, not to bring the athlete to a too low level of tension, or he or she may not become able to visualize skills effectively. A moderate level of relaxation is usually best when it is accompanied by skill imagery, and mental rehearsal of tactics.

Other Methods

As was pointed out in the previous section, athletes often reject operational methods used to relax them, in lieu of simply filling their time prior to contests with distracting activities intended to distract them from the stresses ahead of them. These methods included:

Time Filling. This method is often mentioned by athletes. And as athletes become more experienced they seem to be more structured in how they are likely to spend their pre-contest time. Often these methods, working well for them, are looked upon negatively by their coaches. A mentor may just understand how listening to music prior to a game is helping the athlete prepare. Rather he or she may think that the athlete somehow does not care. Often severe inter-personal conflicts may arise between coach and athlete when there is no mutual agreement upon what constitutes appropriate time-filling activities. When coach and athlete communicate well, mutual agreements may be formulated about this important pre-competition strategy. Often talks about skill and strategy permit the athlete to focus upon meaningful thoughts, thoughts which replace the negative images which may accompany fear during the pre-contest periods.

Sleep, as has been mentioned, represents an important and often-employed time filler. While a too-late awakening may have disastrous results when competition is engaged in, both the coach and athlete may cooperate in planning the sleep schedule of the latter, prior to contests. In this way the late-awakening athlete is not perceived as "lazy" or not caring by the coach, during the pre-game periods.

Selective Association. Selective association was also mentioned as a method by which the athletes we interviewed dealt with activation adjustment prior to contests. Even the casual observer, is aware of the fact that social association ingenders the "catching of behaviors." Social psychologists have also confirmed this kind of tendency for someone to "catch" the behaviors and moods of others with whom they are in close contact. Studies in the 1960s with rowing crews in the Ivy League, produced findings which indicated that the crews who rowed best together, were those whose levels of activation were similar among members. It is often difficult to be around an excited person without being affected by him or her. While the opposite is also true; a "down, or calm" person's mood rubs off on others.

The coach, sensitive to this kind of social contagion, should take it into account during the pre-competition phase. Athletes should be paired with roommates, when possible, who enhance each other's states prior to competition. Coaches, having staffs numbering several assistants, may also "selectively associate" with various athletes prior to contests in efforts to either calm them or relax them to levels which are considered optimum. An overly excited player should go to a movie with a calm coach, and with calm teammates. While a too-calm athlete may also be encouraged to "hang-around" with a more inspiring mentor, before a game.

Often the nature of the tasks will dictate the best associations to be formed before competitions. A few years ago in Canada, two coaches approached me after I had spoken on this topic. These two figure-skating mentors said that they would in the future follow the principles outlined. One believed himself to be excitable, and thus he said that he would associate most with the national team just prior to the execution of their compulsory routines, routines which require energy and strength. On the other hand, mused the quieter of the two, he said that he would talk most to the team prior to the execution of the precise school-figure phase of the competition.

OVERVIEW

Levels of activation experienced by an athlete are likely to exert obvious influences upon subsequent performances. High levels of arousal may improve direct forceful acts, and well-learned skills. Whereas, these same high levels are likely to disrupt complex, recently acquired responses among athletes. The adjustment of activation levels must take into account the current level of an athlete, the requirements of a given task, as well as what kind of "activation type" the athlete seems to be. Some athletes usually perform best when excited, while others consistently radiate a calmer exterior, and yet perform well.

Muscular tension activities have been traditionally used to lower levels of activation. More recently these techniques have been employed in combinations of methods including visual imagery, as well as various efforts to mentally adjust the thoughts of athletes. Activation techniques are effectively combined with other kinds of strategies intended to alter physical skills, aggressive content of thoughts, as well as fear and anxiety.

Activation adjustment strategies also include: (a) time-filling techniques intended to distract the athlete from thoughts of an impending contest, (b) selective association, involving the pairing of people socially prior to contests, so that desirable levels of activation are "transmitted" from one to the other, as well as (c) the adjustment of sleep-awake patterns before games and contests. In this third strategy, the effort is made to fill "worry time" before competition, with useful and restful sleep, and to awake with enough time to engage in proper activation techniques.

REFERENCES

Cratty, B.J., Chapter 10, "Anxiety, stress and tension," *Movement Behavior and Motor Learning,* Lea and Febiger, 3rd Ed., Philadelphia, PA, 1973.

Jacobson, E., *Muscular Relaxation,* University of Chicago Press, Chicago Illinois, 1938.

Kauss, D., *Peak Performance,* Prentice-Hall, Englewood Cliffs, NJ, 1981.

Lazarus, R.S., *Psychological Stress and the Coping Process,* McGraw-Hill, New York, 1966.

Shelton, T.O., and M.J. Mahoney, "The content and effect of psyching-up strategies in weight lifters," *Cognitive Therapy and Research,* 1978, 2 (3), pp. 275-284.

Vanek M. and B.J. Cratty, *The Psychology of the Superior Athlete,* MacMillan Co., New York, 1970.

Weinberg, R.S., D. Gould, and A. Jackson, "Cognitive and motor performance; effect of psyching-up strategies on three motor tasks," *Cognitive Therapy and Research,* 1980, 4 (2), pp. 239-84.

CHAPTER 5

THE CONTROL AND ADJUSTMENT OF AGGRESSION

The word aggression appears frequently on the pages of our daily newspaper. On the front pages the term may be used to denote the savagery of a war, or of the currently "popular" mini-war! In the business section the word might refer to how the stock market is acting, or perhaps used to descibe the merger of two companies. On the sport page, the words anger and aggression may be given either negative or positive meanings. On the one hand, aggression may refer to highly motivated effort by an athlete. In contrast, anger and aggression may be used in a story describing how a fight interfered with the orderly progression of a game.

The psychological literature also differentiates between anger and aggression which denotes trying hard, and the use of these same words, to denote attempts at mayhem and murder. "Instrumental aggression" is used to signify behavior which infers that people are simply striving to their ultimate, but within socially acceptable rules. "Retaliatory aggression" on the other hand, is used by social psychologists to refer to intentions to inflict either bodily harm, or psychological embarassment to another person.

When we questioned athletes, they seldom denied that they were "aggressive." This was particularly noticeable in interviews held with athletes in sports in which effort against others is called for, including waterpolo, karate, football, boxing, and the like. The folklore of these and many similar sports includes demands for intense effort, and athletes are well aware of what is expected of them in these kinds of competitions. When questioned in depth, however, these same athletes usually explained that they used the word aggression to mean that they always tried as hard as they could. Most, however, hastened to explain that "aggression" to him or her did not mean hurting someone else in ways which were not condoned within the rules of their sport. A few, however, admitted that they often aggressed in ways which were not acceptable to many. One athlete explained tht he would, at times, attempt to block an opponent's throwing motion just as it started, in an effort to dislocate his opponent's shoulder!

Often, however, the athletes we questioned described aggression in ways which met the demands of their sport. Thus, the directions and methods of aggression, within the rules, may vary from competitor to competitor. A few years ago I developed a "scale" upon which sports may be contrasted, relative to the nature of the aggression sanctioned, as well as to the direction that anger may be expressed. For example:

1. Direct aggression against another person may be part of the sport. Examples of activities in this category include boxing, some skills in American football, kick-

boxing, and the like.

2. Limited aggression is sanctioned against the person of another. These semi-contact sports include waterpolo, basketball, team handball, as well as soccer football.

3. Indirect aggression is seen in many sports efforts against balls in ways which then transfer an athlete's power against his or her opponent. These include volleyball, tennis, and the like in which force is "felt" indirectly by one's opponent.

4. Aggression may only be directed against objects or apparatus. Golf and other sports involving giving impetus to objects, without those objects then imposing upon another person directly, are examples.

5. Sports may involve relatively little aggression, and mainly consist of aesthetic expression. These include ice-skating, rhythmic (modern) gymnastics, and the like. Even in these activities however, it is not uncommon to hear a competitor describe the ways in which they "attack" their routine aggressively.

In general, there is a rough correspondence between the kinds of aggression expressed by athletes as the describe themselves in their sport, and the degree and type of aggression required in that sport.

When athletes are asked to describe the content of their mental lives which revolve around sport, aggression and anger occupies various "niches" within their psyches. Dreams may contain aggressive content, for example. Athletes may also say that they often try to "think aggressively" just before a game. This attempt to "get themselves up" by thinking aggressively may take the form of anger directed toward a specific team or player, or consist of angry thoughts about more general components of an upcoming contest. Reports about focusing aggressive thoughts against specific people are often obtained from athletes in contact sports. "I hate quarterbacks," a defensive back in American Football recently informed us. Questioned further, he admitted that his hatred was irrational. However, he insisted that he detested anyone who happened to occupy that position on an opposing team!

Mental "game plans" formulated by athletes prior to important competitions, will usually not include aggressive acts which are in excess of what is permitted by the rules. However, these same athletes will invariably say that if excess physical force is used against them, they will instantly retaliate.

The words aggression and anger, do not as often "pop up," in conversation with athletes whose sports do not involve direct physical contact. But at times, after some indepth questioning even "lady" distance runners will admit that sometimes they may try to "destroy" another competitor as they pass her in an important race.

Scholars from a number of subject areas, ranging from philosophy to neurology and bio-chemistry, have been interested in the concepts and manifestation of aggression and anger. Over the years several useful psychological models have been formulated in an attempt to explain and predict aggression in humans. Some of these theories have useful implications for those dealing with aggression in athletics and athletes.

Naturalists for decades have explored the causes and forms of aggression seen in various animal groups. Often the parallels for the causes of animal and human aggression are striking. Overcrowding, for example, seems to elicit inter-personal anger in both animals and humans.

Psychologists interested in the developing child have also devoted a great deal of study to the formation of aggressive content within the immature personality. The effects of children viewing films of aggressive acts, for example, are a frequent focus of their efforts. The ways in which aggressive human "models" may trigger anger by children viewing this kind of "mature" aggressor, have important implications for those trying to optimize the emotional values in "little league" types of sport.

More recently attention by writers and researchers has become laden with ideas about how one may control aggression, that is in excess of what is useful to one's functioning. One of the more useful strategies to emerge has been the use of cognitive adjustments, modifications of thought, usually accomplished through the use of ways to change how an individual talks to himself . . . or herself. These studies have been summarized by Novaco in 1979. The content of these investigations has provided information and methods which are drawn upon, within other parts of this chapter.

The subject of aggression in athletes and athletics has disturbed many throughout the world, during the past several decades. The aggressive acts of sport "fans" have also concerned many observers of the "passing scene." Numerous conferences have devoted a considerable amount of time and effort discussing ways of dealing with the problems of violence in sports and in sport stadia. In the late 1970s for example, a convention of leaders from fifteen international sports federations met in Europe to discuss the reduction of violence in sporting environments. Similar conferences have been held in this country also.

The ways in which societal aggression and violence in general and violence in sport intermingle are difficult to objectify and untangle. Among the difficult questions which beg answers include: Are riots in stadia reflections of, or instigators of violence in a given culture? Would the use of pre-Olympic meetings among social psychologists of sport from various countries help to dispel the combinations of situations and people in Olympic competitions which often trigger overly aggressive acts?

Questions regarding aggression and anger at the level of the single athlete also are important to ask. For example, how much aggressive thought is desirable and undesirable in the athletes competing in various sports? And perhaps most important . . . how might aggression in the thoughts and acts of athletes be kept within reasonable and useful boundaries? For the most part the focus of this chapter is upon answers to these latter queries. However, understanding the broader questions linking violence in sport and society form the bases of attempts to deal with anger within the heart of the individual athlete.

WHAT THE RESEARCH SAYS

The first scientific interest in aggression often revolved around behaviors observed in the animal kingdom. For many decades naturalists concluded that aggression in humans was instinctual and inbred, because angry competition was so often observed among animals at many levels on the evolutionary scale. Some, who advance that sport as a useful way to re-direct aggression, base their suggestions upon this kind of "instinctual" theorizing. They reason that it is truly impossible to ever eliminate aggression in sport and in life, and therefore the best one is able to accomplish is to simply reduce the way in which anger is expressed by providing athletics as a re-directing mechanism.

This kind of model is also transfered in other ways to sport. Parallels between the aggressive territory-seeking seen in many animals and the ways in which football teams push each other up and down the field seeking territory has been discussed in

some books. The ways both athletes and animals often seek to intimidate each other by leveling unwavering "hate-looks" at each other, has often been noted. While the ways in which status hierarchies in both sports teams, and in animal groups resemble each other, has been written about by more than one sociologist and social psychologist studying the inter-personal dynamics within athletics. Animals in the farmyards and on the plains of Africa try to intimidate and to best each other physically in ways which are remarkably similar to activities found within tennis and basketball tournaments.

Later, more sophisticated attempts to determine the causes of human aggression, resulted in a expanded list of reasons. Frustration was identified by many as a major cause of excessive anger. Others observed that aggression also seemed to be learned by children during their formative years, as they watched parents express anger. Contemporary lists of the instigators of aggression include: (a) Changes in activation level of the one annoyed seem to make a difference. Generally higher levels of activation, sometimes the result of exercise, may serve to heighten aggressive tendencies. (b) Thoughts an individual has about his or her annoyer also seem to make a difference as to whether any retaliation is engaged in. (c) Various kinds of demonstrations, and films may trigger violent reactions by onlookers. (d) An individual's childhood experiences often are predictors of aggression seen in adolescence and adulthood. Generally a childhood in which one has either been the focus of a great deal of parental aggression or which has been marked by parental leniency toward aggression expressed by a child are likely to result in later unvented anger of a high level. (e) Fitness levels have recently been studied as a predictor of aggression, as have athletic experiences in both contact and non-contact sports.

As can be seen, many of these potential "triggers" of aggression have implications for sport and for the athlete. Also containing useful guidelines for athletes is recent literature dealing with how one might place aggressive thoughts and actions within useful limits. This same research indicates ways in which athletes may potentially channel aggressive feelings into constructive improvements in skill and well-focused effort. In the following section some of the research about aggression in sport will be discussed.

Aggression in Sport

Some sport psychologists have written in theoretical ways about aggression and its manifestation in athletics. Others, however, have gone directly to team situations, or to individual athletes and studied anger in "real life" settings. For example, a Russian social psychologist with whom I have worked has identified aggression among team members. He identifies the presence of what he terms "victims" and "aggressors" within teams; these consist of some individuals who "lord it over" others, and aggress psychologically against other team members and others who are "victims" of this kind of oppressive behavior. In our writings on the subject we have attempted to portray how these inter-personal differences might be resolved (Cratty and Hanin 1980).

Other psychologists in Europe have placed themselves next to soccer football games, recording the number of fouls committed under various circumstances. The "closeness" of a game, the presence of hostile spectators, as well as the standings of the two teams involved all have been shown to have elevated the number of personal contact of an illegal nature which have been recorded.

Recent investigations in this country have contrasted various groups, to determine differences in the amount of aggression they evidence. Contact sport athletes, for example, seem to be more able to control their aggressions, than do those in non-contact sports when both groups are annoyed in various ways. The more fit athlete also seems to somehow be able to calm himself or herself quicker and more effectively than is true of the less fit performer.

Taken together these lists of variables have begun to provide a reasonably clear picture of the reasons which, if combined, are highly likely to trigger "retaliatory" aggression in sport. What is not clear, however, is the relative importance of the various causes. Also still under investigation are the influences of various thoughts upon aggression. It is probable that more aggression will occur when the one annoyed believes that retaliation will not likely be directed his or her way. Likewise, what an athlete believes about his or her own capacities for retaliation seem important as a molder for subsequent expressions of anger. However, the interaction of these kinds of thoughts with other factors within the environment are still under study.

Recent research, however, makes it rather clear that previously held ideas about aggression in athletics are probably not true. For example, the assertion that sport somehow may channel unwanted anger, and act as a "safety valve" for excess aggression is highly questionable. When fans are interviewed, for example, after watching an aggressive sporting contest, their anger is likely to be heightened. The statement that one may somehow direct aggressions against something or someone other than the annoyer, is also open to question. Research has found, for example, that major satisfaction when annoyed, may be gained primarily by retaliating in a direct way against the person of the annoyer, rather than by "kicking a locker."

Another difficult problem area concerns the manner in which an athlete may somehow manage aggressive tendencies after his or her career ends. The special help that many athletes may need at this terminal point in their careers, has been outlined in a splendid book by Arnold Beisser, titled: *The Madness in Sport.*

The instigators of aggression in young ice hockey players has been explored in several studies supported by the Canadian government. Fights on television among major professional teams, for example, have been contrasted to aggressive incidents occurring among youngsters the next day in junior competitions. In a similar vein the manner in which various "others" associated with junior ice-hockey may influence youthful anger in practices and games has also been studied. In one investigation, for example, it was found that young boys believed that hitting outside the rules was all right, because of pressures from their own young friends. In this same investigation, pressures from their coaches and family were not blamed for the boys' aggression on the ice.

Finally, the assumption by some coaches that "if I can just get my player(s) mad enough he/she (they) will perform well," has come under scrutiny. Effective coaches have come to realize that an overly aggressive player will manifest behaviors which are not only out of control, but also may markedly blunt game skills.

Currently, therefore, the "picture" the research "paints" about aggression in sport, is not a simple graphic. Single sentence platitudes, sometimes searched for by coaches, will not suffice to explain how aggression takes place in sport; who is likely to be an aggressor, why it occurs, as well as when such incidents are likely to happen. It is becoming increasingly apparent that when trying to explain the intricate intertwining of aggression and athletic competition, several groups of causes must be examined. These categories include: (a) The sanctions the society (and sub-culture) in which the athlete performs, places on aggression, as well as the prohibitions against aggression which may also be present. (b) The nature of the annoyance is also important. Both the intensity and type, as well as the source of annoyance is vital to consider. (c) The fitness and physiological make-up of the individual annoyed are in a third critical category. The individual's fitness seems to reflect how well the person's body can somehow "calm itself" after an annoying incident has taken place. (d) Finally, the thoughts the athlete dwells upon when annoyed are critical. What the athlete thinks about his/her personal capacities for retaliation, and about the capacities of the annoyer for further aggression are both important. The athlete's interpretations of the nature of the situation in which annoyance takes place, are also useful variables to consider when formulating the probabilities that aggression will likely occur.

Among the social variables to consider, research has shown, include whether or not the athlete aggressed against, and is performing in front of a home or visiting crowd More aggression is likely if the athlete is not only assailed physically by an opponent, but also if he or she is performing in front of a hostile visiting group of spectators. Strenuous re-aggression, against an annoyer, is more likely when an athlete is in a hostile social setting, as he or she may be "taking out" anger on an opposing player, anger which is actually being felt against spectators in the stands.

Fit athletes seem to be better able to resist overly aggressive retaliation if they are annoyed. Their arousal-activation mechanism seem to gain a harmonious balance, rather quickly after an imbalance has taken place. On the other hand, the less fit performer may remain angry longer, and may be less likely to channel emotional upset experienced into useful manifestations of effort and skill. In a similar manner, the coach who is less fit may remain agitated longer after a decision has gone against the team, than is true of one whose cardio-vascular system is stronger. The "out-of-control," unfit coach may also be one whose decisions under stress are less likely to help the team's performance!

The process of aggression may be looked upon as occurring over time, following an annoyance in competition. This process involves a number of thoughts to be weighed in the mind of the athlete, including whether to aggress physically and immediately, whether to postpone aggression, or to defer aggression indefinitely and perhaps channel the emotional activation experienced into improved effort and skill performed within the rules of the game. These decisions are based upon the athlete's evaluations of: (a) the capacity of the annoyer to retaliate, (b) the athlete's assessments of his or her own capacities to retaliate, (c) whether or not the annoyer intended to aggress (evaluating the motivation of the annoyer is important), (d) the possible amount of guilt that may be experienced if retaliation does not occur, as well as guilt that may be connected with subsequent injury to the annoyer as the result of retaliation, and (e) whether or not someone else, an official or teammate may make the annoyer "pay" for the transgression.

The interactions of these various psychological "forces" may be diagrammed as seen on page 63.

An Aggressive Situation

Considered collectively, the available data suggests that a situation containing several conditions might yield a high probability that an act of aggression will occur. An example of a situation containing this group of explosive variables might consist of the following.

An athlete enters a game in a semi-contact sport, involving two teams from sections of a country that have been political rivals for centuries. The athlete is not very fit, and is nearing the end of his career. He has a powerful physique like his father,

CHART 7

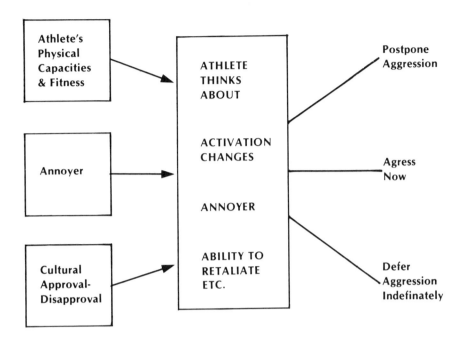

who often beat him when he was a child for the least transgression. The game is being played in front of his opponent's home crowd. The teams are close in the standings, with our athlete's team slightly ahead of their opponents at the time the athlete comes in. The coach and other players on the team expect our athlete to act as an "enforcer" for personal fouls that were committed against team members earlier in the contest.

During the first part of the game, as the player sat on the bench, he noticed that the referees were not very capable or courageous. Their decisions seemed to favor the home team, his opponents. Just after a goal is scored against his team making the score 1-2, a smaller player on the opposing team unexpectedly hits "our hero" a foul blow, and then manages to get away unnoticed by the referees. At this point our hero "boils over" and, as his heart rate rises sharply, he storms after the other player. But before he reaches the annoyer, he is taken out of the game by the coach for a "rest."

As our player sits on the side lines, he remains angry and aroused. His thoughts are grim, and focused upon the player who fouled him illegally and continues to do so to other members of his team without being punished by the referees. Ten minutes later our player, still furious, enters the game and immediately stalks his annoyer, and hits him, putting him out for the remainder of the contest.

An Interpretation

In the situation described the conditions collectively optimized (negativized!), in a way which heightened probabilities that undue aggression would occur. The fitness of the athlete was low, while the threat of the annoyer's ability to retaliate was slight. He was small. The possibility of others, the weak referees, disciplining the annoyer was not good. The annoyer was not being disciplined by teammates. Various social conditions also invited aggression, including the presence of hostile fans, the coach's attitude toward aggression, as well as sanctions apparent from his teammates. The long-time rivalry between "traditionally" political sports opponents would also likely raise chances of aggression occurring.

Additionally, the situation described illustrates what is termed a "delayed reaction" frequently encountered in sport. Our athlete smoldered on the side lines, while his poor fitness level did little to turn on "self-calming" mechanisms which might have been present in the physiological make-ups of more fit players. Thus, as the athlete, while on the side lines, continued to monitor and interpret the internal signs of arousal he felt as meaning "I am very mad." His side line "smolder" was "fanned" by his observation that his annoyer continued to aggress against others.

In the situation described, the prognosis was a rather bleak one, relative to halting aggression. In the real world there are often opportunities for both athletes and coaches to both monitor the possible accumulation of "signs" such as those just described, and at the same time to take positive actions which will forestall the occurrence of violent behaviors. These methods may serve to help the athlete place himself or herself under good control, and to perform better. Some of the more promising of these methods involve "cognitive behavioral therapy." Examples of this technique are found in the final section of the chapter. The often subtle ways in which aggression enters our thoughts and those of athletes is explained in the following section labeled "What Athletes Say." Consideration of this information with the "state of the art" research which has been reviewed are intended to aid both athletes and coaches alike to place anger and aggressive behaviors into proper perspective.

What Athletes Say

Our first studies of the mental lives of athletes contained only general questions delving into aggressive thoughts and behavior. As my staff and I gained more sophistication, and greater insight, we posed our questions so that responses might be placed on various scales. One of these dimensions reflected locations and situations in which aggresstion might occur. A second "intensity" scale was also used. Additiontionally there were three inter-personal dimensions, consisting of categories into which aggressive reports might be placed. An athlete might direct aggressive thoughts or actions against "general others" to give one example. This person would not have a name, but would consist of a "faceless" member of an opposing team. A second inter-personal category involved aggression toward a specifically named other person. Often it was a player on the opposing team who seemed to pose a threat to the athlete about to enter a contest. A third inter-personal dimension, involving direction of aggression, was anger that athlete directed toward himself or herself.

Intensity of aggression was thus scored using the following scale. It was originally used in the research to score aggression people reported in dreams. The scale consists of the following parts.

0 — No aggressive feelings consciously expressed or felt.

1 — Aggression only in terms of trying harder. "Instrumental aggression according to the psychologists.

2 — Aggression in personal terms, which is intended to psychologically embarass the other person.

3. —Aggression occurring physically, but expressed as retribution for physical

acts which first come toward the athlete involved.

4 — Aggression to cause physical harm. This may be the result of an initial annoyance, or simply engendered by the athlete without apparent cause.

5 — Aggression involving the imagery of killing another.

Situational dimensions of our questions included:

(a) Practice sessions: Aggression actually directed toward teammates, or imagery of that nature.

(b) In games and competitions: Physical acts, as well as imagery containing aggression.

(c) In dreams: Aggression observed, felt, or administered during a "typical sport dream."

(d) When being annoyed, while outside a practice or game. The aggression imagery in this "situation" was among the most intense we obtained from athletes.

(e) When imagining competitions: Imagery related to sporting competitions, contests, and meets.

(f) When "just walking around," in the absence of an obvious annoyer, or annoyance.

Our first interviews focused on aggression reported by athletes while engaged in their sport, during competition, and practices. Later, however, we found that often the most intense aggression and anger occurred within the thoughts of athletes when they were "just walking around," and particularly when they were confronted with some kind of "annoyer." Often competitors said that during competitions and even during practices they controlled aggressive thoughts, and focused upon improved effort and skill. In contrast, these same athletes often engaged in highly aggressive imagery when they were insulted, or otherwise affronted by situations in other facets of their lives.

This dichotomy was quite obvious when we interviewed athletes training in the martial arts. Because of the tranquility that is supposed to surround the execution of their skills, they consistently informed us that they did not imagine excess hostility toward their opponents during competition or practices. Rather they said they executed their skills dispassionately, and effectively. On the other hand, these same athletes said that they often imagined themselves physically dismembering and destroying people who irritated them in situations they encountered in every-day life.

When we asked competitors in various sports about aggression their first answers often reflected stereotypes that usually surround their sport, or the positions they played. American football players would tell us that "I must be aggressive in order to play well." However, when more penetrating questions were posed, subtle dimensions of their aggressive thoughts and imagery emerged. For example, quarterbacks and pass-catchers in American football usually said that they directed their aggressive feelings in ways that would improve their skill, rather than against specific opponents or an opposing team as a whole. Linemen in this same sport, however, often reported that they felt anger, and "turned on mental pictures" of specific opponents in order to heighten that anger, and thus produce greater effort in a forthcoming contest.

Athletes in semi-contact sports such as basketball and waterpolo also reported aggressive thoughts, but they also realized that these thoughts, if out of control, would likely disrupt skill. For the most part they said that "aggression" in the form of physical retribution only entered their heads when an opponent had first fouled them outside the rules. Like the "skill" players in football, these other athletes said that they also channeled their anger into improved effort in such skills as rebounding and the like.

Often athletes in various aesthetic non-aggressive sporting activities denied harboring any overly aggressive feelings about their sport. Competitors in figure skating, gymnastics and the like said, however, that they often tend to attack their routines "aggressively." When interviews were conducted in more depth these same athletes often admitted that at times they will select specific opponents and direct various amounts of hatred and anger against him or her. They reported that sometimes imagining undesirable qualities in their opponents helped them do better in certain competitions. Endurance runners have also told us that as they expend effort and encounter fatigue during races, they will sometimes imagine themselves physically harming an opponent as they pass him or her.

The most vivid and interesting account of feelings and images of aggression were obtained from athletes engaged in the martial arts sports. As has been pointed out, the most intense aggression they would often report, was imagery against anyone who insulted them, as they "just walked around." In contrast the imagery the reported during practices and competitions reflected the tranquility that permeates the original philosophies which surround such activities. The attitude that many of these athletes seemed to have adopted was a schizophrenic mentality that on one hand permitted the individual to aggress physically with great vigor, while remaining outwardly calm and peaceful (Cratty, Lange and Whipple 1984).

Many of the female karate competitors had little reluctance to discuss the aggression they imagined during their everyday experiences. Some, as might be expected, had entered the sport because they had been physically attacked on the streets. They thus harbored rather dark thoughts about their previous attackers, and others who might harm their person. For the most part, however, they channeled this anger into very intense practices and competitions. They thus believed, probably correctly, that these skills would make future attacks upon them less likely.

Collectively, karate competitors said that the intent in this sport is to explode vigorously and at the same time exhibit few outward signs of aggression. Enhancing these outbursts of effort are noises which they emit (called "kaki"). These noises they believe, will help them to strike harder. They also said that they tried to keep aggressive feelings, and other emotions from being reflected in their faces as they compete. In this way they believed that they would not "tip off" an opponent to their future intentions in a contest. Thus, their opponent was unlikely to know when they would counter-attack. They said that keeping this outward calm on their faces, contributed to an inner serenity, and thus helped them to heighten the levels of skill they might display.

Karate competitors also reported upon another dimension of aggression which we had not obtained from athletes in other sports. Virtually all reported that as they achieved higher levels of skill, they began to present a more self-confident image to others. Thus, they believed, that as they began to walk and to move in more self-assured ways they were less likely to attack the aggression of others. Thus, they believed that karate practice had helped them in several ways: (a) it had provided them with physical skills needed to fend off others, (b) it had given them internal security, calm and self-assurance, and (c) it has made them appear to others to be more impregnable and thus less likely to be an easy victim of an attack.

For example, one young woman who had been in the sport of karate for four years said that "Prior to my participation in karate, people said that my appearance invited antagonism from others, however, after taking up the sport and gaining skills, I am told that I present a more serene and confidence "picture" to others. I thus feel that I do not give off as many negative and insecure "vibrations," and thus am less likely to antagonize others."

Gaining these skills, these athletes further informed us, made them more aware of what was going on around them, and of people and situations which might endanger them. Thus, they reported that in the future they would tend to act effectively when dangerous situations occurred, rather than in a passive manner as they had done in the past. One woman informed us that "If I am threatened in the future, I am sure that I will *not* do nothing."

Furthermore, the dream content of women who participated in karate, changed as they gained proficiency in the skills involved. The dreams of these well-tained women contained "scenes" of them dealing out, rather than accepting aggression. More is said about the dream content of these competitors in Chapter 8.

In summary, our studies of athletes indicated that the nature of the aggression they engaged in mentally generally reflected both the demands of the sport, as well as the philosophy and folklore which surrounded their sport. Aggression was experienced by athletes in many ways, and was used by them in ways which were often creative. Some used anger to channel and improve concentration and skill. Others employed aggression as ways of heightened all-out physical effort; while still others while reducing aggressive thoughts in competitions, often reported that these same thoughts seemed to "spill over" into their daily lives, and into their dreams.

For the most part successful athletes said that they had devised strategies which helped *them to use aggression* in useful and positive ways as they enhanced their performance. In contrast, it was found that often less successful athletes reported that at times *aggressive thoughts seemed to consume and to use them* in ways that were less than useful. In the following section are contained implications, as well as specific strategies for re-directing anger which may be potentially disruptive to the athlete's endeavors.

IMPLICATIONS FOR COACHES AND ATHLETES

Generally, the available research indicates that what an athlete thinks about an aggressor, or a situation in which aggression is likely to take place, greatly influences what the athlete is likely to feel and thus to do. Further, when trying to modify the aggressive imagery of an athlete, one should thoroughly understand all the possible components of a situation which are likely to process excess anger. The modification of aggression so that the anger is either displaced or focused upon skill performance and maximum effort, should be predicted upon several principles. These ideas and guidelines have been suggested by advocates of both cognitive-behavioral therapy, and its close cousin, "rational-emotive therapy."

1. The athlete can often do little to alter situations which are likely to cause stress and anger. What the athlete *can* accomplish, however, is to learn to control his or her *feelings* about what is, or will likely occur in a given situation. The competitor may thus learn to reduce his or her over-reactions to annoyers encountered in sport, and to acquire behaviors which positively contribute to the sport, and which positively influence the actions of others in close proximity.

2. The anger seen in an athlete does not occur unsupported by thought. Thus, to

modify levels of aggression and anger one must learn how to change how one thinks.

3. Thoughts like other forms of behavior may be learned, forgotten, modified, and remembered. Thus, an athlete who is plagued by too frequent outbursts of anger in sport, should learn to replace overly aggressive thoughts with those reflecting careful and calm appraisals of stressful situations and thoughts, which undergird positive forms of action. Forming thoughts which encourage concentration, rather than those involving the striking of an opponent, would be an example of this kind of re-adjustment process.

4. Often overly aggressive feelings, and feelings of anxiety and frustration stem from various irrational beliefs about one's apparent need for perfection. Other irrational beliefs that may plague an individual who constantly displays angry outbursts, include feelings that all people and situations must be perfectly in tune with his or her needs and expectations. Acceptance of this principle thus suggests that an athlete should expect, and not be surprised when an opponent acts in an overly angry manner in a game. An athlete, should strive for excellence and to demonstrate maximum effort, but should not expect the outcome to always be a perfect score, and a winning competition.

5. Thus, for an athlete to control his or her own aggressions an effort should be made to place competition into perspective, and to make rational and reasonable judgements about the actions of one's opponents and coaches, as well as about the social context in which athletics occurs.

6. The athlete should also learn to work on aggression control along a time continuum. The athlete should learn to predict what future situations might trigger excess anger. Then an effort should be made to adjust the possible changes in activation and arousal which these feelings of impending confrontation may engender. Next, the athlete must learn how to manage aggression during a contest; his or her personal aggressive feelings, as well as the aggression that is directed toward him or her. Finally, the athlete should become able to reflect back upon anger which may have been manifested within a previous contest. This reflection backward in time, should include a reasonable appraisal of what occurred, and thoughts about how future situations may be better "managed."

7. One may also deal with aggression at several levels, levels which have been previously refered to. These include attempts at modifying muscular and physiological responses; the production and focusing of visual imagery, and finally the re-structuring of thought. Thoughts which often must be re-structured include those involving the athlete's perceptions about an annoyer and his or her motives, perceptions of changes in the athlete's own activation system, and the meanings these may have, as well as thoughts the athlete might have about the results of his or her retaliation against an annoyer. Often the athlete may need to, sometimes with the help of another, employ two or more of these "levels" when attempting to curb and re-direct aggression.

8. Often aggression reduction is not the only answer. Anger must often be re-directed. It has been found, for example, that often when aggression cannot be acted upon, or re-directed in useful ways the individual may suffer from anxiety and depression. Thus, when an athlete is extremely agitated, trying merely to subordinate aggressive emotions may lead to problems greater than the problem originally being dealt with.

In the paragraphs which follow several courses of action to reduce and re-direct aggression are outlined. A major emphasis will be placed upon the adjustment of thinking and of thoughts and imagery which support anger.

Cognitive Adjustments

A primary tool of cognitive behavioral therapy is the use of "self-talk." The procedures followed, essentially involve encouraging someone to:

(a) Suppress things that they may say to themselves which are negative, and/or may support behaviors which are undesirable. In the case of an overly aggressive athlete, these kinds of negative "self-talk" might consist of angry phrases muttered under his or her breath describing physical acts to be committed against another player.

CHART Q

Chains of Thoughts and Behavior Assumed by Cognitive Behavioral Therapists.

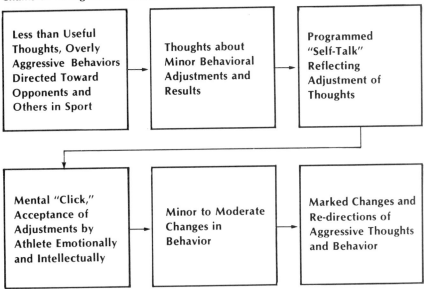

(b) Next positive "self-talk" is substituted. In this case an athlete might be encouraged to voice positive and useful statements, when angered by another in a game. These might include phrases reflecting how the athlete might be attempting to calm himself or herself; or perhaps other "internal" statements which indicate that the athlete is going to try harder to win after being annoyed.

Initially these positive "self-talk" statements are repeated in a parrot-like fashion, usually at the suggestion of another. However, with time, it is suggested by cognitive behavioral therapists, the user may come to believe them, and to act in different ways supported by a real belief in the efficiency of the new behaviors. This internal cognitive adjustment is sometimes referred to as a "cognitive click" by those writing about this useful form of intellectual intervention. The chance of this change occurring, is of course enhanced if the new "internal speech" leads initially to changes in behaviors which are obviously useful and satisfying.

It is decided that an athlete needs help to control aggression, and that cognitive adjustment techniques may prove useful; there are several important next steps to be taken. These include: (a) discussing the general causes of anger and of aggression responses, (b) deciding just what situationally specific "things" in a forthcoming contest will likely trigger too much anger, and (c) formulating a plan of action, a strategy for changing both angry thoughts and the aggressive behaviors which these thoughts may trigger.

After these general steps are taken, a more specific plan of action is needed. This plan should include attempts to modify the athlete's thoughts and feelings before the contest, ways to change the athlete's thinking during the competition, and lastly dealing with the thoughts that occur after the contest is over. The precise components of this "specific plan" are discussed below.

Discussing Causes.

First the athlete should be encouraged to think about what generally causes overly aggressive reactions in him or her, as well as to dwell upon how often and in what form these kinds of aggression-triggering situations take place in his or her sport. This phase is usually facilitated by the help of a psychologist. In this way the athlete should be better prepared to meet possible "surprises" which may arise in an impending contest, as well as sudden changes in activation the athlete may experience as a competition approaches. The causes discussed can include the appearance of "certain" opponents, as well as the presence of the athlete within threatening or stressful environments.

Situationally Specific Conditions

Next the athlete should be guided toward grasping and innumerating the specific conditions in a forthcoming contest that may "trigger" aggressive emotions and actions. Analyses should be made, for example, of what has caused the athlete to become mad in the past, in a same or in a similar competition. These causes might include the arrogance of an opposing player, the coach from the other team, a poor or biased official, unruly fans from the opposing team, or perhaps the behaviors from the athlete's own teammates when they are under stress.

During this detailed pre-contest appraisal, the athlete should be encouraged to consider also what the past consequences were for engaging in an aggressive act. Both favorable as well as unfavorable outcomes for past aggressions may be discussed, and listed. If in the past, for example, the athlete has scored when angry, this should be noted. On the other hand, expulsion from a game, as an outcome of anger should also be discussed.

The Formulation of a Plan

Next, both the athlete and his or her "helper" (coach and/or psychologist) should formulate a detailed plan for confronting and adjusting aggressive emotions and behaviors which may occur as the result of a forthcoming competition. This plan should involve specific "self-talk" statements which reflect the athlete's attempts to:

(a) Prepare for a stressful confrontation. This kind of self-talk phrase might include: "It will be difficult, but I can handle it."

(b) Self-talk statements which will be useful when the athlete confronts his or her opponents should also be planned for. One might include: "The sight of him will not trip me up this time, I should just step-up my efforts to concentrate on what I am to do in the game."

(c) Internal speech which should aid in the adjustment of activation the athlete might feel should also be planned for. Such a statement as "I feel angry. Now it is time to take a deep breath, and try to relax my muscles," might prove useful during competition.

(d) "Self-talk" which encourages the athlete to reflect back upon his or her efforts to "manage aggression" should be also planned for in advance of a contest. This might include such thoughts (words) as "My pride started to get me in trouble, but I relaxed and concentrated upon giving more effort." Perhaps statements which involve self-reward will prove useful, such as "Although I got upset inside, I didn't let it show in my performance."

An Example of These Plans in Action.

The following example should clarify how some of the previously discussed principles, guidelines, and plans might be applied. The "case study" involves an ice-hockey player from a semi-professional team in Moose Gap, Canada, "Big Red."

Twice last year the rugged hockey player from Moose Gap injured other players by "high-sticking" them. This kind of illegal blow, administered with end of the hockey stick was accompanied by verbal outbursts of temper on Red's part. As a result, the league administrator suspended Red for a short period of time, two games. Finally, toward the end of last season, a longer suspension denied the team the use of Big Red, in the playoffs. His team lost in the playoffs. This year, in two games, Big Red hurt other players so seriously that they required hospitalization. Throughout the league he is feared, and considered the team's "enforcer!" Red's coach is a relatively mild man, and encourages his players to play hard, but to stay within the rules. The coach is concerned with Red's behavior, both this year and last, and is worried that Red will not be available for the playoffs this year. After a short suspension this year, Red has just been reinstated, and is not in top condition. His regular job is sedentary and he appears a bit "rusty" when practicing with the team again. His teammates, however, are glad to see Red return and to have his skill and muscle back on the ice. They greet him in recent workouts with shouts that reflect his "enforcer role." "That's the way your gon'a bang them . . . " they might call after Red has executed a hard body-check during a practice.

Red has had one brief confrontation and near fight with a younger member of the team, during practice. This younger member has taken Red's place, while he was away. However, the other team members did not even seem to notice this problem. Only the coach seemed to feel that it was cause for concern.

The first team to be played in the tournament ending this year, contains several players whom Red has injured in the past. The team also is a long-time rival of Red's Moose Gap team. The referees selected for the tournament are the best from that part of the country. Most of the players and coaches respect them.

Red's coach, after some talks with his "problem player" consults a local psychologist who has worked with other team members. He agrees to work with Red. After meeting with the psychologist Red also agrees to try to do something about "controlling myself." He hopes to play better in the tournament game, as the result of some help, but does not really believe that he can change a great deal.

However, the coach, psychologist and Red decided upon a plan of action. It is intended to keep Red in the games as his defensive skills are needed. Additionally, another serious fight or injury as the result of his temper should result not only in a suspension but in his removal from the league permanently. Red is aware of this possible penalty, and wishes to avoid it.

First, the coach and psychologist try to help Red make what is called a "primary appraisal" of the forthcoming game. They wish to aid him to judge the severity of the threat of the contest to his emotional control, and to specify the people and situations which may "set him off." Secondly, they decide to help him make a secondary appraisal, to aid him to formulate things to do when he faces various situations and annoyers, in the form of specific opponents and their behaviors. An effort is made, at this point, to help Red to understand the consequences of any useful and new coping strategies he might adopt. This second step has been called a "skill acquisition stage," one which involves trying to "innoculate" Red against the stresses he will face, stresses which in the past have caused him to lose control.

This second stage involves giving Red an idea of alternative methods he may use when confronting games and opponents. It requires mentally rehearsing both what might happen, as well as, how he might deal with annoyances which provoke him to anger. Within this "skill acquisition stage," Red will be given "self-talk" ideas and phrases directed toward control of his temper. Also during this time the psychologist plans to aid Red through the use of various kinds of role playing strategies. Red will be confronted with statements that his opponents might "throw" at him during warmups and games, phrases intended to upset him. Role playing in this context might even employ another player who insults Red, both verbally and physically (via a hard body check) while on the ice. Also during this phase, Red will be given phrases which enable him to deal with signs that his bodily feelings are becoming aroused to anger. Muscular relaxation training is also a part of this phase of Red's meetings with the psychologist. This preparatory period lasts several weeks, but could well have lasted a month or more.

The time to the final game and tournament, however, is short. During this time, Red and the coach and psychologist engage in the following exchange of ideas and thoughts.

Red: "This is really going to be tough on me, I really hate those guys and particularly John . . . smart-ass foward thinks he can have me every time he comes down the ice. You should hear what he says to me out there!!! He even insults mother! I hate their fans too, throwing that beer on me when I leave the arena. I hate that stuff in my eyes. I think I will kill that son-of-a-bitch, when I get him on the ice next week."

Psychologist-Coach: "We know that it is difficult for you to change your feelings. And we both know how the fans treat us in "Snow Shoe." But when John and his rooters get you angry they are winning the mental game, they own you. You should remember that John and the others on the team are like you are. They have families, and are trying to get by in the game and in their work just like you are.

"Don't let John beat you by helping you to beat yourself. Use him. Use John to make yourself play harder, and better. Don't let him use you. You might tell yourself this before a game: "I know this will be tough, a difficult situation. I am beginning to learn how to handle it, though. I should be good enough to handle myself. I am going to let my anger help me, not hurt me. I am going to "block off" John, and the things he says. I am going to remove the faces from the other members of the team, and just play hard."

Psychologist-Coach: "Remember don't take John's checks personally, as insults to you. If he scores on someone else, or even on you, play harder. Don't try to hurt him. Hurting him will be easy, but you will defeat your own team, and be off the ice for good."

Red: "I'll try, but I may not be able to show much improvement."

Psychologist-Coach: "We know you'll try. But after the first game of the tournament we will sit down and talk some more. We'll decide what happened in this first game, and how you might have improved. We'll decide how you might improve more in the second game. During this first game things might happen which "set you off," which make you mad. You are not in top shape, and you'll be substituted for during the second and third periods. When you are sitting on the bench you should think about ways to stay calm.[2] You'll be given things to say to yourself to control any anger you might have as the result of previous plays. Some of the words you might use include:

"As long as I keep control of myself, I am in control out there on the ice. I am in charge of John and his scoring if I keep my head.

or perhaps

"I don't need to prove myself tough, the players in this league already know that. I need to prove I am an asset to the team. I need to prove that I can play under control, and to work hard within the rules. I can display my emotional as well as my physical strength by the way I control myself.

or maybe

"I am controlling myself quite well so far. I am sure that I am contributing to the team's success. Sitting down on the bench is useful, because when I get in again I can go at top speed, and play hard and well.

or possibly, if it is needed

"I got mad out there. I didn't foul out, however. I just got upset when I got checked hard, and want to hit back. I am glad that I didn't."

Coach-Psychologist: "Some more specific things you might say to yourself as you enter the arena, at the beginning of the warm-ups could include. "My muscles are getting tight, slow down and relax, everything will go just fine. I am spending too much time looking for John during the warmup, and for the other opponents too. Let them look for me, and worry about me!"

Coach-Psychologist: "You must be careful about trying to say things to yourself as you play, rather you should concentrate upon the game. But just as the game begins you might think: I'll take a deep breath. I am excited, but that is good. It is not that I am getting mad, but that it is a sign that I will skate hard, and keep my stick on the ice.

or perhaps after a hard-body check you might remind yourself . . .

They must be worried about me. They are trying to get me made, but that won't work. If they get me angry, they are in trouble because I'll play harder. Then *they* will be in trouble."

Thus, in these ways Red is being given positive kinds of "self-talk" equipping him for pre-game thoughts and feelings, provocations occurring during the game, as well as for the time he will spend on the bench.

Finally, Red is given positive ways of thinking after the game. These ideas should be talked about with the psychologist or coach after the contest. The phrases

---

[2] Klinger and his colleagues have studied what they call "thought content" as players sat on benches while playing basketball. Periodically, players' thoughts were obtained using a tape recorder; they were then analyzed for content. Time on the bench is a critical period for players who may be over anxious, or too aggressive. It is time for them to sort out their thoughts in positive ways, or it may be a time during which their aggressions and fears "take over" and blunt their subsequent efforts in the contest. (Klinger, Barta and Glas, 1981)

73

Figure 4 Often an athlete can dispel fear, or other unwanted emotions, by exaggerating an emotion and its results until the exercise becomes ridiculous, and the unwanted emotion dissipates. This is termed *paradoxical intention*.

may be reflections of how he resolved conflicts experienced during the game, how he met and controlled his anger, and perhaps about problems which still remained. First, the coach or psychologist might draw out from him, how he felt about the game, and about his behavior and feelings while playing. Examples of these discussions are as follows.

Coach-Psychologist: "Red, how did you feel about the game. How did you do?

Red: "Well I think I did pretty good. I played hard while I was in there. I didn't hurt anyone, and had no major penalties. The two infractions I did commit might have been avoided. I am glad that we won."

Coach: "Your performance was good, particularly when we were short handed in the last period. Did the rest you got at the beginning of that period help?"

Red: "Yeah, but I had some bad thoughts about John as he scored the tying point, I thought about smashing him, so that he couldn't score again."

Coach-Psychologist: "Well there were some positive and negative things happening!"

Red: "Yeah, I guess I did well in the game. But I had some thoughts which could have gotten me into trouble while I watched. My thoughts during the game, however, were positive. I had trouble thinking about anything but hockey during the game. But your thoughts and sentences helped me during the time I spent on the bench helped me."

Coach-Psychologist: "You might think over some phrases which will sum up where you are not, and which might help you before the next game. I hope they will help."

"I still have some things to work out, but I have made some progress.

"I should "shake off" thoughts about hurting people. I must relax and calm down during the breaks, concentrate upon what is happening during the game, and not upon people.

"I should remember that hockey is not war. I am not a brain surgeon out there. I should relax and have fun."

Some positive statements which consist of "rewards" should also be dealt upon. These might include:

"I handled myself pretty well in the final game. The team won and I helped in the final period a lot.

"My teammates appreciated my help a lot, and want me to stay inside the rules while I try hard.

Even though I have negative, aggressive thoughts on the bench during the last quarter, when I got in the game I played hard and well.

"I know that trying to keep my "enforcer" reputation may get me into trouble. I can put that behind me, and play well with intensity and concentration in the future."

Thus, within the hypothetical example outlined, it has been shown how a coach, perhaps with the aid of a psychologist may help an athlete to control and re-direct angry thoughts. In the brief explanations which follow several other techniques will be discussed, techniques involving visual imagery.

IMAGERY AND AGGRESSION REDUCTION

Throughout the book various ways in which visual imagery may aid in the formulation of the "mental game" are discussed. Imagery may also be used to control and reduce aggression. Anger is often accompanied by internal images reflecting how the individual wishes to physically or psychologically hurt another person. Often changing these images is an important first step to be taken prior to the real reduction of both aggressive thoughts and actions. Athletes vary as to how much they employ visual imagery, as well as to the clarity of the visual images they habitually "turn on" inside their heads. Thus, the "visual channel" may not be best for aggression modification in all athletes. Some of the variations of imagery which may be employed in this context, are as follows.

Paradoxical Intention in Imagery

Paradoxical intention is a strategy which is sometimes used by athletes and their psychologists to reduce anxiety, as well as to control and focus other emotions. Essentially the strategy involves mentally exaggerating a feeling, to heights which result in the emotion somehow reversing itself, and either "turning off" or becoming greatly reduced. An athlete, for example who appears fearful may be asked to sit on a chair and try to become as frightened as possible. As this exercise is engaged in for a period of time, the athlete soon realizes the absurdity of what he or she is trying to do. Laughter may replace fear, and the athlete returns to a calmer state.

This same method may be used to place excess anger under control. An athlete may be asked to imagine himself/herself aggressing against opponents in a highly intense manner. The athlete may thus, for a period of time, "call up" intense imagery involving this suggestion. The imagery furthermore, might include some of the results of this kind of physical aggression, including even the legal consequences which might befall the athlete, arrest, trial, and jail! Finally, when the athlete has seemed to have exhausted this "theme," and perhaps played the scenario until a height of absurdity has been reached, the imaginary "tape" might be erased and changed. The athlete might be encouraged to play a more positive scene within his or her "inside recorder." The athlete should be asked to "run through" the sport scenario again, replacing aggressive imagery with more positive alternatives. This revised and positive "film" might consist of ignoring an opponent who was aggressed against in the first "run-through." Scoring a goal might be substituted for a physical or psychological injury inflicted in the initial "program" of imagery. Positive imagery in this latter exercise might also include various kinds of "success imagery" depicting the athlete receiving an award for either performing well or even for sportsmanship. (Sportswomenship!!)

Thus, this program of paradoxical intention, tries to accomplish two things: (a) it attempts to exaggerate various expressions of aggression which may have "flooded" the imagery of the athlete previously, and (b) replace fruitless and negative get-mad pictures with more positive ones including those depicting success.

Relax and Re-Direct Aggression

Visual imagery of a positive nature may accompany the kind of relaxation training that has previously described (Chapter 4). Initially, after an athlete has been moderately relaxed, general success images may be "turned on" replacing visual impressions of angry and hostile acts. Next, while moderately relaxed, the athlete may be encouraged to imagine specific skill situations found in the sport. These second types of images might include both precise as well as powerful acts required. Finally, an effort should be made by the athlete to re-activate, and to duplicate the activation levels usually experienced as one is angry. While at this higher level the athlete again should try to concentrate upon skill and success, rather than upon acts which are marked by anger. The sprinter might try to view himself/herself running hard. The

76

shot putter might imaginally explode, as the shot is released. The basketball player might visualize fighting for and obtaining rebounds. In this manner higher levels of activation, instead of being paired with aggressive acts, become aligned with positive expressions of skill and power.

Other Methods

Other approaches may be used alone, or combined with some of the previous strategies when trying to curb and focus aggression. The athlete may be encouraged to "selectively associate" with calm non-aggressive coaches or teammates prior to contests. Moreover, relaxation training, visual imagery, and cognitive readjustment may be used serially instead of in combinations. That is, a period of time might first be devoted to only relaxation work, followed by a second separate session involving visual imagery. This approach concludes with a period of time devoted only to cognitive adjustments using the self-talk procedures outlined previously.

OVERVIEW

A case might be made for the hypothesis that the major problem in the world today is the identification and control of aggression in the human community. Aggression in athletics is both a reflection of, as well as, a further impetus to aggression seen in dealings between people and nations. The athlete should take an interest in adjusting and reducing anger in that vital part of the world which he or she can exert some control over, himself or herself! Blaming others for outbursts of violence is too frequently practiced between the leaders of countries. Athletes should try to take responsibility for their own anger, and by their examples, provide positive models of behavior for others to emulate.

REFERENCES

Berkowitz, L., *Aggression: A Social Psychological Analysis,* McGraw-Hill, New York, 1972.

Cratty, B.J., Chapter 8, "Aggression" in B.J. Cratty, *Social Psychology in Athletics,* Prentice-Hall, Englewood Cliffs, NJ, 1981.

Cratty, B.J. and P. Carpinter, "Mental activity in team sport athletics," publication pending, *Sportswissenschaft,* 1983.

Klinger, Eric, S.V. Barta, and R.A. Glas, "Thought content, and gap time, in basketball," *Cognitive Therapy and Research,* 5, 1, 1981, pp. 109-114.

McCarthy, J.F., and B. Kelly, "Aggression, performance variables, and anger, self-report in ice hockey players," *Journal of Psychology,* 1978, 99, 97-101.

Nosanchuk, T., "The way of the warrior," *Human Relations,* 1981, 34, 6, pp. 435-444.

Novaco, R.W., Chapter 8, "The cognitive regulation of anger and stress." in Kendall, P.C. and S.D. Hollon, *Cognitive-Behavioral Interventions, Theory, Research and Procedures,* Academic Press, 1979, pp. 241-278.

Zillman, D., R.C. Johnson, and K.D. Day, "Provoked and unprovoked aggression in athletes," *Journal of Research in Personality,* 1974, V. 12, pp. 112-116.

Beisser, A., *The Madness in Sport,* Appleton-Century Crofts, New York, 1952.

CHAPTER 6

THE MANAGEMENT OF FEAR AND ANXIETY

The study of fear and anxiety has been a major topic in psychological journals for decades. Psychologists working in clinics have often devoted a major part of their practice to calming the fears of their patients. Over the years such words as fear, anxiety, and related terms have taken on a variety of meanings, both within the scientific community and when used in daily conversation.

One of the general assumptions people make is that fear is undesirable and should be eliminated whenever possible. However, some psychologists distinguish between what they term fear, a healthy respect for a potentially threatening situation and what they call "anxiety" or an unreasonable feeling of dread, a feeling that is not warranted by the actual characteristics of the situation. So that on one hand, it would be said that if one runs when a lion breaks loose in the circus, he or she is exhibiting healthy fear; while if a person becomes frightened at the sight of a small cat, anxiety is being evidenced.

Sport psychologists and athletes themselves devote a great deal of time and energy trying to understand fears connected with sport, and in trying to place them into proper perspective, and at times to reduce or eliminate these disquieting feelings. The efforts of sport psychologists have been directed both toward the formulation of helpful theories about sport anxiety, as well as, toward the construction of useful testing instruments to evaluate this often elusive concept. An equal amount of energy has also been devoted toward formulating various ways to reduce anxiety and its accompanying stress.

In the following sections we will first sketch briefly some of the more important research findings relating anxiety to sports competition. Next, a survey of the ways in which athletes speak about and attempt to reduce their fears, usually prior to sporting competition, will be presented. Finally, some of the more useful "mental" ways of adjusting the fears of athletes will be covered.

WHAT THE RESEARCH SAYS

As has been pointed out, researchers interested in sport have, during the past several decades, devoted a great deal of energy toward understanding the fears of athletes. Often their endeavors have evidenced a healthy inter-change of ideas between psychologists and psychiatry in general. For example, one of the primary ideas that has emerged is that individuals, athletes as well as others, carry around with them two types of fears or anxieties; on one hand, is a person's general level of anxiety, a personality trait. Thus, one may be generally fearful in a variety of situations, or lack fear in general, or may evidence moderate fears in more than one situation. On the other hand, behavioral scientists have identified and sought to measure what they term "situational anxiety" (sometimes called state anxiety), a sometimes rather short-term condition of fearfulness which reflects an individual's reaction to specific situations. Sometimes this condition is called a temporary mood.

General anxiety and situational anxiety are important ideas to deal with when attempting to understand the athlete. Particularly important is the idea of "situational anxiety," when assessing the athlete's feelings prior to, during, and following competition. In general it is found that athletes who are generally fearful are often most upset and fearful when confronting competition, a stress situation; while conversely those of us who are relatively tranquil in general, when confronting stress situations are less likely to show "jumps" in signs of fear. Often sport psychologists working with physiologists have plotted changes in signs of the body's readiness to react to threat, changes in heart-rate and blood pressure and the like, for periods of time lasting as long as a year prior to important competitions. In this way, an attempt is made to determine just how the individual's mechanisms for meeting fear fluctuate as important contests are anticipated and then participated in.

In general, the research dealing with anxiety in sport may be classified into four general areas. Initially, attempts have been made to understand the *causes* of anxiety and stress. Next, there is a considerable amount of research, some of which is from physiological laboratories, which has focused upon physical signs associated with anxiety.

Work has also been carried out dealing with the manner in which performance is likely to change under conditions which are emotionally stressful to athletes. And finally, work has been done, sometimes by clinical psychologists and psychiatrists, to find out how best to reduce an athlete's fears.

One of the most promising directions in the research has been to study the interaction of more than one factor at a time, when trying to "get a handle" on anxiety in sport. That is, it has been assumed that to understand the reactions of a specific athlete, one must acquire information concerning the manner in which that athlete's physiological reactions change when confronted with certain kinds of stresses, both social and situational (a game and a yelling coach), in order to later remediate or adjust the fears of the athlete in question.

Causes

Athletic competition is an extremely public endeavor. People other than those directly involved are either spectators, or will later make some evaluation of the performance results. It is not surprising that fears revolving around social criticisms and evaluation are likely to cause athletes the most concern. Often the athlete is far more concerned, even in a contact sport, about the social consequences of his or her efforts than about the potential for injury. The social censure and judgements that are often of most concern to the athlete, are those coming from people the athlete values most, close friends and teammates. Often the cheers of the fans, as well as their boss, both of which the athlete knows to be realatively transitory, are not as important judgements as are the feelings of their family, friends, and teammates.

A second, sometimes hidden source of anxiety and stress in athletics, are conditions which are sometimes quite removed from the athletic environment. At times, athletes do quite well handling the stress of athletics, and other conditions in their personal and social lives. However, the death of a loved one, the departing of a girl or boy friend, or some other stress in life, coupled with athletic demands, often combine to cause performance fluctuations which are sometimes puzzling to the coach. That is, the athlete never performs in a social vacuum. The athlete, like all of us, is surrounded by potentially stressful conditions, and when another component of

Success phobia, the need to continue to maintain excellence after a winning effort

Crisis in one's personal life

Fear of not being perfect

S. Salmela

Unusual fears of not pleasing others

Fear of bodily harm

his/her life becomes disruptive, the stress of athletics often becomes too much for the athlete to deal with. It is for this reason that coaches should carefully nurture lines of communication between themselves and their athletes, communication which may serve both parties well as the athlete undergoes the stress of life.

There are other sources of potential fear and anxiety to the athlete. Some athletes harbor great fears of injury and of potential, temporary or permanent damage to the vehicle with which they perform, their body.

Pain, connected either with physical contact or physiological overloads, constitutes another source of fear and anxiety. Often these sources combine in subtle ways, as an athlete approaches an important contest, to engender fear which the athlete may have difficulty in understanding.

An important source of fear, related to the social consequences of performance previously discussed, is the threat which failure in competition may pose to the athlete's feelings about himself or herself. All of us, and athletes in particular, harbor relatively complex, but nevertheless real "self-concepts." This feeling we have for ourself becomes fragmented and rather specialized as we mature; that is, we set goals and standards for ourselves in rather specific ways and in designated situations with increasing precision as we mature. The athlete is usually proud, for without pride little in the way of superior performance will likely transpire. When an important competition is imminent, the athlete may perceive a threat to his or her pride. This perception of threat, whether real or imagined, is likely to produce a fearful athlete, a person judged anxious by those who observe him or her. It is for this reason that the coach may perform a useful function by helping athletes to realize that their "self" is dependent upon capabilities other than those exhibited on the athletic field, or in the gymnasium.

If the coach can in this way help the athlete to achieve a more secure personal self-concept, the participant in athletics may then view the possibilities of losing in less threatening terms, and assess the reasons for winning and losing in more realistic and less emotional ways.

EFFECTS OF ANXIETY AND FEAR-PRODUCING SITUATIONS

If the athlete confronts a situation which he or she perceives as threatening, a number of changes may occur, both prior to and during performance.

Initially the athlete may experience sanctions related to physiology. The body prepares for a threat by activating systems and sub-systems which support and enhance physical performance, and by shutting down systems which are not contributing to physical performance. This "fight-or-flight" reaction is coordinated by unconscious mechanisms within the nervous system, and include such movement enhancing changes as increasing blood pressure and breathing rate. Generally, there are positive increases in muscular tension, but at times, if anxiety is quite high the athlete experiences first a rise and then a lessening of muscular tension with accompanying feelings of weakness.

Subsequent experiences which are likely to occur, are not as easy to predict. Whether there is an improvement or a diminuition of performance depends upon a number of factors, including the athlete's background in similar stress situations. The type of skill or task required of the athlete in the competition also influences whether or not performance will improve or decline. Generally, a relatively simple forceful action, particularly one which has been well learned (a simple straightforward charge in football, or the well learned movements of a champion weightlifter) will be improved. On the other hand, an action or skill, or team strategy, which has not been well learned and/or is extremely complex will often be performed at less than optimum levels by a fearful athlete or a team composed of more than one scared performer.

Recent research has indicated that subtle "personal" factors also influence whether or not these activation responses are helpful to performance. Some athletes, it has been found, habitually perform better if they function at a somewhat scared level. They are either accustomed to this feeling in themselves or at least perform best when activated in this way. Other athletes need to achieve a calmer state in order to optimally perform their skills. It thus appears that each athlete should be considered as an individual and should be helped either to "get up" or "calm down" as their unique disposition dictates. Ways of accomplishing these kinds of adjustments are covered in more detail at the conclusion of this chapter.

One of the more important recent trends in the research suggests that feelings of anxiety are largely based upon what an individual thinks about when confronting a threatening situation. Thoughts which trigger anxiety can include those which evaluate the situation in fearful ways or those which involve perceptions of physical harm or social consequences of athletic participation. Similarly, what the athlete believes the changes in his or her physiology mean are of critical importance. Does the athlete view these as positive or negative signs, as indications that his or her body is "running-away-with-itself," or that they are "out-of-control" or that the body is reacting in useful ways to enhance performance? The athlete's careful and conceptual evaluation of the total threat-activation change and performance chain of events dictates both immediate reactions to the situation, as well as long-term learned responses to the later threat situations encountered in sport.

Diagrammed, this important thought-interpretative quality inserted with the performance-anxiety may be depicted as follows.

CHART 9

Thus, the cognitive or thoughtful activity the athlete engages in, forms a critical linkage between events and outcomes. More will be said about this quality in a section which follows. Important here, however, is the suggestion that to modify how an athlete feels, how frightened they are, one had best attend to changing how an athlete interprets the situation.

WHAT ATHLETES SAY

When interviewing athletes for our research, an early question in our interview form asked whether or not the athlete consciously planned their "mental activity" relative to their sport. The athletes were asked, for example, whether or not they carefully planned just how they consciously "managed" their thinking about emotional states such as fear, concentration, and aggression. When this kind of planning question was asked in a general manner, over half the athletes queried said that they did not consciously plan their thinking processes, but rather they dealt with thoughts that came to them in a random manner.

Initially they stated that they rarely spent time analyzing their thinking. To a later question, however, the athletes seemed to reverse themselves. When asked how they dealt with fears they encountered in competition, almost all carefully chronicled just how they dealt with anxiety prior to a game. Thus, when they were confronted with situations which caused fear, they seemingly were forced to think their way out of it. On the other hand, when they were not threatened or seemingly had the opportunity to carefully plan their skills in unemotional ways, they apparently did not engage in careful planning.

In several studies we carefully attempted to determine if significant relationships existed between the strategies of mental planning adopted by athletes, their coaches ratings of their motivation, intensity and performance. In general, we failed to discover meaningful correlations between these kinds of variables. Additionally, as is true when discussing aggression with athletes, it is often difficult to arrive at common definitions for the term "anxiety" when confering with athletes. Some, for example, view anxiety in close proximity to the word activation; while others view it as a totally negative performance-paralyzing phenomena.

Overall, we were struck with (a) the great diversity of strategies reported to us by athletes, (b) the highly creative nature of some of these strategies, and finally (c) the manner in which the athlete often had to somehow mentally "neutralize" the coach and his or her behavior prior to contests, in order to achieve some kind of mental state conducive to optimum performance. Some of the more creative strategies and useful findings from these studies follows.

About 20% or more reported that they viewed their anxiety as a positive feeling, one which would help them perform better. Some even stated that they were anxious if they did not feel anxious![1] These same athletes stated that they tried to achieve an optimum anxiety prior to competition in order that they would perform better. One female gymnast said that she tried to achieve a "buzz state" prior to a competition, and that if she did, she knew she would do well. Thus, many probably enjoyed, understood, and otherwise felt positively about the feelings of activation that moderate fear brought to them. If coaches would understand that helping athletes to understand this positive aspect of moderate fear, many of the negative side-effects from anxiety-states would not be present to impede performance. "I like to be scared, if I'm not, I'm worried," is a typical report.

At least one sport psychologist (Klauss, 1980) has spent a considerable amount of time outlining just how an athlete should prepare for competition; and as an important part of that preparation it was suggested that a "special place" be sought, in order to mentally reflect upon the forthcoming stress and to mentally reduce that

---

[1] I once talked to an agitated female distance runner, just prior to a national competition, who was highly anxious because "she was not anxious . . ." she knew she would not do well, she informed me. The next day she performed poorly.

stress. Thus, it was asked whether or not an athlete tended to retire to a special "planning place" prior to a competition. This query was usually answered to the negative. Only 1.2% said that they withdrew to special places, i.e., to bed, to a room and the like. Many athletes correctly pointed out that retirement to a specific location is often impractical or impossible, given the highly mobile athletes and athletic teams in today's world of sport.

More intriguing, and seemingly creative were attempts by athletes to remove or transport themselves mentally, when confronted with anxiety producing competitions. At times this attempt involved shutting others and "other things" off. "I shut everything out," or "I just think about my job, not the people or the game;" "I relax and forget about the game" is another typical report. Some designate given time periods to thoughts about impending competition . . . "I think about the game only 10 minutes and then get it out of my mind."

One of the more creative strategies, according to one gymnast, was to transport himself in time and in space, when confronting performance difficulties. "After completing several events in a foreign meet," he recounted, "I was doing poorly, I became concerned and then scared that the next event and those afterward, would be affected by my fears and feelings." It was just then he decided to "move out" of the gymnasium and competition, or as he put it; "I took myself back to the practice situation at the university in the United States where I train. I imagined my teammates around me, it was a workout, a practice." He apparently was successful in this mental time-space transformation, as he reported that "in the next event and those afterward I did not see or hear the crowd in Germany, and felt the close support of my teammates in my home gym . . . I did well."

An often reported strategy was the use of positive imagery i.e., successful "self-talk" relative to their own performance. This positive imagery was of several types including (a) positive thoughts, often accompanied by "self-talk" concerning successful completion of the athlete's own skills and team contribution, (b) positive imagery concerning the successful outcome of the total team competition and (c) success imagery focused upon the athlete's preparation and level of training leading up to the competition.

In this context therefore, the athlete might report, "thinking about being successful;" or the athlete might say that, "good workouts best resolve fear . . . I just think about the end of the game, past the work, about the payoff for winning." Sometimes this success imagery reflects upon past successful experience. For example, more than one university athlete reported reflecting back in time to a highly successful high school performance. A distance runner, for example, said that "I often think about successful races in high school when I was far ahead, when I worry about races at the university." A male waterpolo player likewise thought about, "tearing up a high school game, I could do anything . . . It helps me reduce my worries before a game at the university." Or perhaps as another athlete put it, "good workouts best resolve fear . . . I know that I have done all I can."

Another frequently reported strategy involved complete removal (mentally) from the athlete context. The athlete essentially reported thinking about other things, about keeping busy, often times in a set routine prior to a contest, so that there was little time to become afraid. These athletes reported that they sought perceptual-experiences, as represented by music, "I have a set routine . . . I listen to music in my room." While others even engaged in other physical experiences to reduce anxiety, for example one athlete said that, "I race motorcycles . . . I keep a motorcycle in the gymnasium with me during workouts . . . thinking about racing them calms me down!''

There were often social implications embedded within the athlete's stress reduction statements and strategies. They often viewed opponents, or their teammates in personal ways, and through thought, carefully worked out ways to reduce fear. For example, they often dealt personally (although mentally) with opponents. One athlete said, "I let opponents know who is boss . . . there is no reason, I tell myself, that the other team is different, and I come on strong at the beginning of the game." Further, from another athlete, "I find out just who to beat, I find out their marks, and then concentrate upon beating them, as I think about the contest." While another said, "If there is an awesome player publicized on the other team, he has to prove it to me . . . I tell myself before the game."

Other social content in athlete's thoughts before games, which is related to "calming" self-talk, included references to teammates and audiences. One said that he used his duties as a team captain to keep his mind and thoughts occupied in ways which would reduce his anxiety; another said that, "I avoid teammates who are anxious, as then I am anxious" . . . another said that "When teammates are worried, then I am worried . . . I leave the nervous ones alone." This "selective social association" strategy has been documented in the literature, as a means of reducing pre-contest anxiety.

Finally, the athletes reported using another strategy which has been previously written about by those interested in anxiety reduction in athletes. They said that they reduce the importance of the contest in their minds. "This is no big deal!" one athlete tells himself before a game; while another reported that she thinks . . . "this race is only for the experience," before a competition; while another stated to himself that "athletics are not important . . . It's like putting on a show" . . .

Overall there were several anxiety reduction strategies which predominated in the athlete's reports. In general, some of these strategies have been discussed in previous sport psychology literature, while others have not been accorded a great deal of attention.

Methods involved some type of self-applied "mental counseling," which sometimes was and at other times was not accompanied by counseling from a psychologist or psychiatrist.

Notably absent in the report of the athletes we polled, were descriptions of relaxation methods, and other tension adjustment techniques frequently recommended in books written by sport psychologists. Only the members of one team, a womens' track and field group, reported that anyone had ever come to their team in an attempt to enable them to relax and perform better. Group methods were applied, and the women viewed the attempt not only as ineffective, but as actually interfering with their workouts and performances.

While other athletes had heard of, or read of various relaxation methods, they unanimously reported that they did not participate in them now, nor did they plan to do so in the future. For the most part, the athletes reported that they thought their way into a more tranquil state, often substituting mental practice of skill, or the types of mental transfer in time and place described earlier.

In general, about one-third of the athletes in our investigations performed at the national level, while an additional third performed at international levels. If any trend could be ascertained in their reports, trends reflecting correlations between superior performance and those of average ability, it was the tendency of the better athletes to reduce anxiety in very positive ways, by telling themselves that they had no reason to be fearful, that they had prepared well, that their workouts the previous weeks and months had been hard and effective. Thus, they seemed to be saying that it is the opposition that had better be anxious about me, "I am ready," they asserted and "they must prove that they can beat me." It would thus seem that hard effective workouts are one of the primary types of "armour" by which an athlete may be protected. An ill-prepared athlete, according to our investigations, is likely to be an anxious one.

ANXIETY ADJUSTMENT

Taking into consideration our data and that of the literature, as well as suggestions by clinicians who have worked with athletes on a one-to-one basis, several primary guidelines suggest themselves as effective ones in the reduction and/or adjustment of fear and anxiety. It should also be emphasized at this point that some athletes, even with the help of a knowledgeable coach cannot effectively adjust anxiety. Often the help of a mental health professional (psychologist or psychiatrist) is called for.

COGNITIVE BEHAVIORAL THERAPY

It has only been in recent years, primarily during the latter part of the 1970s that both psychologists and those interested specifically in sport, have focused upon how the adjustment of an athlete's thoughts may in turn modify their physical performance in positive ways.

The suggestions which follow primarily arise from work carried out in the past ten years, dealing with what is called "cognitive-behavioral therapy" or the use of thoughts to change how people feel, and/or behave. It is believed that this approach is valid when working with athletes both because the athletes in our research reported playing various "mind-games" with themselves involving thought and the re-structuring of situations and themselves by thinking. An increasingly positive group of findings has arisen from applications of this type of thought-therapy, which suggest that the method and operations suggested by this approach have important uses within sports environments. The observation that attitudes and thoughts have important effects upon emotion and behavior is not new, and indeed the generalization has appeared in various forms, both in psychological and philosophical literature for decades. However, several years ago, Albert Ellis, refined this broad assumption by suggesting that several forms of anxiety and emotional disturbances related to fears are based upon illogical ideas, or irrational ways of thinking. Stemming from this assumption was his second premise; that if anxiety is caused by less than useful thoughts then it follows that anxiety may be modified if one can change how one views threatening situations, events, and people. To put it briefly, you can reduce fears by changing how people think about fearful things.

Fear may be considered as occurring within a time framework, consisting of three interlocking phases. First, there is the threatening situation, followed by a personal-physiological reaction. Finally, the person's perceptions of the outcomes of his or her interaction with the threatening situation are formulated.

A broad assumption postulated by many mental health specialists is that sound emotional health rests upon the individual feeling that they are both lovable and competent. A person must feel capable of doing something well, as well as being capable of being loved for his/her own sake relatively independent of objective performance capabilities. The converse of this assumption is that when individuals feel less than adequate during the performance of important tasks, and also harbor feelings if being unworthy of attracting unselfish love, they are likely also to evidence signs of poor mental health.

Lovability and success, however, are highly subjective phenomena, both in the eyes of the receiver, and in the eyes of those making judgements about these qualities in others. Perfection is seldom achieved; while few of us are revered by all with whom we come in contact. It is thus often found that the more anxious among us are those who feel that all must love us; and/or those who believe that any effort on their part which is less than an expression of the ultimate in perfection is not worthy of consideration. Indeed, most psychologists who work with the disturbed attempt to promote good mental health by adjusting the thoughts of their clients. They must overcome the irrational belief that their client holds concerning the assumption that everyone must find them attractive and worthy of affection, or the equally irrational supposition that the client may hold that he must achieve a high level of expertise in everything undertaken.

It is not too difficult to translate these basic principles into situations and people found in sport. While it is equally easy to hypothesize just how an athlete may experience an inordinate level of fear as a competitive event (or season) approaches.

For example, an athlete reared among perfectionist parents, who either obviously or subtly indicates that his or her lovability is dependent upon expertise, may come to the athletic arena with unrealistic and irrational assumptions. That is, the boy, approaching his first high school football game in which he has a major role, may harbor feelings of dread concerning the perfect way in which he must conduct himself as quarterback as well as the forboding dread that not only his parents, relatives, girl friend, and perhaps the coach and the townspeople will not like him (or love him depending upon the relationship) if he fails to do well. That he is overly anxious in the locker room prior to the first contest is understandable, and more than that, these feelings are likely to impede his efforts on the field. To fail in the situation outlined will bring down two curses upon the head of our hapless athlete; these important "others" in his life will hypothetically fail to find him lovable, or at least not as highly likeable as he might have been had the game been successful. And also, failure to win or to do well, will demonstrate to others that he is not expert, as perfect as he perceived himself in his athletic endeavors.

Similar situations are multiplied time and time again within a variety of athletic situations and competitions. Moreover, athletic participation is something a lot of people are likely to care about, and additionally, a type of display of one's expertise (or lack of it), which is highly visible and understandable to many. It is no wonder that high levels of "failure anxiety" exist in the hearts of many athletes.

A major tool used by contemporary "cognitive-behavioral" therapists is what they term "self-talk." They attempt to encourage the client-athlete to voice, usually to themselves, rational assessments of potentially confusing and/or threatening situations, events, or people. Self-talk techniques are employed to help athletes and others in stressful situations to adjust their belief systems about their own possibly unrealistic feelings about perfection in performance, and about other unrealistic perceptions about how people may view them during and after winning and losing.

This kind of strategy has great potential when working with the often irrational beliefs of athletes concerning their invincibility and whether or not others will like, accept, or even love them following losses or displays of ineptitude. Helping the anxious athlete to adjust thoughts leading to anxiety, in this manner, is usually a two phase process. During the first phase the athlete must engage in what has been termed primary assessment; that is, he or she must be helped to accurately guage the "real" threat of the situation. Secondary assessment involves various kinds of self-talk which attempts to change thoughts to ones which trigger emotions and rational interpretations of previously anxiety producing situations. Thus, primary assessment involves interpretation and logical evaluations of what is really going on in objective ways; whereas secondary assessments are the steps toward remediation.

Often these stages in the re-structuring of thoughts cannot be "handled" by the athlete or by the coach. One cannot always think their way out of problems; fear may be so overpowering that any kind of rational change in thinking is difficult. While on the other hand, the coach, due to his previous association with the athlete may not only have difficulty relating to the athlete in rational ways, but he similarly constrained as to objective interrelation of just what is going on. Moreover, the coach may be caught at cross-purposes. For example, it may be difficult to help the athlete realistically reduce the importance of the contest, having already spent a great deal of time "blowing up" the importance of the contest in the "locker room pep talk." It is for this reason that the reader, be he or she a coach or athlete, should consider the following suggestions as guidelines which might be followed by a psychologist-psychiatrist attached to the team, rather than as a recipe of "cookbook methods" to apply directly.

Mahoney and others have refered to what they term a "cognitive click" (Mahoney 1974) occurring when an individual suddenly and deeply accepts some internal change in their belief system as a result of changes in "self-talk" or what others have refered to as an "internal dialogue." This kind of real change in thinking, which hopefully leads to positive changes in emotions and behaviors, may or may not come after prolonged periods of time; whereas valid changes in attitudes, emotions, and thoughts about situations in sport may occur with or without the help of professionally trained others.

In general, athletes should attempt to re-structure and re-adjust thoughts which may not be entirely logical, but are probably impediments to healthy emotions and efforts within three main aspects of the situation in which they find themselves. These include: (1) Rational assessment and re-adjustment of the nature of the impending competition. (2) Rational and realistic assessment and modification of "internal-dialogue" concerning the athlete's own emotional and physiological reactions to athletic situations, both general and specific. And finally, (3) Try to help the athlete modify how they perceive the outcomes of athletic competition, both successful and unsuccessful. Within the final phase are attempts to aid the individual to accurately appraise just how others are likely to react to their winning or losing efforts.

In general, the self-talk techniques and strategies outlined in the following examples are effectively applied if several guidelines are followed. Initially and most important, the person helping the athlete (or the athlete himself or herself) should try to determine just what kinds of irrational beliefs concerning perfection and lovability seem to be the primary and direct causes of apprehension. Next, the athlete should be aided to pinpoint when these beliefs are most prevalent, prior to, during, or following contests; as well as at what locations these less than useful beliefs seem to reside, i.e., within situations, within other people, or within emotions of the athletes themselves. Finally, it is usually helpful if the type of self-talk first encouraged involves more general statements, ones which are more impersonal than personal. Later, the internal dialogue encouraged may be more personal and specific to the individual and sport situations which are being confronted.

With these guidelines in mind, it is helpful to list some of the potentially irrational beliefs that an athlete may have, and thus needs to adjust, relative to the three components of the athletic situation described (the event, the the athlete's body, and the outcome. Following the innumeration, various case studies will be described, outlining how the athlete may talk to himself (or herself), as well as the kinds of internal dialogue which may be encouraged by others.

Among the untenable beliefs and irrational thoughts one may have about impending athletic competition(s) include the following:

1. The other team will injure us, they are large enough to kill us.
2. The opponent will beat me so badly, that I'll never be able to play again.
3. I have not practiced hard enough, I will lose badly, and I will feel crushed.
4. Our team is not good enough to be playing these people.
5. The other team, or individual, will ridicule me while I play.
6. They will make me so mad that I will lose my head, and play badly, or hit a member of the other team.
7. This is the most important event in my life; if I fail, I will carry the stigma the rest of my life.

Among the irrational beliefs, that the athlete may have about his own body and emotions as the contest approaches include these:

1. My heart is really beating fast, I will blow it, I am really scared!
2. I can't seem to calm down, I am too nervous to play well.
3. They are making me so nervous and mad, that I will lose my head and foul out.
4. They are bigger and better than I am, I have no chance against them.
5. Everyone is watching me, and will see me fail, and think that I am lousy.
6. I am perspiring so much I can't even handle the ball. How can I stop it?

And finally, thoughts about the post-competition period, which may occur prior to, and also during the game include the following:

1. After I lose this, nobody will speak to me any more.
2. I will let everyone know if I lose, nobody will think I am any good anymore.
3. My girl will not care about me if he beats me.
4. My father will be embarrassed; he has everyone from work watching the game.
5. I'll be disgraced in this community; I'll never be able to hold my head up again.
6. If I play badly, I'll let the team down and they'll hate me; the team has worked so hard for this win.

As can be seen, these statements are for the most part irrational and illogical. The athlete might begin by determining which thoughts of this nature are most believed and which thoughts bring about the greatest concern. Having ascertained this, the next step is to formulate *general* statements, and formulate internal dialogue(s) which counteract them. Some of the general, and somewhat impersonal statements which might be used, include those counteracting some of the pre-competition assumptions listed previously. For example:

1. The other team may injure or kill us, they are so good and big. (Injuries are rare in well conditioned athletes, and even rarer are deaths in sport . . .)

I have not practiced hard enough, and will lose. (People practice as hard as they are able, and are often limited by conditions, coaching, and other things beyond their control; the players on the other team are likely to be as limited in conditioning at this time of the year.)

3. This is a most important event in my life. I'll never live it down when I do badly. (Most people blow up athletic competitions all out of proportion to their real importance; later in life one is able to place youthful athletic competitions into true perspective and some of the so-called important ones are even forgotten 5-10 years later.)

Still later, after these statements seem to be gaining some inroads into the athlete's consciousness, and the truth of them begins to dawn upon the individual engaging in "self-talk," more specific statements counteracting pre-competition assumptions, which are less than helpful, may be "spoken" inside the head of the athlete. These replacement statements might include:

1. Instead of, "people practice as hard as the can" . . . the statement should be, "*I've* practiced as hard as I can and realize my limitations. For the next game I will put in more work, on my own if necessary, to be even better prepared."

2. Instead of, "the other team may injure us . . ." the statement should be made more pointed . . . "I have never been injured. Worrying about injuries will likely bring some on. If I hit hard, I will not get hurt; and they had better be careful and worried about me.

Most important are "corrective" statements, signaling more useful self-talk involving feelings the athlete may have within his own emotional and physical constitution which often accompany feelings of anxiety. The following useful statements may be substituted for the false and counterproductive statements previously listed.

1. Instead of worried thoughts accompanied by "self-talk" regarding the body, i.e., "My heart is beating fast . . . I am perspiring . . . I can't catch my breath . . ." Substitute, "I am glad that my body is reacting well to the effort I must give. A fast heart and deep breathing are signs that I am getting ready to do my best . . . these are good indications that I will do well."

2. Instead of, "I am perspiring so much . . ." "People wet their hands to grip axe handles better, perspiration will help things stick in my hands, and help me play better . . ." or "I can wipe them off. Perspiration is a sign that my body is ready to act, I hope the other team and players are ready for me."

Negative self-talk following contests, or thoughts of the social implications after the game is over, are perhaps the most restrictive and impeding types of thoughts. The ones previously listed may be counteracted by the following substitutions.

1. Instead of "After I lose this, nobody will speak to me again . . ." substitute, "although some people may react differently after I do not win, I know what I have done in the game and practice, practices they have not shared with me. Their after-the-game treatment is of no consequences to me."

2. "I'll let the team down . . ." substitute, "I know how hard I've worked and so do my teammates; most of them at one time or another will do poorly and yet they are still hardworking, worthwhile people . . . Maybe in the future I can be kind to one of them if they do badly in a game . . . Teammates who hold some fault against me, will soon be forgotten as I grow throughout life . . . teammates who value me, above my athletic contributions, will remain my friends for a long time."

Strategies of this sort may be applied at specific times during the day, and in specific places, i.e., 20 minutes just before going to sleep.

Some athletes have discovered that it is effective to apply positive self-talk whenever negative thoughts "pop up." When anxiety threatens, if possible, the athlete should take a deep breath, stop what they are doing, or retire to a quiet place, and slowly and carefully think through sentences which are appropriate to the kind of fear which may be engendered. For the most part, fears may be traced to specific kinds of negativisms and irrational beliefs, as has been pointed out. At times the athlete must seek professional help in order to (a) identify the source or belief which seems to trigger anxiety about sport, and (b) to formulate and help him or her rehearse appropriate positive and useful internal dialogue or self-talk, in the manner described.

In summary, the basic tenants upon which this kind of thoughtful readjustments are based consist of:

1. Most sources of anxiety are based upon irrational, illogical beliefs about performance perfection and social acceptability. Specifically, when people believe that they must perform perfectly at all times, and also be liked and accepted by all, they are likely to be anxious when less than perfect performance is imminent and/or there is a likelihood that all people will not like or even accept them.

2. Thus, to counteract these fallacies, one should formulate thoughts crystallized in internal speech, which are based upon logical assumptions about the performance and social value. These basically include the idea that for the most part people do not perform in ways which are perfect, and that most of us are not highly valued all the time by all those with whom we come in contact. One must accept the obvious conclusion that much of the time an individual performs in imperfect ways, and that many times people will not like you, independent of how you perform and of your worth as a person.

3. A first step in correcting these fallacies is to formulate general statements and then more sport and competition specific statements, which are more rational than those which trigger anxiety. These include those indicating that losing an athletic competition is not like dying.

4. Application of self-talk techniques are likely to modify emotions, and thoughts about things which formally made the athlete anxious. This is particularly true if the athlete applies them whenever fear-arousing thoughts arise in his or her consciousness.

A review of the following has obvious implications for the coach, some of which are listed below.

1. The coach should not contribute to the irrationality of athlete invincibility and perfectionism, by charging the athlete to win and be perfect all the time. One of the most successful coaches in California habitually charged athletes with doing their best, of approaching perfection, even if not reaching it; that success is performing to one's optimum.

2. The coach should not contribute to the irrationality of relaitonships between real liking and athletic success. The coach should try to be one of several who contact the athletes who let him or her know that they are a worthy and likeable person independent of their athletic prowess.

92

PARADOXICAL INTENTION

I once heard a diving coach of a national team say that in order to overcome the anxiety of a girl he was coaching, he told her to go over to a chair and make herself as frightened as she could. She did as he instructed, and soon dissolved into laughter. What she was trying to do to herself was so ridiculous that she could not keep it up with a straight face. Her anxiety seemed to disappear.

This strategy was first advanced by a follower of Sigmund Freud, Victor Frankel, who suggested the term "paradoxical intention." Essentially it is the exaggeration of some feeling or emotion to the point where it becomes obvious, exaggerated, and a satire on itself. Often this strategy dissipates the emotion, and changes an unwanted mood state.

Once when working with Yuri Hanin, a social psychologist of sport in Leningrad, he informed me about a similar strategy he had attempted with the captain of a girl's basketball team. This girl had been, what he had termed, an "oppressor" to the other girls on the team. Her temper and temperament had made her an obnoxious companion to the other members of the team. She oppressed others, both verbally and with her expressions and gestures, during games and practices. Her exaggerated feelings and behaviors were a problem both to her coach, as well as to the players.

Hanin informed me that he and two other girls on the team formed a strategy in an attempt to solve the problem by changing the "oppressor's" attitudes and behaviors. The other two were coached to imitate *her* behavior during practice, at times, even to emit the exact exasperating expression as the "oppressor" had used. After several weeks, the "oppressor" got the point; she became aware of the "behavioral mirror" that was being held up before her. Realization brought change. After that time she began to change markedly in her feelings and expressions towards others on the team. The transformation was obvious to all, and resulted in a more productive team.

This latter "acting out" therapy could also be named a type of paradoxical intention, but in an indirect manner. The focus of the change was not saddled with the job of exaggerating feelings and behavior, but instead others did it. At the same time, this social acting out resulted in the focus of the change, really modifying her behavior.

In still another instance, within a Russian women's national team, Hanin informed me that an "oppressor" was dealt with, in the direct ways infered by the terms "paradoxical intention." That is, the girl herself was first counseled concerning her obnoxious ways of dealing with others on the team including the coach. Then the girl, having tentatively accepted the psychological diagnosis, was coached to exaggerate her authoritarian and punative behaviors. Soon the other team members got the point and began to laugh with her. Real change took place, both in the behaviors emitted by the "leader-oppressor" as well as in the attitudes others took toward her.

OTHER METHODS

Numerous other methods, as varied as those used by psychiatrists and psychologists on patients with anxiety who are not athletes, have been applied to those engaging in athletic competition. Bio-feedback accompanied by various forms of psycho-therapy may be used in positive ways, by those trained in their use. These methods have been successfully employed with athletes.

Psycho-dramas have been successfully employed by sport psychologists both in the United States and abroad. This technique involves "acting out" aggressions and anxiety, sometimes with the assistance and cooperation of others. Analyses of these "dramas" may lead the athlete toward understanding the sources of his/her own fears.

Various forms of meditation have also been used with some positive effects to calm athletes. This type of intervention, in which an athlete may repeat a "mantra" (a special phrase or word) for a period of time each day (usually 20 minutes), has been reported as helpful in inducing muscular relaxation, as well as in improving motor performance scores within laboratories. Care should be taken when using this method, that prolonged exposure does not produce a "too calm" individual, unable to get himself/herself "up" for strenuous competition, however.

Often the reduction of anxiety in athletes is a long-term undertaking. If the athlete is suffering from severe problems, the intervention should only be attempted by a trained professional (an individual within the mental health field) and one who is familiar with the special needs of athletes.

OVERVIEW

One of the most important problems facing an athlete, and thus his/her coach is the reduction of anxiety relative to impending competition. Anxiety is generally a mental interpretation on the part of the athlete about the degree of threat which an impending event or opponent is about to impose, coupled with changes (usually heightened) in activation-arousal levels. Higher levels of anxiety are often useful to an athlete and enable him/her to do better under stressful circumstances, to exert more force and/or to endure longer in events which require physiological power.

Athletes report a variety of coping strategies when asked what they do about performance anxiety. And for the most part it is difficult to identify a "best" solution which will serve all performers. Most useful in the literature are principles derived from Ellis' concepts of rational-emotive-therapy. The athlete must restructure emotional beliefs concerning perfection of performance and whether he will be liked for his performance. Thus, examples in the chapter have drawn heavily upon these principles, presenting various situations in which "self-talk" was suggested for athletes in an attempt to correct "irrational beliefs."

Still another strategy suggested was termed "paradoxical intention." In this method, an attempt is made to have the athlete exaggerate the emotion of an effort to somehow break through the fear and to view the mood state as somehow absurd, one which is not worthwhile sustaining.

In addition to the methods proposed in this chapter, there are others, often aligned with specific "schools" of psycho-therapy. Often these are complex, and need prolonged periods of time to accomplish. Usually they are effective only in the hands of a therapist well grounded in their use and rationale.

REFERENCES

Cratty, B.J., "Anxiety," *Psychology in Contemporary Sport,* 2nd Edition, Prentice-Hall Inc., Englewood Cliffs, N.J., 1983, pp. 114-143.

Fenz, W.D. and G.B. Jones, "Individual differences in physiological arousal and performance in sport parachutists," *Psychosomatic Medicine,* 1972, 34(1), pp. 1-8.

Kauss, D., *Peak Performance.* Prentice-Hall, Englewood Cliffs, N.J., 1980.

Klavora, P. and J. Daniel, (eds.), "Customary arousal for peak performance," *Coach, Athlete and Sport Psychologist,* Human Kinetics Publishers, Champaign, Il., 1977.

Miechenbaum, D., *Cognitive-behavior and modification.* New York, Plenum, 1977.

Nideffer, R.M., "The relation of attention and anxiety to performance," *Sport Psychology: An Analysis of Athletic Behavior,* Mouvement Publications, Ithaca, N.Y. 1978.

Smith, R.E., "Development of an integrating coping response through cognitive-affective stress management training," *Stress and Anxiety,* Hemisphere, Washington, D.C., 1979, Vol. 7.

Suinn, R.N. and R. Richardson, "Anxiety management training, a non-specific behavior therapy program for anxiety control," *Behavior Therapy,* 1971, 4, pp. 498-510.

CHAPTER 7

CONCENTRATION, FOCUSING AND MAINTAINING ATTENTION

Athletes often mention concentration as an important quality when they are interviewed by newspaper people. Close attention to the task at hand, performers reiterate, enables them to do well in a number of sports ranging from those which require aiming (archery or pistol shooting), to those of a more vigorous nature (most team and individual sports). "I let my mind wander, at the close of the game," a football player may be quoted as he tries to explain a "mental lapse," or how he was injured. While still another might report that their tournament tennis improved when "I learned to concentrate for the entire match."

Attention as an important pre-requisite to learning and as a pre-condition for various perceptual judgements has occupied the time of numerous experimental psychologists for several decades. The "mental fatigue" that soldiers encountered as they were forced to observe radar scopes during the war, was studied by some in order to prolong attention in this and similar tasks. Other experimenters studied both the amount of information, as well as conflicting information which individuals could attend in both distracting and distraction-free conditions. Child psychologists have been interested in attentional behaviors on the part of youngsters within school room settings. However, relatively little concrete work has been carried out by sport psychologists on the nature of athletes' attention in various sports, and how to heighten attention in order to improve performance. The work that has been carried out in sport often takes the form of interesting theoretical and practical models, with little accompanying data which either confirms or negates the various assumptions made.

Attention remains a relatively unexplored area. At the same time, both athletes and sport psychologists intuitively recognize the importance of this human quality. Attention infers that the athlete is focusing on the important elements within the game, and at the same time exluding extraneous stimulation, including fan noise or distractions emitted by other players. Breakdown in attention can usually result in performance disruption, in behaving inapproriately or even dangerously in numerous sporting situations.

WHAT THE RESEARCH SAYS

Research dealing with the general problem of attention in humans encompasses a broad spectrum of studies. The findings of many of these studies have prompted the formulation of what has been termed "information theory." This theory and the sub-models which constitute it have dealt with such problems as the amount of information or "information load" which may be born by an individual in various situations. Generally, there are vast individual differences in the ability to attend to a broad spectrum of stimuli. This ability also differs greatly depending upon the amount of tension-anxiety exhibited by the individual. Thus, in sport it has been assumed by more than one current writer, that with increased anxiety in a game or competition, the athlete is likely to attend to a narrower range of information, than is true when the performer is more relaxed. In the case of basketball, for example, one is familar with the high strung high school forward who at the end of a close game seems only to see the basket, rather than open teammates who might have scored easily had they been pressed to.

Information theory also deals with the concept of "noise" within the information processing "network." In common terms this concept refers to distractions which plague both athletes as well as bus drivers, when they may be both trying to perform some difficult maneuver, one with his body, the other with his vehicle. Individuals differ also in the amount of "noise" they can tolerate while maintaining attention to important components of the performance situation. Athletes are believed by some to become able to better block off noise, in the form of fan reaction, as they acquire increased experience in their sport. Forms of "noise" in an athletic context, according to some information theorists, would include more subtle distractions including: thoughts that a parent will be upset with performance, slight movements to either side of the field, the presence of a girl friend in the stands, or even perhaps negative kinds of internal speech to which the athlete subjects himself or herself.

Klinger and his colleagues periodically interrupted basketball players both while they were sitting on the bench during a game and immediately as they came out of a game, in order to evaluate various aspects of attention in athletes (1981). As a result he found that distracting thoughts of the athletes were able to be categorized into five groupings, including:

1. Thoughts completely unrelated to the game.

2. Thoughts about the game, unrelated to doing a good job, i.e. "When will I get into the game?"

3. Thoughts related to the game, but focused upon general qualities, including the ease or difficulty of winning, or general wishes to do better, or anger or joy over things happening in the game.

4. Exhortations and evaluations of the subjects own play, or the play of the whole team, trying to increase their own or a teammates motivation.

5. Problem solving thoughts about play, or focusing on specific strategies of one's own personal functions or future actions.

Thus, for the most part the first three categories were unlikely to improve the athlete's play, while only the 5th category of thoughts were likely to have any marked beneficial effect upon the athlete's play.

One of the more remarkable findings from this study was that when the team was not doing well (during a period in which the other team scored 2 or more consecutive baskets) the player's thoughts were never on various problem solving strategies, category 5. Rather their thoughts gathered within categories three and four, involving general exhortation, and about the general qualities apparent in the game. Only when the team may have needed the thoughts in category 5 the least (when *they* were scoring two or more consecutive goals) did the players attend to specific strategies and tactics dealing with the situation at hand. Thus, strong focus of attention on the important elements in the game at hand seemed to take place primarily when the team was in a favorable position; while at other times relatively little thought was concentrated upon important elements, elements necessary to do better.

This same kind of phenemona was noted in research carried out by my colleague Yuri Hanin, when evaluating inter-personal communication among numerous sports teams in the Soviet Union. It was consistently found that when a team began to lose, inter-personal communications tended to quickly drop into a "negative" category; teammates started to berate each other instead of generally encouraging each other, and/or helping each other to do better in specific helpful ways. It is difficult to assign a cause-effect status to these findings i.e., does losing trigger negative communication, or does the reverse happen? In any case negative comments coupled with losing efforts certainly tend to summate to produce increasingly negative results. Klinger and his colleagues suggest this same negative chain of events are suggested by their findings. That is, when a team may need the attention and concentration of players the most, attention seemed most likely to wain. Irrelevant thoughts intruded into the consciousness of athletes he studied, more when the other team was doing well, a combination of factors which would make it likely that even less able performances would be forthcoming.

Numerous theorizers have speculated about the dimensions of human attention in sport as well as in other aspects of life. Nideffer in several publications has suggested that an athlete may be characterized by two types of attention that he or she may be "paying" to the situation. One dimension he terms "breadth" denoting the range of cues to which the individual may be attending; the second is an "inward-outward" dichotomy, which suggests that the athlete may be either "listening" to himself or herself to the internal cues perhaps in the form of "self-talk," or the athlete may be attending outwardly to cues and speech emitted from others. Thus, an athlete may be attending inwardly to a wide or narrow range of cues, or may be attending outwardly—again to a wide or to a narrow range of information—the game or competition. Nideffer, perhaps correctly, suggests that the athlete's range of attentional behavior is likely to be reduced when anxiety or tension are present. In other words, the athlete may literally not see as much or hear as much when he or she is frightened. In some cases this "narrowing" may be useful, such as when performing a simple direct act in which numerous cues may not be important; while in other cases, this "narrowing" may be highly detrimental as in the case of a boxer or an athlete in a complicated team sport.

Others have suggested that "flexibility" of attention may be more important than simply whether an athlete is listening to himself or to others, or attending to a narrow or wide range of cues. In many team sports, particularly those which involve reactions to others whose movements are relatively unpredictable, the athlete must quickly transfer his or her attention from one specific piece of information to a large "field" of cues. The basketball player on offense or defense must, for example, keep in mind the location of numerous other players, together with the location of the ball; and at the same time the player must suddenly focus in on a single cue, the basket, just before taking a shot. Numerous other examples of perceptual flexibility or attentional flexibility in sport could be given.

Concepts used by educators to describe attention in school children may be useful for consideration by sport psychologists and athletes. The ideas "general" and "close" attention are used. Close attention, for example, is seen for only a minute or two at a time in younger school children, while general attention to a lesson is a more frequent and prolonged condition. Athletes, too, may pay close attention to important relevant cues, while at the same time maintaining general attention to a broader range of information in the competitive context. Athletes, as well as others, probably vary greatly in the degree to which they can maintain both types of attention in various situations. Likely, the more experienced athletes can not only concentrate for prolonged periods of time, but also can demonstrate the presence of both general and close attention, by attending to various cues in ways which are flexible, and which meet their needs and the demands of the performance situations in which they find themselves.

Attention is not difficult to talk about and to theorize about, but is a more difficult quality to evaluate well in athletes. Klinger and his colleagues periodically tapped their basketball player-subjects on the shoulders during the course of a game, but for the most part each player was only asked to report "what you were just thinking" from once to twice a game. For the most part, athletes' attention may be inferred from various performance qualities. Psychologists for decades in Eastern Europe have attempted to determine concentration qualities in athletes by giving them tasks which are irrelevant to their sport to complete the evening before or even a few hours before their competition. A typical one is to ask the athlete to quickly make dots into numbered squares on a small grid. If an athlete did well on this type of task, it was inferred that he had good concentrational qualities. However, some might assert that doing well in this type of task which had no connection to his sport inferred that the athlete was not concentrating upon the sport as he or she might do prior to the contest, or that the athlete was extremely tolerant to apparently insensitive psychologists during stressful pre-competition periods.[1]

Sport psychologists in Eastern Europe, and to a lesser degree on this side of the Atlantic, have carefully clocked the duration of times athletes wait between trials, for such efforts as high jumping, weightlifting, pole vaulting and the like, in an effort to correlate inter-trial waiting time with subsequent performance. The findings usually point to some optimimal time between trials, often referred to as "concentration time," which is productive of the best effort in a given type of performance. Often, however, such findings are difficult to interpret and particularly difficult to transfer to other sports, and from athlete to athlete. Often confounding such results is the fact that in several sports the waiting time is carefully prescribed by the rules; weightlifting is one case in point. Thus, the "true" waiting time is some compromise arrived at by the coach-athlete, when confronted by the restrictive rules. Even more difficult to interpret, when viewing such findings, is just *what* the athlete *is* doing between trials. The researchers infer that he or she is "concentrating" on the forthcoming trial; however, what the athlete is really doing, remains in the head of the athlete and may only be guessed at by those conducting the research, and those viewing the data which emerges.

Sport psychologists who carefully clock waiting time for a given athlete, and then contrast it to performance efforts, may serve that athlete in useful ways after careful conferences with both that athlete and the coach involved. That is, for a given athlete, an optimum waiting-concentration time, may be useful to achieve high

---

[1]One Finnish psychologist reported that when he did this to the Finnish team, several Olympics ago, during the night prior to their competition, some of them were reduced to tears . . . no wonder!

Figure 5   The athlete often imagines a cocoon placed over him/her in ways which exclude all but important performance qualities. In karate this is sometimes reported, and the athlete thus reacts to the limbs of the opponent entering this imaginary psychological covering.

level performance, if both the coach and athlete agree upon what the athlete is likely doing mentally during this interval. Drawing broad generalizations from this type of data to apply in meaningful ways to athletes in several sports and within other social and emotional contexts, however, seems frought with peril.

For decades psychologists interested in perception have formulated a dichotomy which infers that individuals tend to be either "figure" oriented or "ground" oriented, as they view complex situations. In more simple terms, some people focus best on the central part of their space field, upon the ball coming to them from across the tennis net, rather than upon the "ground" (the entire scope of the situation: the net, the other player, and other important cues in the background). Some educators have suggested that children who are too "ground" oriented may not correctly select out words in a sentence to correctly interpret. Likewise, the athlete who is too "figure" oriented may not correctly "organize" the totality of the opposing team, and its members' locations. Thus, the concept is similar to the broad, versus narrow attentional qualities as proposed by Nideffer and discussed earlier.

In recent pilot investigations this problem has been studied in an athletic context. For example, it was hypothesized by one student of mine that athletes who are too figure oriented, who focus upon a central component, rather than the wholeness of the situation, may have problems when attempting to score goals against goal keepers as found in waterpolo, soccer-football, and lacrosse. The figure-oriented athlete, it could be argued, might tend to look at and then hit the goalie with the ball in these situations, rather than perceiving the broad context, including: the location of the goalie, the size of the goal, and the location of other important defensive players. Numerous coaches of these sports often experience frustration when strong scorers with apparently "free and easy goals" hit the goalie with the ball, instead of kicking (or throwing) the ball away from the goalie and into the goal! Some experimental evidence is present which backs up this assumption; indeed some players will tend to throw to the goalie, the central figure, more often than others, not because of stupidity, or in an effort to give the coach a nervous breakdown, but because of unique perceptual tendencies which seem to mold their behavior in ways which are inappropriate to the situation.

Thus, at this point, the available research points to numerous dimensions of attention, most of which have a high degree of relevance to sport and to athletic performance. These dimensions include:

1. Quality of the attention being given by the athlete: is it general, or a high quality "close attention?"

2. Duration of Attention: How long should the athlete be able to concentrate within a given sport context, to optimize his or her skill? How can this prolongation best be accomplished?

3. Breadth of Attention: Is the athlete attending to a broad range of cues, to the "ground," or to a narrow range of cues, to a single figure?

4. Inward-Outward: Is the athlete attending to information external to his person and mind, including words from the coach, as well as to visual and auditory information which may be eminating from the sports situation . . . or to his own thoughts, to internal feelings and images?

5. Flexibility of Attention: Is the athlete attending to a variety of cues, to a broad range, as well as quickly changing to a narrow range of cues? Can he or she make this transition appropriately and quickly, or does the athlete demonstrate perceptual and attentional inflexibility and appears to be "stuck" on cues which may

alternately gain and then lose relevance in the context of the performance?

WHAT ATHLETES SAY

Many of our interview questions did not hinge directly upon the problems of concentration in athletics. However, despite this, many athletes referred to concentration and its problems when speaking to us. Others told us of highly creative and potentially useful intellectual strategies, "mental games" they played in their heads to help them to focus in on the important components of their skills and their sport.

One of the more common reports, heard from a variety of athletes in which skill ws highly important in their sport, involved pre-competition concentration sessions. At times, particularly in gymnastics, these athletes told us that they spent a considerable amount of time, just before competition, thinking and concentrating upon the skills of their sport. Often this concentrated thought resulted in a semi- or complete trance state, a state of mind involving a cutting off of other stimuli.

Some atheltes told us of ways of "cutting off distractions," which enabled them to concentrate better, involving the forming of a "bubble" over themselves and other important aspects of their performance. This was reported by karate performers, for example, who explained that they attempted to place a mental bubble, an opaque canopy over themselves and their opponent. In this way the believed that they could concentrate better. At times this bubble extended over their own bodies and they concentrated upon reacting to their opponent's hands which would flash into their "bubble." Similar strategies were reported to us by gymnasts who placed themselves in mentally "empty rooms" in the middle of a bustling gymnasium. In this way they concentrated only upon their own reactions, skills, and apparatus, remaining relatively oblivious to distractions provided by spectators and others who might be performing at the same time.

Etzel in a recent study (1979) also used the "ask them" approach in order to ascertain the types of problems athletes seemed to be having relative to attention. Seventy-one world class athletes were polled in an effort to determine what kinds of "self-talk" reflected various categories of attentional problems. He found that five types of attentional problems were prevalent in the athletes questioned. These included:

1. Thoughts about attentional capacities: such "self-talk" statements as, "I must exert high levels of attention when I am under pressure," reflected this initial category.

2. Thoughts about duration of attention, an endurance dimension of attention. Thus, such "self-talk statements" as "I have difficulty keeping my attention for the entire contest" . . . or "I have trouble keeping my attention on the game, during the final stages," reflected this type of quality.

3. Thoughts about flexibility of attention included various introspective statements such as, "I have difficulty shifting my attention to details and then to the big picture" . . . or perhaps, "I have difficulty giving my attention to the basket when shooting and then to the entire team when I come down on offense," reflect this highly important flexibility quality. Flexibility is essential to many interdependent team sports in which players must alternate from a perceptual "set" involving precise passing and shooting, to a broader attentional spectrum which requires perceiving a general pattern of players confronted on defense and their own players when on offense.

4. Intensity thought are reflected in such self-administered statements as, "I feel better about shooting when I am alert and well rested?"

5. Attentional selectivity was seen when athletes reported that at times they said to themselves, "When I shoot, I shut out all thoughts except those dealing with my performance."

IMPLICATIONS FOR COACHES AND ATHLETES

Overall, the "athlete-centered" research reveals that there is more than one dimension of attention and thus an athlete may need to be questioned closely when he/she simply states, "I have trouble with my attention." To help such an athlete, one needs to know precisely just what kinds of attentional problem(s) the athlete may be incurring.

Further, it seems important to be aware that various sports, by their very nature, contain their own unique or combination of unique attentional requirements and demands. Thus, a shooter may, for example, confront major attentional problems such as selecting the target out of distracting backgrounds (high levels of visual and auditory "noise" being present). Further, the athlete in this same sport may incur attentional problems involving duration and intensity as the competition wears on into its latter stages. This prolongation of attention is encountered by athletes in endurance sports which are highly "loaded" with elements of pain and stress, as exemplified by long distance running, cross-country skiing, and the like. However, athletes in this latter type of endurance sport rarely mention problems of attempting to focus visually upon a specific object, person, or target as is often talked about by archers and pistol shooters.

One may construct a chart-diagram depicting hypothetical attentional demands of various sports. I have attempted to do so, however, it should be emphasized that for the most part the diagram is based upon hypothetical assumptions as yet untested by objective studies.

Numerous other examples could be given, in addition to those on the preceeding chart. In general, however, it is apparent that many sports have a variety of attentional demands, particularly those involving complex and variable team interactions, interpolated by target-goal throwing (making). Sports which are relatively "closed," in which the individual does not have to react to the often unpredictable efforts of others, i.e. gymnastics, target shooting, and the like, may require fewer types of attentional demands.

After polling athletes and reviewing the efforts of others who have done so, it becomes apparent that if an athlete is aware that there are attentional demands and perhaps he/she is having problems, he/she will generally engage in two general types of strategies. One approach by the athlete is to exclude distracting conditions: people, noise, or other confusion. This is generally done via self-talk or some kind of creative imagery (i.e. imagining the gymnasium empty, or a canopy placed over the competing place/apparatus, etc.). The second approach involves an effort to "self-talk" one's way to more critical and intense attention by focusing upon some (or the) important component in the task. That is, this second method, instead of consisting of negative exclusion consists of positive inclusion. Occasionally an athlete will report engaging in both methods, first attempting to exclude distractions, and then concentrating upon critical performance qualities.

ATTENTIONAL DEMANDS OF VARIOUS SPORTS

	Intensity	Duration	Flexibility	Center Figure Selected, A Central Focus
1. Team Sports: basketball, ice-hockey, team hand ball, etc.	at times	at end of contest	yes, from offense to defense to shooting	yes, when shooting, passing to one man
2. Endurance running skiing, swimming	at times	for long races	not generally	not usually, unless passed by opponent
3. Shooting: rifles pistols, archery	at times	at end of competition	no, not usually	yes, at target
4. Field events in track and field	yes, usually	not always	no	yes, upon skill as a focus, at times at target, i.e. bar to be jumped, distance line in shot putting, etc.
5. American football	at times	at completion of game	yes, frequently on defense	in some positions, i.e. targets to pass to, intercepting balls
6. Baseball	at times	as game is prolonged	yes, on defense primarily	frequently, when pitching, attempting to hit ball, throwing to base, catching ball
7. Gymnastics	yes	as events are prolonged	not usually	yes, upon specific skill, or skill pattern

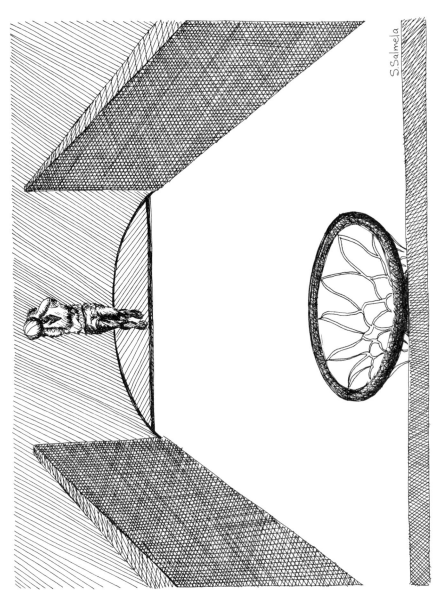

Figure 6 Concentration may be enhanced when the athlete places imaginary walls which serve to block off distracting conditions, as when a basketball player attempts to shoot a free-throw.

THREE CASE STUDIES

Now three case studies are presented, reflecting what one might do to enhance the attentional capacities of an athlete. These methods are generally either self-administrated, or may be suggested by the coach and then self-administered by the athlete. In general, they require the athlete to first adjust his/her activation level at optimum, and then to engage in various kinds of "self-talk," sometimes coupled with visual imagery.

These case studies differ along important dimensions, some of which have been referred to before. (a) Some athletes may have unique attentional problems consisting of a specific kind of inability to prolong or otherwise deal with attention in a given component of a sport. (2) The case studies reflect different sports, and thus different attentional demands placed upon athletes because of the very nature of the demands inherent in the sport. (3) Finally, the case studies differ according to whether the athlete is applying attentional strategies, during the break in a sport (i.e. between events in gymnastics or trials in track-and-field) or during the time the athlete is actually participating (i.e. while running, or swimming).

Case 1 The "Shakey" Shooter

Tim, a pistol shooter, generally posts excellent scores during the beginning levels of competition each year. As he ascends higher and higher in various tournaments he begins to have problems during the latter stages of the tournaments. At times, his attempts to focus attention result in extreme tension. "My hand shakes at times," and this tension acts in a negative-feedback system, that is, increased tension engenders more tension and less steadiness as critical parts of matches are reached. He seems to have problems prolonging attention and of maintaining that attentional level in ways which permit muscular tension to be at an optimum.

Several strategies in combination may be used to help "shakey." These include attempts to exclude distractions, as well as ways to adjust intensity and to prolong optimum attention, by taking attentional "breaks." Thus, this athlete may be told to: (1) Pretend that you are shooting down a long hall with high walls which are thick and prevent the noise of other shooters to get to you. Build this wall in your mind before you shoot, and imagine it while you are shooting. (2) Imagine your shooting wrist suspended from a wire so that a minimum of muscular tension is needed to hold it in place. Relax your arm muscles as much as you can, while shooting, during the initial parts of the match. Pretend that your arm-wire is on an over-head pully and that between groups of shots it is lowered (your arm), permitting it to relax and rest. Slowly raise it again, but let it float to a horizontal position, being pulled there by others working the pully. During the final portions of the match take an "attentional time out." Purposely let your attention wander to a pleasant outcome of your sport (imagine yourself receiving the medal) . . . or to a completely unrelated success experience outside of sport, being awarded a scholarship! Now bring your attention back to the match. First slowly, and then with intensity, work hard to get it back and keep it back for shorter periods of time, during the end of the match. To win, all you need are short, intense periods of close attention. Near the end imagine your bullet going toward the center of the target on a string . . . imagine your target's center larger and larger as bullets traveling down the string in precise ways as the last shots are made. Toward the end concentrate upon a larger target center, your arm suspended by others, and make your wall thick and sound proof. Block out your scores, other's scores, and the noise made by others!

Case 2   The Nervous Gymnast

The gymnast has had problems concentrating upon her performance, particularly after early and often successful performances. The scores of her teammates often distract her, because if they are low she must somehow make up for their deficiencies in her own performance. Also, when she scores high at the beginning (9.6's and 9.7's) she mentally adds up totals and becomes anxious, and thus, her attention falters as she sees pressure upon herself to achieve a total of 38 or above (10 x 4 events). As subsequent events are confronted she is able to pay less and less attention to her own performance and sub-skills as she worries more and more about her previous scores and the scores of her teammates.

Attention and anxiety are intertwined. Increased worry can unfocus attention, shift attention to qualities extraneous to good performance, and/or cause the athlete (in this case gymnast) to break off prolonged attention during subsequent stages of a competition. Several of these problems seem to be afflicting this gymnast. To counteract these attentional problems in this context, this gymnast may be encouraged to engage in the following imaginal and cognitive strategies.

1. The gymnast may be encouraged to reduce fears of failure with reference to cognitive-emotive-therapy. That is, she may be encouraged to "self-talk" such messages as, "If I do not do well, the rest of the team will not foreshake me; most will feel that I am a worthwhile person." On the positive vein, the gymnast may be encouraged to think (self-talk), "If I forget the others and their scores, and concentrate upon only my own performance, I will do better. I cannot carry the whole team on my shoulders and if I try to do so the worry will hurt my attention." Or perhaps, "I should not worry about how I score on each event and how that score may influence my totals, or the team total; but instead I should focus upon the movement patterns and sequences needed in my routines."

2. Exclusionary imagery may be useful. The gymnast may be encouraged to "imagine the gymnasium empty; an empty gymnasium in an empty college in a town without anyone in it." Not only is the gymnasium empty and quiet — but also a circus has been to town and a tent has been left, which may be placed over each apparatus as I come to it. A large crane will move it from apparatus to apparatus, as I perform. The tent excludes everyone, even judges; it just covers me and the beam, the uneven parallel bars, the free-exercise mat and the horse, as I use them."

"I have no adding machine in my head adding up scores . . ." The gymnast may be encouraged to think . . . "I only have patterns of exact and beautiful movements, movements necessary to complete my routines well. Between events, in a special house I will build for myself, I will sit and think about patterns of skills to come in my next routine." These are suggestions for thoughts which might occupy the gymnast in positive ways. Between events, the coach or psychologist who has collaborated in these kinds of imagery might remind the gymnast, "now relax and go to your thinking house, everyone else is doing fine in this meet; you will do fine if you concentrate upon your movement patterns, not upon numbers." Successful culmination of a meet in which this type of imagery is encouraged, may encourage the girl to continue with this type of thinking, imagining and planning in future competition. Periodic checks should be made, either formally or informally, to determine if attentional problems may be reoccurring, particularly if a decrease in performance efficiency may reflect a subsequent retrogression in attentional quality.

Case Study 3   The Basketball Player and His Free-Throws

The basketball player *is* exceptional, his field goal scoring is excellent, both in percentage and in numbers, an 18 plus average per game, with a percentage of better than 55%. He often plays deep, posting up as center, and his jump shot from in-deep usually goes in. But free-throws are another matter, his percentage is often below his field goal percentage; he seems to freeze, to shoot a shallow shot, a "brick" with no trajectory. This often increases as a problem late in the contest. His mind wanders, he says, during the early parts of the game and after missing one or more he becomes anxious and tightens up and misses more. Distracting crowd noise really bothers him, as do crowds who wave their arms, banners, and other implements to visually distract him as he starts to shoot. Hostile crowds know of his problems, and he knows they know!

This player has several problems, some of which are related to stress and anxiety. The cues which he attends to are not appropriate when under stress (both crowd stress and the stress to win and make free throws), while at the same time he has difficulties both focusing upon the central figure (a basket) and in blocking out extraneous cues (fan noise and visual distractions). He may have problems in attentional flexibility, in quickly changing from a broad-width of attention needed as he comes down a court on offense, watching and knowing where other players are, and the narrow range of attention he needs when coming up to free throw. A number of kinds of interventions may be attempted, as his attentional problems are multifaceted. For example:

1. Stress modeling may be used with positive effects in this situation. During practice, free-throws should be periodically attempted while the athlete is moderately fatigued. These should be accompanied by a loud "blast" of crowd noise (taped and played by a student manager). These noises should be intermittent, coming and going in quick succession, as he prepares to shoot. Others, perhaps substitutes should place themselves under the basket during a practice free-throw and yell, wave towels, and otherwise provide the same or similar visual distractions as those which will be encountered in the competition arena.

2. Specific focusing imagery should also be employed. That is, the athlete should be given a specific ritual to engage in, one which will calm him prior to attempting to free throw. The ritual should contain one or more deep breaths, and a certain number of bounces of the ball. This ritual is designed to make each free throw attempt similar, no matter what the situation.

3. Target(s) of attention should be provided. For example, the player should be required to first focus upon the center of the basket's rim . . . then imagine a point just behind it (4-6'') and then shoot the ball at that point (the athlete may also be asked to imagine the center of the back of the rim and then imagine a point just in front of it, if this is more comfortable to him). Perhaps an imaginary spot within the basket should be shot at, rather than some diffuse or undefined target within the larger target of the basket. A basket may be given to the basketball player with a suspended "spot" within it, attached to a rod, a basket which he may hang in his room and focus upon, while he imagines himself shooting throws successfully as he goes to sleep each night.

4. Exclusionary imagery may also be employed, as has been the case in other case studies covered. This imagery may be more efficient, if some real experience is first given to the basketball player, involving exclusion of distractions. That is, the player may be kept after practice, the gymnasium emptied, for from 2-3 times a week. An assistant coach may ask him to practice free-throwing with the attentional (target) conditions described in (3) above. Then later during practice, as it begins, a

free throw or two may be attempted with the athlete encouraged to imaginally or mentally "empty the gymnasium" before shooting. "Imagine the gymnasium empty, as when we practice after practice . . ." the helper-coach may suggest . . . "now shoot . . . no one can get to you, no one is watching, no one will know . . . no one will care what you do."

Exclusionary imagery may also be used to block off noise. The free thrower may first practice with ear-plugs after practice, excluding noise. Then after an "image" model has been acquired by the athlete (as an "empty gym" model has been acquired), the player may be asked to imagine the ear-plugs in place before throwing.

Finally, partial visual exclusion may be imagined, in order to cognitively "block-off" visual distractions which may occur behind the basket. That is, the player may be asked to imagine a large iron door dropping down from the top of the arena, just prior to free-throws occurring during practice, after practice, and finally during games. In this way the athlete may learn to cut off these kinds of distractions during games.

Obviously the coach-psychologist (or the athlete himself) may evolve too many ways to focus attention in free-throwing. In this case the athlete may be so busy imagining ways to focus attention that the skill of the throw is somehow lost in the shuffle. Likewise, the athlete is unable to both imagine a wall blocking off visual distractors, while on the other hand, learning to handle visual stresses imposed by managers waving towels during practices while he throws. In any case, this case study illustrates specific examples of how attention may be improved with two major types of strategies-exclusionary and focusing.

OVERVIEW

Description of the attention and concentration abilities in athletics has occupied the time of sport psychologists for several decades within the countries of Eastern Europe. Only recently has that interest been seen on this side of the Atlantic. A number of variables and relationships are important to consider when attempting to assess an athlete's attentional abilities and to determine how they might be refined, if necessary.

Attentional demands of various sports range from those which require close attention for only brief periods to others whose requirements involved prolonged periods of concentration, often lasting several hours. For the most part, anxiety and attention are closely associated with fear-producing situations or emotions, serving to shorten or ease the athlete's attentional abilities.

Models to explain attention have included several dimensions: (1) breadth of attention, (2) whether it is directed inward or outward, (3) flexibility of attention required, (4) and other attributes including "close" versus "general" attention.

Attention heightening strategies include relaxation training coupled with various kinds of imagery, and self-talk. The strategies proposed in this chapter include those which attempt to exclude distracting conditions, as well as ways of helping the athlete focus in on the "target" or the center of the skilled act. Case studies of various athletes have been presented, including a pistol shooter, a gymnast and a basketball player attempting to improve free-throws. In each case, a variety of imagery is suggested.

REFERENCES

Cratty, B.J. and Y. Hanin, *The Athlete and the Sport Team,* Love Publications, Denver, Co., 1980.

Etzel, E.F., "Validation of a conceptual model characterizing attention among international rifle shooters," *Journal of Sport Psychology,* 1979, 1, pp. 281-290.

Klinger, E., S.V. Barta and R.A. Glass, "Thought content and gap time in basketball," *Cognitive Therapy and Research,* 1981, 5, 1, pp. 109-114.

Nideffer, R.M., "Relationship of attention and anxiety to performance," *Sport Psychology: An Analysis of Athletic Behavior.* Mouvement Publications, Ithaca, N.Y. 1978.

CHAPTER 8

DREAMS AND OTHER "SPECIAL STATES"

Dreams and other special "mental" states are a pervasive part of the lives of many. It is virtually impossible to delve even superficially into the religions and customs of the world's people without encountering the manner in which trance states, meditation, and imagery of unusual kinds invade all cultures of the world, and are found within all societal levels.

Although undoubtedly these special feelings and experiences have been present in the heads of athletes over the centuries, it is only recently that writers and scientists have paid much attention to the "unusual experiences" reported by many, if not most sports competitiors. These first efforts, by scholars interested in this potentially exciting topic, have been primarily involved in attempts to classify the experiences of athletes rather than investigations into the meaning and relationships which these "special states" may hold for the improvement of athletic performance.

In one of the more recent energetic treatments of this topic, Murphy and White (1978), dealing with reports of athletics reflecting "the psychic side of sport," grouped quotes from athletes into several categories. These included experiences which involved distortions of the athlete's perceptions, those which seemed to enable (or accompanied) unusually great efforts and high marks, as well as those which involved some kind of apparent transformation of the athlete's body (e.g., floating over ones-self). Although the study of dreams has been a major scientific exercise for decades, investigations of the dreams of athletes are represented in only a handful of papers (Mahoney and Avener, 1977; Cratty et al. 1983). Here again the data involves so few athletes in a limited number of sports, that drawing valid meanings and conclusions from the information these studies contain is an extremely shakey undertaking.

The sport of running, achieving heightened popularity in recent years, has triggered an interest in what kinds of special mental experiences seem to beset those who pound the tracks for prolonged periods of time. Runners themselves, as well as writers, have become intrigued with what is termed a "runner's high," or a kind of "spinning out" that may occur as the runner extends his/her efforts over prolonged times and/or distances.

The superficial information that is available, suggests that the answers to several questions could have important ramifications for the improvement of athletic performance. These questions include:

1. In what ways might these special states be triggered? and further, in what ways might the athlete either supress, or instigate these "conditions" to his/her advantage?

2. In what ways might some kinds of special states, when they appear "spontaneously," be harmful to athletic performance? Might a runner who is running

"out of his/her head" be less involved with the careful monitoring of physical feelings important to useful pacing of efforts?

3. To what degree might the athlete exert control over these special feelings? To what degree may (or should) someone else (a hypnotist?) aid an athlete to achieve these states?

4. In what ways do these "special feelings or unusual pictures" interact with such feelings or unusual pictures interact with such feelings and emotions as anxiety, aggression, concentration, tolerance of fatigue, pain, as well as the production of physical skill and effort?

The answers to these questions are far from clear at this point. However, in this chapter some tentative suggestions will be made. Only the athlete can accurately "feel" these experiences, and thus judge their worth to his/her athletic efforts. It is hoped that the following information may aid the athlete to understand more about the manner in which the mind seems at times to be "on a lark," as competition takes place.

WHAT THE RESEARCH SAYS

Dreams

Dreams have intrigued writers, scholars and philosophers for centuries. Pre-scientific societies often placed a great deal of emphasis upon dreams, and attended to them closely, feeling that their content and messages were communications from the gods. With the rise of scientific inquiry, following the middle ages, the study of dreams continued to languish as it was found that they were not easily measured. It was not until the early part of this century that Sigmund Freud's speculations gave legitimacy to the study of dreams. He and his followers believed that dreams were important windows into the sub-conscious and that relationships between dream life and conscious experiences when understood, provided meaningful insights into the psychodynamics of the individual.

Scientists, during the decades which followed, have studied dreams for reasons which reflect their varied backgrounds. Sociologists and anthropologists have explored dream content of primitive people to determine the manner in which the individual integrates with society, and the impact of the society upon its members. Psychiatrists and some experimental psychologists have employed dream reports as a kind of projective test, similar to the Rorschach ink-blot test, as a way to reveal parts of the dreamer's personality which are often hidden and difficult to understand.

In the 1950s, a number of researchers observed that the dream experience occurred during periods of what they termed "a unique organismic state" which was accompanied by rapid flickerings of the eyes. At last, dreams seemed more amenable to collection and classification. Later, in the 1960s, it was found that the mental content of dreams could be retrieved from a number of periods of sleep, periods which were well defined by obtaining measures of electric activity coming from the brain. This pairing of objective brain activity with apparent dream incidence and content prompted an even greater interest in the night pictures of men and women.

At the present time there are hundreds of studies of dream content in the literature. One current reference lists at least 132 questionnaire and rating forms to facilitate their collection (Winget and Kramer, 1979). These investigations sometimes have taken place within highly sophisticated "sleep laboratories" in which subject's are often "wired up" to obtain parallel electric-physiological information. However, researchers continued to obtain information from direct interviews of people, in circumstances which are relaxed and normal for the subjects (in a living room). It is often found that the reports obtained in such circumstances are not distorted by the often usual conditions the dreamer must deal with in an (often threatening) environment presented by a medical center, i.e., physicians in white smocks, and wires extending to his/her scalp! In contrast, the research we have conducted with athletes is based upon interviews carried out in "natural" settings.

In studies which have taken place generally have attempted to:

1. Determine differences in dream content reported by people of different ages, sex, race, occupational preference, religion, and philosophical orientation.

2. Determine what special emotional states might elicit changes in dream content.

3. Discover possible relationships between various kinds and degrees of mental disturbances and dream content.

Few studies have made an attempt to modify dream content, i.e., by engaging in some kind of mental activity just before sleep. Research which looks at the dreams of athlete's for meaning is virtually non-existant. Thus, hypotheses which relate dream content to athletic peformance must be formed with reference to the general findings of the dream researchers rather than being based upon information gained directly from athletes themselves.

Generally the available information from the dream studies indicate that:

1. Dream content is a continuation of the dreamer's conscious awake life. When the dream is a moderate distortion it may reveal somewhat the same information as is gained when a psychologist or psychiatrist administers some kind of projective test.[1]

2. In healthy adolescents, dream content is often of the "wish-fulfillment" type, in which the dreamer experiences a sought after reward. Many of the younger university athletes we interviewed reported this type of dream to us. (Cratty et al, 1983).

3. The dream content gained from reports from people in "normal" environments (e.g., their living room) is likely to be freer of distortions than that gained from a "sleep laboratory setting." However, in this latter environment more information may be obtained about more dreams.

4. Aggressive thoughts enter dreams frequently. Younger people and older people are usually the recipients of aggression, or simply observe aggression. A "chase dream" often enters the dreams of younger children, relfecting the child's fears of someone or something. Likewise, women are more likely to be the receivers of aggression than the opposite.

5. Males from 18 to 30 are more likely to dream about aggressing against others than are younger or older men, or than females of all ages.

6. Numerous variables may alter the report of a dream given to a scientist. These include the setting, the rapport (or relationship) between the scientist and reporter, as well as the age, sex, nationality, religious orientation, and mood of the dreamer. People not only vary in the number of dreams remembered, but also in the facility

---

[1]Projective tests include those which encourage the client to project themselves into various kinds of test materials . . . i.e., to complete a sentence which might have several kinds of endings . . . or to interpret an ink blot, or perhaps to complete a story whose beginning is supplied by the psychologist or psychiatrist.

Figure 7   Athletes often dream of successful situations, of winning important competitions. This type of wish-fulfillment dream is most common among athletes from 12-16 or 18 years of age.

with which they are able to translate their visual-dream experience into a verbal report. The clarity, reality, as well as the duration of a dream may vary greatly, thus modifying reports obtained by the scientist recording a verbal report.

The collection of and analysis of the dreams of athletes is just beginning (Mahoney and Avener 1978, Cratty et al. 1983). The aspiration of young athletes are often said to include "dreams of making the Olympic team." Indeed some of the reports we have obtained include dreams about just that. These dreams are commonly reported by athletes in late adolescence, when such "wish-fulfillment dreams" are most prevalent. Older athletes often report dream fragments, partial pictures of games, in which sometimes others are present, and sometimes they are the sole focus of attention.

Trance States, Special "Out-Of-Contact Experiences"

The research dealing with various "special states" of athletes is in its infancy. The investigations, which have been carried out are good first attempts, but consist primarily of efforts to classify and count, rather than to interpret the meaning of various kinds of "buzz states" which athletes reportedly experience. Murphy and White, writing about the psychic side of sport, present a wide variety of "special experiences" encountered by, and reported by athletes. These range from those which have accompanied or seemingly facilitated unusual athletic efforts, to those which may be termed unusual but not likely to have greatly modified athletic participation.

Within a more narrow conceptual focus, Carmack and Martens reported a study of what they (or their subjects) reported as "spinning out" during long distance running. They found that about 250 males and 65 females reported running in at least a moderately dissociative "mind" set, and that this apparent frame of mind occurred most often after about forty minutes into their runs. Sachs and Pargman in a further attempt to more precisely classify these types of thoughts in runners, found that they may be placed into three categories: (a) those reflecting a division, completely different from running, as when a runner, for example, would imagine himself building a house while running, (b) thoughts representing some kind of problem solving behavior, and a less defined category, (c) those involving relatively rapid and spontaneous thoughts on the part of runners.

In interviews with football players conducted recently, we found that virtually all of the linemen interviewed reported having deja-vu experiences; occurrences in games which they declared had apparently happened to them before, in dreams or in their imagination. They would say, for example, that often during play they would feel as though they had made the same exact play in the past. The same colors, the numbers on their opponents were the same and otherwise they seemed to be "replaying" something that had happened to them in the past. Furthermore, they usually had trouble pinpointing the time and place of the past experiences.

A case could be made for the fact that all athletes, at one time or another, have experienced special states or distortions of perceptions of thoughts and/or imagery which ranged from bizarre to mildly disturbing. Those of us interviewing athletes are likely to find out about these "special states" if we are careful not to voice (or by gesture) any negative judgement concerning our feelings and interpretations of these reports. However, it is difficult to "get an objective measure" or a "handle" on these reports, in so far as the terminology that the interviewer might use versus the "name" given the experience by that athlete may not reflect the same type of occurrence. That is, some athletes may refer to the same kind of flowing, effortless, floating experience as a "buzz state" . . . "flow" . . . "floating" . . . or perhaps some other less descriptive term. More difficulty is encountered when attempting to attach these experiences to positive or negative changes in performance, or when trying to determine just what causes them to occur.

Finally, difficulties lie when counseling athletes about whether they should somehow seek to "enter" these special perceptual or conceptual worlds, or whether they should avoid them. A case could be made, for example, that a dissociative mind set while distance running is counter-productive. Published research (Morgan 1979), as well as pilot studies we have carried out (unpublished, by Albert Marquez), indicate that most high quality distance runners, at distances over 5,000 . . . and particularly up to 10,000 km. and the marathon, do best when they consciously and closely monitor the various bodily sub-systems (heart-rate, muscular tensions, respiration etc.) as they change themselves during the rigors of running. Those runners who apparently do not, are not as successful, or may be running simply to achieve a runner's high rather than to achieve low times.

In contrast to this apparent counter-productivity of a "runner's high" are reports we have heard from gymnasts (Cratty, Lange, and O'Neil 1983) who reported that they often entered a "buzz state" prior to competition, and furthermore sought to do so, in so far as they attached better performance to this state. When pressed for exactly what the state felt like, or how they "entered" such an altered condition, they were less communicative, and would report vaguely, for example, that "I don't know . . . it's just a feeling I get . . ." or perhaps "I seem relaxed and not really aware of others . . ."

This contradiction and contrast in the apparent occurrence, reasons for occurrence, and value attached to these apparently "altered states" by athletes indicate that two, almost opposable kinds of hypotheses might be formulated for their presence and existence. (1) Athletes who are extremely over-activated, and/or fearful may enter this kind of "altered state" as their psyche almost seems to be tranquilizing itself, much as the body's physiology seems to "kick in" tranquilizers when the body has been stressed. The athlete who enters such a state and who has achieved a high skill level, simply relaxes as the "programs" flow out of their neuromotor system, thus leading to apparently effortless and superior performance. (2) A second hypothesis may also be suggested, as was mentioned above. That is, an athlete who may be over-stressed physiologically, as when running or swimming a long distance, and is experiencing pain, may simply begin to tranquilize himself via hormonal tranquilizers, and possible increases of specific brain enzymes which tend to mask pain. This second hypothesis may explain the runner's high, and its masking effect upon both thought and pain experiences.

A positive "flow state" has been reported to us by several athletes in recent interview studies. These reports seem to substantiate a performance-state hypothesis; that is, their good performance seemed to trigger a useful "flowing" or floating state. In one case, a woman softball competitor reported that she would seem at times to float, in slow motion, to first base when she had just hit the ball well in an important game. "I seemed to move slowly, as did all around me, and yet I was running at my maximum." Still other reports from distance runners seem to also substantiate the existence of first performance and then an altered state. One distance runner reported to us that he would enter a state when he was in the middle one-third of a race, particularly when he was in good condition, and when he was running efficiently. "I seem to float along, slightly above the ground; I cannot feel my legs or the contact and jarring when my feet hit the ground," he said. He continued by explaining that he would remain in this state until another runner would pass him. At that point either of two things was likely to happen: (a) If he permitted the opponent to pass without doing anything, he would suddenly leave his altered state, and be seemingly jarred awake, and then would pursue his competition. On the other hand, if he quickly changes his pace to meet a passer's challenge and did so successfully, or even remained behind his opponent the previously felt euphoric state would continue and be sustained. That is, he would suddenly "wake up" if his race and position was both threatened, and he was passed easily, however if the challenge was met by his body his "flowing" altered state would remain.[2]

WHAT ATHLETES TELL US ABOUT THEIR DREAMS

In one of the few previous studies of dream reports by athletes it was found that the frequency of dreams, on the part of eight athletes, somehow differentiated the better performers from the less able. This information gained from gymnasts, however, is not in accord with some we have obtained (Mahoney and Avener 1978), and which will be reviewed shortly. However, this kind of finding about so few athletes, points up the scarcity of valid information concerning the dreams of athletes, and prompted questions about dreams in the interview forms we administered for a period of two years. (Cratty and Carpinter, 1983, Cratty, Lange and O'Neill, 1983; Cratty, Lange and Whipple, Carpinter and Cratty, 1983 etc.). As our studies continued, our questions regarding dream and dream content reflected more sophistication. However our efforts represent only brief glimpses into what is likely to be an increasingly popular and fascinating area of inquiry for sport psychologists.

In one of our first studies of the "mental life of athletes" we simply asked university-level football players if they ever dreamed about their sport, and whether these dream experiences reflected positive or negative performance or emotions (Cratty and Carpinter 1983). These same questions were also asked of men and women gymnasts and of women track and field performers (Cratty, Lange and O'Neill 1983). Later studies of waterpolo players included additional questions: we asked about the frequency of "sports dreams," as well as about the presence of others (who?) in the dream, and whether the dream was positive or negative in its impact upon the athlete. Additionally, we were curious about whether the dreamer awakened upset-tired or refreshed as the result of the dream. Finally, we were interested in whether the frequency of a "sports dream" increased as the season (and thus purportedly the tensions) progressed.

In one recent investigation, our study focused upon aggressive content in sports dreams of men and women karate competitors. We contrasted these reports to dream reports obtained from non-competitive women; and within the karate population we contrasted the dream content of those with more and less experience at the sport (Cratty, Lange, and Whipple 1983). Finally, in an investigation of team sport athletes we were curious as to relationships between the type and frequency of dreams

---

[2]We were surprised when this runner informed us that he would also engage in a fair amount of "success imagery" during the initial parts of a race, imagine himself breaking the finish line first. When other distance runners were asked about the incidence of success imagery of this type in their thoughts during races, they responded in a similar fashion.

reported and the coach's ratings of the athlete's "intensity-motivation," and of his "performance and ability" (Carpinter and Cratty 1983).

The following represent some of the conclusions we reached in these preliminary studies:

1. It was found that the type of dream tended to differ fom sport to sport. For example, in the individual sports of track and field and gymnastics, dreams involving positive experiences usually prevailed. However, within individual sport groups, more "negative experiences" were evidenced in dreams than was true among team sport athletes. Typical of a "negative experience" in a dream reported by an individual sport athlete was being able to stop giant swings on the hi-bar, or having the apparatus somehow capture and retain the performer when he/she wanted to get off! Distance runners reported frequent dreams of being unable to run through heavy sand or in water which was knee-deep. While discus throwers, javelin throwers, and shot-putters would dream of holding excessively heavy implements and being unable to propel them any distance! The common observation that individual sport athletes may have to overcome more anxiety than team sport athletes could have resulted in these differences. The team sport athlete is often not responsible for the total win or loss . . . and is somehow "hidden" within the total team effort. The individual sport athlete on the other hand, often feels extremely exposed, vulnerable to ridicule, and visible to all when performing. This increased visability and responsibility for success and failure, may make these kinds of "negative dreams" more frequent in these latter competitors.

2. For the most part, younger team sport athletes reported numerous dreams of the "wish-fulfillment" type. The athlete pictured himself or herself as the center of success with surprising regularity. In one team, a succession of college-age freshmen reported that they were winning the nationals in their sport, an identical dream eminating from four consecutive athletes! More mature athletes, however, repeatedly dream about (or) of fragments of their sport, of success and failure, and of partial success not total over-powering victory. Thus, with maturity it appears that the imagery in dream content reflects a more realistic orientation than is true among the younger peformers. This finding is parallel with previous work in dream control and wish-fulfillment episodes reported by late adolescents in general.

3. Athletes whose skills may be simple or extremely well learned, and whose activation levels are extremely high often reported that they remembered little of relatively prolonged athletic contests. For example, most of a group of superior high school linemen (in American football) told us that they rarely remembered what happened in a game; that they performed powerfully and instinctively, and learned of their successes and failures either during films viewed later, or when people informed them of what they did!

4. This same group of football players also reported that they frequently had deja-vu experiences when playing; feelings that the exact competitive incidence had occurred earlier in their dreams. The parallels were often striking, including the same numbers on players, colors, and actions.

5. Athletes generally reported that they observed the action of their dreams, while looking out of their own eyes. However, when the manner in which they experienced their dreams (observing themselves or viewing themselves in a normal way, from within) was contrasted to the type of imagery they engaged in when mentally practicing skills, no relationships were obtained (Cratty and Carpinter 1983).

6. Virtually all athletes told us that the frequency of their "sport related

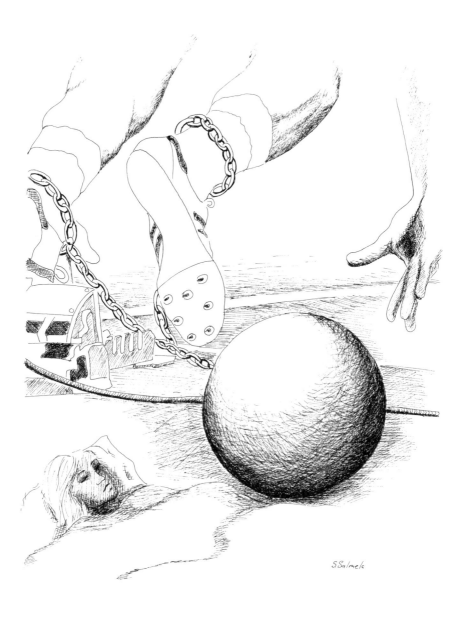

Figure 8   Athletes often report performance problems in their dreams of trying to run through deep sand or through the surf; or of the gymnastic apparatus refusing to let them dismount.

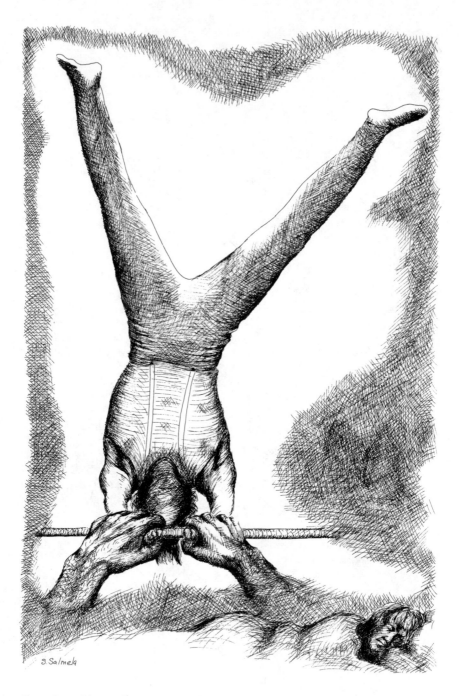

Figure 9 Athletes often report performance problems in their dreams of trying to run through deep sand or through the surf; or of the gymnastic apparatus refusing to let them dismount.

dreams'' increased as the critical parts of the season were approaching. This increased incidence of sports dreams could have reflected heightened anxiety about their sport, as the final parts of their season approached.

7. Perhaps the most important find arising from this research was the negative relationships we obtained when contrasting coach's ratings of ability and the athlete's frequency of dreams. In one larger group we polled, the athletes rated lower in ability, dreamed more. Whether this increased incidence of dreaming reflected anxiety which in turn negatively affected performance we could not tell. However, this kind of relationship is possible.

8. We were struck with the fact that a considerable percentage of the athletes in all sports we polled reported that they had not been able to remember a single "sports dream." Whether dreams obtained via the sleep laboratory on these same "dreamless" athletes would have elicited a different result, we don't know. Future studies might explore this possibility.

9. The athletes often dreamed about significant others. The coach was the most frequent figure, followed by other players, and friends (the girl friend was a frequent visitor). The presence of others in the dreams did not necessarily relate to the athlete's performance; however it is possible that the existence of the coach in an athlete's dream might reflect some inter-personal problem between the two. Further work might explore this possibility.

10. Women who had gained experience and proficiency in the martial arts reported that they dreamed about retaliatory aggression with some frequency, when annoyed in their dreams (being pursued was frequent dream content). On the other hand, women who were not equipped with these skills reported the usual content expected, they were the receivers rather than the initiators of aggression (Cratty, Lange and Whipple 1983). It thus appeared that when women had gained real skills in these defensive and offensive skills, their dream life also changed. Indeed the aggressive content of female karate performer's dreams in terms of their "dishing out" aggression paralleled that expected in males of their age.

Only a few athletes seemed to find their dreams of more than passing interest, although several were intrigued by deja-vu experiences. Some athletes, about 30%, seemed to be aware of "typical" dreams experienced by those in their sport (i.e., apparatus grabbing them in gymnastics), however, most were oblivious to the dreams of others in the sport, nor had they previously discussed dream content with anyone previous to our interviews. Athletes plagued with negative dreams, i.e., missing a trick, or performing poorly, realized that this content may reflect anxiety about a real performance problem. None, however, reported attempting to modify their dream content, in order to positively change performance.

In our first studies, we asked about "unusual trance" states they might have experienced, and only about one-third replied in the positive. However, in subsequent interviews, we quickly learned that one must question carefully, taking a non-judgemental attitude. These unusual experiences of athletes are relatively frequent, but the athlete must be assured that he/she will not somehow be judged "unbalanced" when they relate such an experience to others.

WHAT ATHLETES TELL US ABOUT "SPECIAL STATES"

Virtually all the athletes we have interviewed reported experiencing some kind of "special state" either prior to, or during performance. Less frequent were reports of these kinds of unusual trances occurring after performance.

We were rather surprised, however, to find out that often an athlete was unable to report even one sport-related dream. In one study of gymnasts, for example, less than half the athletes interviewed said that they could remember a single dream with "gymnastic content" in it.

In an effort to bring some order out of the complex and often choatic reports we listened to, I have classified these special "flow" states in the following ways:

1. *"States" which are triggered by highly activated or anxious states prior to performance.* The athlete seems to become so upset that he/she "trances out" and often it is necessary to (a) help the athlete use such states as means to evoke skill rehearsal and/or imagery which reduces pre-competition and/or (b) to later "bring the athlete out" of the "special state" so that he/she will attend to the important details of performance.

2. *"States" caused by extremely good feeling during performance, usually occurring over time in the psyche of a well prepared athlete, one who is well trained both physically and mentally.* These may be classified as "positive in-performance phenomena" and if the "trance state" is not too deeply entered by the athlete (i.e., he comes out of it when an opponent successfully passes him/her), the state may be an advantage to the athlete.

3. *A second kind of in-performance state, however, may be less than useful; the athlete is not simply "floating" or "flowing" in a positive way, but mentally escapes rather dramatically from the immediate demands and possibly the pain of the performance.* An example of this is the "runner's high," a state which probably carries the athlete too far away from the immediate demands of the competition, and from various important "signs" emiting from his/her body while running. This type may thus be termed a "negative in-performance" state, one which the coach ought to know about, and one which may have to be counteracted in rather positive and diligent ways, by both coach-athlete, perhaps with the help of a psychologist.

4. Finally a fourth type of "trance state" is reported with some frequency, but not with the frequency as are the other three types. This type occurs following a contest. *The players report buzzing out, seemingly taking a mental break to recuperate from the physical and psychological rigors of the contest.* During this time, as is often true when the other trance states occur, the athlete may be relatively uncommunicative and may seem to be "unable to be interviewed" by the more aggressive members of the press, if they are present in the locker room. During this time however, the athlete may be encouraged to contemplate in useful and realistic ways the manner in which he/she performed and how that performance might be improved. General reasons as to why success or failure encountered should also be dealt with at this time.

IMPLICATIONS FOR COACHES AND ATHLETES

Hopefully if the communications between the coach and the athlete are good enough the coach will be informed of the type of trance states the athletes is typically encountering. However, often these "special states" are so unbelievable ("I see the players on the other team as suddenly smaller"), that the athlete may be reluctant to communicate their nature and specific content to someone (the coach) who is so obviously able to reward or punish the athlete. Thus, these states, unless entrusted to a special friend or a psychologist in whom the athlete confides, are often the sole purview, and thus the sole "management responsibility" of the athlete.

The most important information the athlete should acquire, as the result of reading this chapter, as well as other publications on the subject, is that the occurrence of these styles is not unusual, indeed most athletes experience one or more types of these states rather frequently! The athlete should then focus upon attempting to classify the unique type he/she is experiencing, as well as attempting to determine whether the state is a positive, neutral, or negative influence upon his/her performance.

After these questions have been answered, the athlete may then wish to attempt to (a) help neutralize possibly negative influences of these states, (b) help induce, and "go-with-the-flow" of the positive ones, and/or (c) fill in seemingly "empty" states of this nature, with positive content—i.e. interject skill imagery into a pre-composition "space out" . . . or engage in positive "self-talk" questions and answers in a seemingly empty post-competition state. Some examples of how these various strategies may work, and at times may backfire, are as follows:

Positive "trance" states in a sport may be identified when the athlete feels, (or reports) that, for example . . . as a gymnast reported to us . . . "I get into it just before every event, when I raise my hand to the judges. It is a self-hypnotic state, and I try to induce it, to help me do better." This falls into the previously identified category of a "pre-competition trance" which is positive. Notice that this comes immediately before competing, occurs cyclically to this gymnast, and at the same time is seen by the performer as a positive experience. "I try to induce it." The implication that such a positive pre-competition state has for the athlete is that he/she should continue to try to induce it, and at times not try too hard. Often when trying hard or thinking too much about such an experience, it does not happen! Also both the athlete and the coach, if he/she is brought into the confidence of the athlete, should manage the environment just before competition so that such a positive trance may occur. For example, the gymnast should be permitted to be by himself/herself if it seems desirable. The coach should not suddenly break into the consciousness of the athlete with hurried and often ineffectual last-minute instructions, if the gymnast seeks and needs solitude during this period of time.

The football players who reported that they frequently "day dream before a game . . .", or "I am in my own world before a game and hard to talk to," or perhaps, "I am so wrapped up in what is happening that I cannot hear anyone talking to me," also are exhibiting pre-competition trance-states which may or may not be positive, and which may or may not be filled with performance related thoughts. These pre-competition trances are common among skilled players, and among players whose sport requires a high degree of skill. Waterpolo players, for example, report these trances to the same degree and in the same terms as do football players.

The coach, if he/she is aware of these states, should respect the athlete's apparent need for them. Time and time again, athletes in a number of sports have told us that the coach's bombastic attempts to "motivate them," break into, and break up such helpful meditative-like experiences. The player also should not feel guilty, or be made to feel guilty by others, that he/she is not engaging in various kinds of social interactions all the time, prior to an important competition; these trance-like states are common, and for the most part apparently useful.

They seem often to have a calming effect upon athletes. However, for the most part those meditative intervals, are best filled with positive imagery ("imagine myself doing well"), as well as specific skill rehearsal, or mental review of tactics. Often this content may be suggested to the athlete with positive results, particularly, if the athlete's apparently "blank" mind during these intervals, is sometimes invaded by negative thoughts (losing, doing poorly) or thoughts which heighten anxiety in various ways.

During performance, trance-like states are more difficult to "handle" in so far as they may accompany the need to monitor in some detail bodily processes, or may be parallel to highly complex skills. Thus, athletes may report (or say to themselves) that, "during competition I am often in a trance, I don't remember what I do, until I can see myself on films afterward . . ." Or perhaps, "I never know what people are talking about when they discuss my performance, until I see the films of my game." The athlete as well as the coach should try to discern between in-performance trance-states which are either positive or negative relative to performance effects and/or their possible influence upon injuries occurring.

For the most part, current thought and research indicates that a relatively disas-sociative state while distance running, a state which is often encountered when the athlete is from 30-40 minutes into a race, is not very useful. The athlete should be en-couraged to "keep in contact" with the race, his/her opponents, and particularly with his/her bodily functions and feelings. At times the coach may wish to verbally remind the athlete during races and during workouts, that "keeping in contact" is useful and helpful to performance.

Other types of flow states may be evaluated, by comparing your own state, its depth and type, with the accompanying performance you experience. If this state is helpful, either let it happen or attempt to induce it, using subtle cues and feelings which are usually non-verbal. If these states seem to interfere with your best per-formance, attempt to anticipate their occurrence and try to reduce, or neutalize them. During workouts, for example, if you feel yourself "slipping into them," stop performing for a brief period, "get your head together," and then continue in an "in contact mode;" rather than continuing in an "out of contact" manner. Indeed in a recent study, we found that more experienced distance runners seemed to be able to take themselves into and out of these during-race trance states, whereas less ex-perienced runners were not as able to do so, and usually spent more time in trance states during races than their more experienced colleagues (Marquez 1983). When these helpful in-performance trances occur, it is not always easy to determine what triggers them. A case could be made for such casual lifestyle changes as slight modi-fications of diet, some unusual emotional situation, the time of day, level of competition, or perhaps something someone has said prior to the competition.

You may also wish to not only discover how to induce them, or at least become able to neutralize things which prevent them, but also to become able to switch them off and on during various phases of your competition. Shooters, track and field per-formers, and weight lifters often perform in cyclic ways with rest and time phases be-tween peak efforts. Often these athletes report themselves slipping into and out of such "special states" in ways which are either helpful or harmful to their perform-ance efforts.

It is highly possible that negative in-performance trances may be triggered by ex-cess activation accompanied by cognitive sets which interpret the activation as excess anxiety. Positive performance accompanying trances are likely triggered by euphoria experienced by the athlete as he/she performs well, together with some optimum level of activation-arousal which is also ideally suited to the task. The athlete should work hard, sometimes with the help of these two types of "in-performance special states," one detrimental and the other a helpful adjunct to optimum physical effort and performance.

In contrast to the difficult-to-manage and interpret "in-performance" trance, the post-competition experience of "detachment" may be relatively easy to interpret and to modify in directions which are helpful. When athletes report that they are "removed, particularly after a big meet . . ." or perhaps, "I slip into a worried trance after each game . . .," they are reporting variations of a post-competition trance. For the most part these states may be classified as "empty" or "filled." They may contain thoughts which are either negative or positive, or they may simply be "empty." In this later case the athlete is experiencing some kind of "removal" from stress in ways which are probably helpful and therapeutic.

The "management" (or self-management) for these post competitive states can include either of two strategies: (a) For the most part during the initial stages of such a state, the athlete should be left alone (or should leave himself/herself alone). Unfilled mental "space" may be just what is needed after minutes or hours of close concentration combined with high levels of physical effort, complex skills, and social threat.

If prolonged, however, the athlete may begin to induce worried thoughts, negative concepts which can be less than beneficial to subsequent competition. Sensitive psychologists for years have known how important the post-competitive period is for the athlete. The athlete, during this post-competition trance period, should seek in rational ways to (a) ascertain the reasons for success or failure experienced, (b) correctly interpret, and define success and failure in rational terms (i.e., success need not be winning. Losing is not always a sign of failure), and finally (c) decide upon personal strategies for the future.

The sensitive coach should attempt to leave the athlete alone with his/her thoughts for a period of time (sometimes more than a day or two), and then when appropriate, schedule a calm private conference which involves assessment of the conditions mentioned above.

Dream management has been suggested in numerous books and articles for many years. The fascination of the ancients with dreams and their meaning prompted the invention of ways to manage dreams and help people in positive ways, usually by thoughts and conditions arranged just prior to sleeping. Several sport psychologists have suggested that dream management may be a positive approach to improving performance.

Relatively objective research, however, indicates that attempts to influence the content of one's dreams is an extremely difficult if not impossible undertaking. Less than 10% of the dreams encountered are likely to be related to the intent of the pre-dream management technique attempted. Our research indicated that "success fulfillment" types of athletic dreams are relatively common among late adolescents participating in high level sports; however, the incidence of these dreams bore little relationship to the performer's ratings by coaches of "intensity motivation" or of performance (Carpinter and Cratty 1983).

It is possible that if an athlete intensely attempts to engage in positive skill imagery just prior to sleep in an attempt to influence a dream in the same direction, that the anxiety generated might indeed produce a dream which contains negative occurrences. It may be useful to place superficial interpretations upon dreams after they happen, and to formulate anxiety management strategies, after, for example, an athlete consistently dreams of missing a critical skill in gymnastics. However, attempting to influence dreams in a post-hoc manner before sleep may usually be counted upon to be non-productive, and may even be counter productive.

OVERVIEW

Although a fair amount of research has been conducted over the decades dealing with dreams and other "special states," sport psychologists have just begun to take an interest in this potentially "gold mine" of information. Dreams, for the most part, echo an athlete's conscious life, and reflect both positive success imagery and anxiety about competition. Trance states seem to "come into" the psyche of athletes under two conditions: (a) when they are experiencing a positive lift because of high levels of skill and conditioning they have reached, and/or (b) when they are highly aroused and activated as they perform some task. Dreams present a window into the deepest thoughts and concerns of athletes, while trance states may either impede or enhance performances.

Athletes are sometimes aware of just how they seem to enter useful trance states, while at other times these "special levels" seem "just to come on." Some athletes, are able to enduce special feelings, bordering on hallucinations, while in other cases these strange experiences unexpectedly plague an athlete. For the most part, when an athlete must closely attend to his/her skills or to bodily processes important to monitor in endurance contests, conscious attention to the situation is required and mental "spin outs" are not very useful. However, at other times an athlete may find himself/herself in a high level performance "groove" and in that case find an unusual state helpful.

Both athletes and coaches should be aware that virtually all athletes encounter these special states, and should become able to understand what instigates them, how to reduce them if warranted, and how to "invite them into" the consciousness if they are helpful.

Recent dream studies have suggested that an excess of "wish fulfillment dreams" may not be useful, as they may reflect unrealistic complacency regarding the sport. While additional data indicates that competencies in the martial arts, among women, may tend to dramatically modify the degree to which they are victims or aggressors in their dream lives.

REFERENCES

Carmack, M.A. and R. Martens. "Motivation, committment to running, and mental states," *Journal of Sport Psychology,* 1979, 1, pp. 25-42.

Cratty, B.J., C. Lange, and M.R. O'Neill, *Mental Activity in Individual Sport Athletes,* publication pending, Sportswissenschaft, 1983.

Cratty, B.J., C. Lange, and P.A. Whipple, "Aggressive imagery of male and female karate performers," publication pending, *International Journal of Physical Education,* 1983.

Mahoney, M.J. and M. Avener, "Psychology of the elite athlete, in exploratory study," *Cognitive Therapy and Research,* 1977, 1, pp. 135-141.

Miller, C., "Focus on Dreams," *The American Journal of Psychoanalysis,* 1978, 38, pp. 163-167.

Morgan, W.P. and D. Costill, "Psychological characteristics of the marathon runner," *Journal of Sport Medicine, and Physical Fitness,* 1972, 12, pp. 42-46.

Marquez, A., "Imagery of distance runners," unpublished study Perceptual-Motor Learning Laboratory, UCLA, 1983.

Murphy, M. and R.A. White, *The Psychic Side of Sports,* Addison Wesley, 1978, Menlo Park, Ca.

Nosanchuk, T., "The way of the warrior," *Human Relations,* 1981, 34, No. 6, pp. 435-444.

Paolino, A., "Dreams: sex differences in aggressive content," *Journal of Projective Techniques,* 1964, 28, pp. 219-226.

Sachs, M.L. and D. Pargman, *Effects of Association/Dissassociation Cognitive Strategies in Regular Runners,* Paper delivered at North American Society of Sport Psychology, Boulder, Co., 1980.

Starker, M., "Positive affects of daydreaming," *Journal of Abnormal Psychology,* 1974, 28, pp. 837-842.

Winget, C. and M. Kramer, *Dimensions of Dreams,* 1979, Gainesville, Fl., pp. 303-306.

CHAPTER 9

SPECIAL HELP FOR CHILDREN IN SPORT

A vast number of studies, clinical observations, and books have been devoted to the manner in which thought develops in the maturing child. Inspired during the first part of this century by the Swiss genius in child development, Jean Piaget, numerous scholars on both sides of the Atlantic Ocean have explored the emergence of cognitive behaviors in infants, children, and youth. Among the findings which have emerged, include the fact that the infant begins learning even prior to birth; and that between the ages of four to seven years the child is not only likely to think in ways which are increasingly sophisticated, but begins also to think about thinking itself. That is, during the latter portion of early childhood, children begin to become concerned with appropriate ways of pairing mental life with problems that confront them.

Despite the literally millions of youth currently engaged in competitive sport in the United States, relatively little work has been carried out which attempts to identify the various kinds of psychological factors at work in youth sport participation. The work that has been carried out consisted of only a handful of studies prior to 1970; while since that time several respectable and comprehensive research programs have been carried out concerning the feelings and emotions, as well as the mental abilities of youngsters. Very few of these investigations have, however, focused upon the central theme of this text, pairing mental activity with physical activity in sport. For the most part these studies have dealt with more general topics involving the child's feelings of stress in sport, their motives, as well as psychological traits which purportedly interact with competition.

It might be assumed that as one questions children of increasing age, one will receive increasingly sophisticated reports concerning the manner in which a child pairs various components of his/her mental life with the demands and intracacies of sport. However, relatively little data is around to confirm or negate this hypothesis.

Much of the information which is available, suggests that the motives and feelings of children in sport are similar to those same qualities in adult athletes. How the child may deal with the stresses of sport, however, are likely to be at marked variation of those strategies employed by university and professional athletes.

Further work comparing the mental strategies and thoughts of adult athletes to those of more youthful competitors seems important. The older performer is often able to dispel anxiety by replacing fearful thoughts with more useful ones, perhaps focusing upon the skills of the sport. Thus, more youthful athletes may also be aided to overcome fears by thinking in positive ways about the skills and strategies of competition, during times when anxious thoughts are likely to occupy their minds.

In the following sections, I will first review pertinent and related studies, pairing the mental life of children and youth, with the physical and emotional demands of sport. Next, a summary of what youth and children have told us, is presented, together with the ways a child seems to differ from a more mature athlete, as he or she tries to "handle" the problems confronted in sport. The final part of the chapter contains useful guidelines when working with children in competitive sport.

WHAT THE RESEARCH SAYS

The research to be reviewed represents a rather comprehensive survey of the various psychological factors in childrens' sport. Studies specific to the intent of this book are largely absent. However, those which are available are discussed, and implications relevant to the "mental life" of the child have been abstracted. As has been true within numerous areas dealing with motor activity, historically the first studies were "one-shot" piece-meal efforts, with little attempt made to follow them up, or to formulate a comprehensive program surrounding a theme or important topic. One is forced to conclude that many of these were carried out by authors trying to earn a degree, or to obtain promotions within a college-university setting. However, within the past decade, it is possible to identify several sustained programs of research within the United States, as well as in other countries. These latter efforts start with rather general problems and then in useful ways gradually crystallize important sub-questions. In this way these programs have produced more important and useful information than did the former superficial approaches to problems within this area of investigation.

The youth sport movement generated force within the United States shortly after World War II. The main sport in which it appeared was baseball, both other sports shortly followed, and now a broad spectrum of often vigorous physical activities are represented, including programs for handicapped children, the sports of rodeo, many Olympic sports, as well as exotic endeavors such as "bashing."[1]

During the first decade of competitive sports for children there are few attempts made to determine what effects this participation might be having upon participants. It was not until the 1960s that one is able to locate one or two investigations which involved boys in little league baseball competition. The boys' responses often indicated that they were even more anxious just after winning a stressful contest, than they were if they had lost. Also during this decade, boys in this same sport were "wired-up" to determine what heart rate changes might be occurring during their actual competition. The researchers found that often the young baseball players experienced higher stress reactions, measured by an elevation of heart rate, while they were awaiting a pitch or standing at the plate, than they evidenced while playing the game on defense. Based upon changes in heart rate, the emotional reactions found in batters seems more pronounced than the stresses of actual physical actions needed when running in the outfield.

During the 1960s, several scholars tried to determine how parental attitudes and influences may impinge upon the youthful competitor. Relatively high correlations were obtained between parental attitudes and the performance evidenced by their children. In the 1970s, the researchers began to focus not only upon parents, but

---

[1]Bashing: is the name given for a group of programs in which youthful competitors don the paraphenalia of the medieval combatant. Authentic garb is coupled with intricate skills and semi-mock wars and duals employing the lance, mace, and sword.

upon an individual who is most important within the youthful sporting environment, the coach.

Among the topics found in research about children in sport, are attempts to find out why they participate, their motivation. Richard Alderman and his students and colleagues in Canada for example, have found that children report participating in sport primarily due to seven major types of incentives. These include:

1. The pursuit of excellence, the desire to be very good in sport.

2. The need to exert social power, to modify the opinions others have.

3. The need to have exciting experiences, experiences which are novel, whose outcomes are uncertain, and which are unreasonably complex.

4. The opportunity to be independent, to do things on one's own, without the advice or criticisms of others.

5. The need to achieve success, to acquire social approval, and prestige for their efforts.

6. The need to express aggression, in the form of domination and intimidation of others.

7. The need to acquire close personal relationships with other athletes and coaches, an affiliation need.

The findings of these studies, involving several thousand youthful competitors, have suggested that the younger athlete competes primarily to satisfy needs for acquiring excellence, to achieve success, to affiliate with others, and finally, to engage in exciting experiences which stimulate their senses. Less important to the participants polled in these investigations were needs to aggress against others or to express independence. However, detailed analysis of inter-sport comparisons, as well as possible shifts in the power of these various motives in children of various ages and of both sexes, continue to be needed.

Sensitive observers of youth have been at times shocked by the powerful social forces which may "come down" upon the young athlete. Parents, coaches, and other "friends" are often heard in the bleachers of the little league contest, alternately offering encouragement and derision in amounts which are often repulsive to those within ear-shot. Many coaches of youthful performers in a variety of sports simply do not allow parents within "ear-shot" or "eye-shot" of their charges during practices; and these same coaches often hold their breadth during competitions as parents or others may heap abuse upon the struggling young athletes.

Many psychologists agree that continual social pressure and psychological abuse from others are likely to lower self-esteem, while heightening feelings of anxiety in younger athletes. Thus, recently, sensitive researchers have focused their attention upon possible relationships between anxiety, self-esteem, and performance in young athletes participating in both team and individual sports. Their findings have confirmed what common sense would dictate. Oppressive coaching and/or overbearing parents are likely to lower the self-esteem of young athletes. Also athletes with low feelings of esteem are more likely to be anxious when approaching and competing in both team and individual sports. Several psychological scales were developed in the 1970s in order to evaluate some of these important qualities in children participating in sport, including their feelings of self-worth, as well as anxiety they might experience.

Using these scales, it has been found that a combination of qualities combine to heighten chances that a child will experience rather marked performance anxiety when confronting "opportunities" to engage in competitive sport. These factors include: (a) low self-esteem, (b) low expectations concerning the possibility of winning and being successful in a forthcoming contest, (c) high levels of general anxiety perhaps triggered by a less-than-secure background involving punative judges of prior attempts to perform, (d) how much "fun" they experience and anticipate experiencing during the game, which is directly related to (e) whether or not they win the contest. Most fearful children and youth, it has been hypothesized by those conducting this type of research, are almost traumatized prior to, during and between athletic performances by the knowledge that those who view them are likely to evaluate them negatively as they display their efforts.

Aggression has also been studied, within several studies of youthful sports competitors. The "favorite" sport for this type of study has been ice hockey, and the most frequent locale has been in Canada. Canadian researchers have been concerned that young ice hockey players might be negatively influenced by the powerful "enforcers" among the players of professional hockey programs.

For the most part these investigations score the kinds of fouls committed, and have concluded that the primary instigators of aggressive behavior are spectators the same age as the youthful participants, rather than over zealous coaches or parents.[2]

Perhaps the most ambitious and useful program of research in youthful sport has focused upon a central figure on the "scene," the coach. Frank Smoll and Richard Smith at the University of Washington in Seattle have conducted a number of studies resulting in findings which suggest that high pressure coaching is likely to influence both the anxiety experienced by younger athletes, as well as their self-esteem. Their research has formalized ways of obtaining samples of coaching behaviors, those which seem to be triggered by an event, a player making a mistake, or those which emerge spontaneously from the coach. Most important in these studies, it has been found that coaches who correct mistakes with non-emotional instructions as to how to do better, have positive effects on young athletes. On the other hand, coaches who ridicule and who socially punish mistakes without giving the youngster an "out," negatively influence the children with whom they work. A promising outcome of this research has been the indication that within a short period of time one is able to exert measurable changes in the behaviors of coaches in children's sport, changes which in turn exert positive effects on young athletes.

As cognitive theorists, Smith and Smoll find that youthful sports participants carefully think about the behaviors projected their way, both the content of the behavior, as well as, the emotional "tone" of what is extended toward them.

After evaluating the kind of coaching behaviors they experienced, youthful competitors then project equally intense feelings, either negative or positive, toward the coaches and others who have projected these feelings. More important it was found that youthful sports participants were likely to be a great deal more discriminating about the types of coaching behaviors engaged in by the mentors, than were

---

[2]Other important work by two social psychologists Carolyn and Mutzfer Sherif, in the 1950s, indicate that two youthful sports teams forced by circumstances to continually compete, are likely to heighten both individual and group aggressions expressed outside the sports situation. In this program of research it was found that only when the two groups were compelled to cooperate in "stressful" group tasks confronting them (and manufactured by the experimenters) was normalcy in human relationships restored.

the coaches themselves! This apparent insensitivity found in these first studies, has also been observed in subsequent investigations. It was indicated that coaches were unlikely to change the ways in which they coached, when confronted with children who evidenced different kinds of motivated behaviors and needs, in practice, eg., those who tried hard, versus those who did not; or those who were confident, and those who were not. Thus, children requiring different kinds of coaching behaviors were apparently not easily perceived by youth coaches.

These studies, however, do not directly focus upon the mental life of younger athletes in a comprehensive manner. They have looked at various "pieces" of thoughts and feelings reported by youngsters, i.e. how they feel about themselves, about coahces, what they think about coaching behaviors, and at times why they participate in sport.

Research in Sweden recently has also taken a look at whether or not school children can successfully "think their way" into relaxation. The conclusions of these researchers hold potentially useful implications for those wishing to adjust the mental-emotional "life" of younger athletes through adjusting thought processes. Setterline and Patriksson applied a six week program of "tension control" to almost three hundred Swedish school children and youth from 12 to 17 years of age. They were taught techniques of muscular relaxation, mental relaxation, and later in the program they were given techniques which enabled them to choose their own methods of reducing stress in their bodies and minds. For the most part, the youths not only evidenced the ability to acquire the techniques taught to them, but reported that they found the experience(s) pleasant and rewarding. The results of this investigation make it apparent that if given the techniques for inducing muscular and emotional relaxation, children and youth of these ages are able to understand and apply them to their own "psyches." What is not clear, however, is the degree to which younger athletes might benefit from these same exercises. Further studies should build upon these promising beginnings.

Just because preliminary studies indicating that positive and modifying "self-talk" may seem to aid older athletes, is no reason to believe that a blanket application of these techniques will have a positive effect upon younger competitors. One should be extremely selective in both how and with whom such methods might be applied. Gravel and his colleagues, for example, found that a "package" of ways to adjust deprecating "ruiminations," (including negative feelings about the enviornment, their own limits, their competitors, their family and even finances) aids the performance of cross-country skiers, of about 21 years of age. However, Mayer et al., surveying the effects of similar methods upon younger gymnasts, averaging about 10 years of age, found no significant results measured by changes in performance of simple gymnastic skills. These two studies employed different types of skills, and involved quite disparate athletic groups. In the second investigation dealing with gymnastic skills and younger competitors, more improvement took place when only mental practice of the skills was involved, rather than when the young girls engaged in more sophisticated thoughts reflecting "self-talk" techniques intended to reduce fear.

Mayer and his colleagues, correctly pointed out that often the effects of relatively subtle cognitive training of athletes' emotions may be over-powered by the simple physical practice of skills. Physical practice of skills, both in individuals and in groups forms a powerful way to improve, certainly more powerful than "pure" mental practice. And while current speculation in the literature indicates that some combination of physical and mental training of skills and attitudes is likely best, it must be remembered that cognitive-mental practice should seldom be engaged in at the expense of the time devoted to physical practice. Mental-cognitive "re-adjustment attempts" both by athletes and psychologists should not interfere with the athlete's primary physical training. Athletes whom we have interviewed consistently tell us of the negative feelings they have when forced to "lie down and relax" . . . etc., prior to practice, for periods of time which are obviously detracting from their physical conditioning, or skill-learning.

Younger children at play are often seen to gleefully engage in vigorous activity for its own sake, independent of any apparent rewards extended by others. Play seemingly is rewarded in and of itself. Likewise, the child's earliest competitive experiences may be accompanied by similar feelings of satisfaction, gained by simply participating in the sport itself. However, there is some research carried out during the past decade that suggests this joy in movement and sport may not be a continuing emotion in children in middle and late childhood, particularly if the sport participation has been accompanied by an inordinate number of rewards given by others, in the form of jackets, trophies, and the like.[3]

It has been found by some researchers, that if rewarded in this manner, children and later youth may persist in sport in a less than self-satisfying manner, encouraged by their own expansion of capacities and by the vigor of the sport itself, but will only exibit continued effort if someone "pays them" in the form of rewards external to the joy of participation. This shift of motivational "perks" from those within the activity, to those outside the sport, may serve to make further participation seem to work. This "work" aspect of sport is in morbid contrast to the joy associated with sport in the early life of the child. The youth may lay back, waiting for others to reward them in the form of a college scholarship, as he or she nears the completion of secondary school. And when researchers questioned university-college athletes who had received scholarships, this lack of pleasure in sport for its own sake was quite apparent. In contrast, athletes who had not received scholarships apparently continued to derive pleasure from mere participation.

This apparent tendency for external rewards to somehow blunt pleasure derived from the sporting activity itself, may be counter-balanced by making sure that the child is only rewarded when real improvement or effort is exhibited, rather than indiscriminately, for more participation as is many times the case. However, this tendency for gift giving may at times be hard to reverse, particularly if the child-youth has been a cynical receiver of "perks" to peform, for prolonged periods of time.

RESEARCH ON CHILDREN AND THOUGHT PROCESSES

There is an enormous volume of research and speculation about the manner in which childrens' thinking matures from early to late childhood. Some of this information has relevance to the "care and preparation" of younger athletes, however, only a brief survey will be conducted here. The research and accompanying speculations generally fall into two major categories: (a) The earlier studies focused either

---

[3]See reference by Deci in the Bibliography of this chapter.

upon the quantity of the child's thought, inspired by the 19th century interest in intelligence measurement. (b) More recent work has dealt with the manner in which children's thoughts may be modified in order to change behaviors important to classroom learning, including attention span, aggression, hyperactivity and the like.[4] The most useful part of this more contemporary thrust has been the work on "cognitive-behavioral" therapy (summarized by Kendall and Hollon, 1979). This type of approach has potentially useful applications for young athletes.

Generally there is a marked change in the manner in which children think, and the amount of thinking about their thinking that transpires from the ages of 5 to 7 years of age. Thus, the degree to which a coach or parent may expect a child of 5 to "concentrate upon skills" or to otherwise analyze his/her performance may vary greatly during these years. Generally, children are far more impulsive at 5, rushing head-long and spontaneously into skill situations, as well as into other problems without bothering to take time to analyze the demands of the tasks or of their capacities to solve it. A child of 5 years, for example, may quickly follow demonstrated skills without much thought. While when an older child views the same skill, kicking a goal in soccer for example, he or she may first hesitate and think through the reasons for various aspects of the action, as well as the mechanics behind the action itself.

Children and youth evidence marked changes in impulsivity as they mature. Indeed neutral processes, which seem to relfect the ability to focus attention and to reflect upon problem situations, continue to mature well past the age of 20. One child may thus be characteristically a person who reflects, who thinks carefully about each sport situation. Whereas another child, even of the same age may evidence little reflection, and rather seems to primarily act upon impulses. Each of these two characteristics may be useful in various sport situations confronting youth. Reflection and analysis are useful qualities to bring to a gymnastic practice when a new routine or skill is presented; undue reflection may hurt the performance of a youth learning to leave the starting blocks in sprinting. Thus, the coach of a younger competitor must at times have to change just how a given youngster deals with situations presenting themselves.

Two studies recently completed in our laboratory, using some of the principles of cognitive-behavioral therapy, have illustrated that it is possible to modify a child from an habitual "mode" of impulsive thoughtless action, to one which involves planning and thought.

We encouraged two children of five, in sessions lasting for six weeks (two a week), to engage in various kinds of "self-talk" which reflected: (a) pre-planning strategies "when I see this problem, I must think about how to do it" . . . (b) strategies which may occur during the performance . . . "there I made an error, I must avoid that error" (Rogers, 1983, and Stanley, 1983). Physical skills were used in this planning, and self-reward . . . "I didn't do too badly that time, but next time I will avoid that error" (Rogers, 1983, and Stanley, $983). Physical skills were used in this work, with those involving the larger muscle groups most helpful, in so far as the time taken to complete each one gave the children more time to "self-talk" their way

[4]See also, a text by B.J. Cratty, *Physical Expressions of Intelligence,* Prentice-Hall, Englewood Cliffs, N.J., 1973 for other mental-motor relationships in children and youth.

through the task. The teacher's evaluations of the children's "attention quality" as well as objective measures of self-control reflected dramatic changes in the children's thoughtful problem-solving behaviors as well as in their attention spans, and control of hyperactivity.[5]

These studies of hyperactive children we have conducted thus indicate that children may be made more thoughtful (reflective) if it is desired to do so. The work we did also suggests that physical skills involving the larger muscle groups may be useful in bringing about these changes, while observations of various sports indicate that the reverse effects may be gained. That is, changing a child's thoughts and ways of habitually approaching tasks may exert positive changes in their coachability, and athletic performance.

Research indicates that the child and youth also change in numerous other ways as they mature. From early to later childhood, for example, more cognitive strategies are adopted as they attempt to learn both academic and cognitive skills. A four-way classification has been used to explain some of these differences, differences which reflect relationships between precision, habitual speed, and accuracy used in various physical tasks by children and youth.

	fast	slow
accurate	fast-accurate (A)	slow-accurate (C)
inaccurate	fast-inaccurate (B)	slow-inaccurate (D)

This chart indicates that children and youth may be roughly classified into four groups, relative to how they seem to prefer to work, and to approach tasks: (a) some are fast and also accorate, (b) others are fast, but apparently do not care to be accurate, (c) others are slow, precise and accurate, while a fourth group (d) are both slow and inaccurate.

These above differences may also reflect a child's personality, and/or perhaps basic capacities for processing information, as well as for producing accurate physical skills. In any case these categories hold importance for people attempting to teach children and youth various skills in different sports.

A more important change in cognitive behaviors occurs in late childhood, from after the 8th year or so in girls, and somewhat later in boys. Their thoughts usually focus more and more during these later years upon the social forces which surround them. In late childhood, more and more time is spent analyzing just who is doing what to whom socially, within their immediate environment. Thus, complex team interactions which might only be apparent to the coach of a boys' soccer team of 5 year olds, come immediately into focus to the members of a team containing 10 and 12 year olds. In these later years, therefore, how and why a team captain is selected may become important issues. Similarly, they may be more likely to take note of those who try to "star," or when teammates reject or accept a newcomer.

---

[5]Tasks evaluating impulsivity included those which asked the child to "move as slowly as you can, while drawing lines, or while walking lines."

In summary, therefore, the studies dealing with various psychological dimensions of youthful sports competitors indicate that emotions and feelings do indeed influence their performance, as do their reasons for competing, and their thoughts about how they are coached. Moreover, youth in early and middle adolescence have been shown to have the ability to take advantage of instructional techniques intended to "calm them down," or/and to "control their tension." This ability to elicit the "relaxation response" seems a useful one for both youth and adult athletes to acquire, as pointed out elsewhere in this and in other texts. However, the degree to which this self-imposed relaxation is able to be "managed" by individuals in early and middle childhood is unclear, given the present evidence. Following talks we have had with younger athletes and their parents, no hard-fast rules emerged which paired in precise ways various conceptual strategies with sports performance. Only general guidelines were able to be formulated as a result of these discussions. These viewpoints are summarized in the following section.

IMPLICATIONS FOR COACHES OF YOUNGER ATHLETES

Numerous suggestions might be made concerning how to "handle" children, or ways which will enable them to "deal" with themselves in more effective manners when confronted with sport competition. Generally, it is assumed that initially at least, the child in sport is a less powerful, and thus a less influential figure, than is the adult-coach confronting him/her. The research is largely absent, concerning how one might help children learn to help themselves mentally and emotionally while in sport; although hopefully in the near future more and more of this type of work will be forthcoming.

Several main guidelines should be kept in mind (in addition to the relatively powerless position of a young child new to sport) when dealing with the psychological preparation of a child in sport. One of these involves the "natural" and spontaneous nature of the child at play. One must walk a narrow line when attempting to channel the child in constricted ways, as they are forced to conform to methods and skills, and at the same time leave the fun and "flow" in the activity. Some types of sports obviously require more confining to norms than do others. However, it should be remembered that the free-spirit of the child should be left unfettered as far as possible, a freedom that much of the time not only helps to nourish a budding personality, but also may contribute to better performance in many sports which require energy and adaptability.

Additionally, one should be aware that stages and limitations in cognitive maturity (maturity of thought processes) may either aid or inhibit one's best efforts to help a child think more deeply about their sport. Perhaps the child, more so than the adult, may be led toward paralysis through over-analysis! One should attempt to be cerebral when practical, while teaching the child, but at the same time develop a low-key soft-sell in the explanation of mechanics and intricacies of sport.

Finally, it should be noted that children, just as is true among adults, may evidence marked differences in the intellectual approaches and strategies each prefers to use when approaching problem solving situations inherent in overcoming obstacles in sport. The trade off between speed and accuracy was previously alluded to. Others may include differences in how a child prefers to imagine the skill. Some may prefer to visually see themselves perform, others may prefer to feel the movements, while others may wish to talk themselves through an action. Some children may be analyzers, carefully taking apart a strategy or a skill, for the close inspection of its parts. Others may be classified as "synthesizers." They habitually look at the big picture, at wholes, placing little emphasis upon taking-apart and inspecting skill components in detail.

Thus, just as is true among adults, one should be flexible when working with children's thoughts and learnings connected to sport. Formulating exact recipes for dealing with a child, teaching them skill, or otherwise attempting to teach them something, is as naive as listing a similar restricted list of "rules" for teaching adults about their sport and about themselves.

EMOTIONS, THEIR CARE AND TREATMENT

Children's earliest sporting experiences, good or bad, are seldom forgotten. Even as adults, most of us can remember pleasant or unpleasant sentences sent our way by coaches in athletic situations. Post game jitters may infect children just as they do adults. Pre-game anxiety is also prevalent in children. To children, however, these feelings may be relatively new and difficult to manage, at least in the context of sport. Moreover, the powerful mentors inhabiting this often frightening new world, may seem relatively oblivious to the nervousness, and even to the terror a child may be experiencing.

It is, therefore, both practical and humane to attempt to find out how the child is reacting to initial sports experiences. This type of survey may be based upon parent's observations, but should include things the parent can see the child do, and more specifically what changes the parent may see in the child, prior to and following a competition. The following kind of checklist should be made available to parents of children. The results contain data important to the coach, as well as to the parent. Moreover, this kind of information may lead the parent to place the child in formal counseling, if the signs of disruption persist, and are marked in nature. Such a checklist should include the following:

	Before Competition	After Competition
1. Change in Eating Habits Refuses meals, concentrates on junk food? Other changes? Other changes, Please explain: ___	yes___no___	yes___no___
2. Changes in Mood Too quiet, sullen, over boisterous, cries, over elated? Or what? Please explain: ___	yes___no___	yes___no___
3. Aggression? Fights with others, overly passive? Argues a great deal? Other changes? Please explain: ___	yes___no___	yes___no___
4. Change in Sleeping Habits Troubles going to sleep? Sleep-walks? Awakened by disturbing dreams? Bed wetting? Other changes? Please explain: ___	yes___no___	yes___no___

5. Other sings of emotional upset you   Before Competition   After Competition
have observed.
Please explain _____

Note that the answers from parents and guardians include observations made before and after competition. It is assumed that the coach will observe the child or youth extensively during competition. It is before and after games and competitions that negative signs of behavior reflecting emotional upset may emerge. These changes can often be best evaluated by parents, who have had a long period of time in which to observe their children both before and during their sports careers. The parent is thus in the best position to observe changes in their offspring's behaviors which occur following a game, and which may not be "normal" for their child.

Some of the guidelines for coaches and parents, to reduce and lessen the emotional impact of sport upon youth and children include the following:

1. It is important for the child to feel that he or she has importance, for reasons not connected with sport. The child should be made to feel lovable for his or her own sake, and should be encouraged to express competence in skills not found in competitive sport. Most important, the parent should recognize the abilities of the child in areas not associated with sports participation.

2. Sibling rivalry should not extend to sport. Whenever possible, place brothers and sisters on different teams, indifferent sports participating at different times under different coaches. Comparative statements concerning the abilities of brothers and sisters should not be made.

3. The coach should come under constant scrutiny by the parents, before the child is placed in his/her hands, and during the time the child competes. The child should be asked for their impressions of the coach, and his/her opinions given validity and consideration. A parent should *never* hesitate removing their child from a noxious and emotionally abrasive coach. The parent should err in the direction of over-protectiveness, rather than thinking they may be making the child tough by exposing them to a "tough coach."

4. The parents themselves should air differences they have about their child's sports participation, and the reasons each parent may have for the child being in sport, *in private,* and not in front of the child . . . In our interviews with parents and children participating in sport, the tendency for the parents to be in agreement when assessing their children's reasons for being in sport, was critical, and usually assured a happy sporting competition for the child. Whereas when the parents are not in accord, and the child knows it, frustration and anxiety on the part of the child was often the outcome.

5. Parents should attempt to become aware, through formal or informal education of what to expect physically and emotionally from their child. Unrealistic parental expectations are a major source of emotional problems in younger athletes. Parents and coaches should work as a cooperative "team" in efforts to help the child set and achieve reasonable goals in practice and competition.

RELAXATION, ANXIETY REDUCTION

Relaxation training such as that described in Chapter 4, may also be realistically applied to children. Upon receiving this help, most children will report the experience pleasant and helpful. A child may be "brought down" by introducing them to muscular relaxation just prior to a contest, by the parent or coach. Often language may be simplified with good effects. Statements like, "make your muscles like macaroni" . . . or perhaps "take all the bones out of your arms . . .," may induce the degree of relaxation required.

Anxiety reduction may also be accomplished by: (a) Helping the child place an impending competition into proper perspective . . . "This is really not the world series today; I will always remember how hard you have worked this season, not how well the team does today" . . . or perhaps, "You know there are thousands of games just like this being played today" . . . or maybe, "You have many more seasons to play, this is not the end today." (b) Helping the child realize that the parent's love, and acceptance, or the coach's feelings about them will not change with a loss . . . "However you do, we'll always remember how hard you tried all season, and we are proud of you in so many ways" . . . or perhaps "I know you will do your best, and that is all we can expect . . . success is doing your best, not always winning" . . . are positive points.

Parents and coaches should be aware of the importance of after-competition conferences, both for the mutual health of the performer, and for future performance success. Such conferences, often carried out without the participation of the child, should reflect: (a) a concern for the child as a person, (b) attempts to help the child place the loss or win into perspective, and finally (c) an attempt to help the child to evaluate the real reasons for the loss, or success, in objective ways. Often this latter kind of "summing up" may come days or even weeks after a particularly important contest, particularly if an apparent "crushing" loss has occurred.

The child should be helped to correct illogical assumptions about (1) achievement, (2) perfection of people and situations, (3) their own social acceptability. Care should be taken to phrase this type of "self-talk," in terms usable and appropriate to the age of the child or youth. Often the correction of these illogical assumptions is more easily accomplished with younger competitors, than with older ones.

REWARDS, WHAT KIND? WHERE? WHEN?, AND WHY?

A considerable amount of research has indicated that great care should be taken when "handing out" rewards to children and youth participating in sport. Overly rewarded children, with reinforcements coming indiscriminately in the form of jackets, trophies and the like, are likely to cause the child to begin to view sport as work, something that one must be paid for. Scholarship athletes at a university in their final years often say that they are continuing the sport they are in, not for any intrinsic satisfactions they obtain from participation, but "to keep my scholarship."

If one is not careful, much younger "scholarship" athletes may be created as younger children compete, and are rewarded too generously with material things. Great care must be taken to offer rewards rather sparingly, and only for real improvement in peformance, effort, or attitude. Most important is to teach a youngster about the inherent satisfaction of performing well for its own sake, to achieve mastery of one's self, and one's skills. A child who begins to understand the value of participation for its own sake, and who never loses that feeling, is more likely to go on to higher levels of competition, and not to "burn out" as he/she reaches college and university level participation.

The child should be taught that it is ok, even desirable at times, to perform to please one's self, rather than always attempting to please others including family, friends, and coach. This selfish motive of excelling is felt by most athletes, young and old. A young child should not be made to feel guilty when the feeling of excelling becomes an important impetus to working hard and competing well.

Most of all children should be taught early, during the years they are most impressionable, that success is not always winning. Success, you might inform the child, is dependent upon relationships between your goals, and your actual participation. Success is also measured by deciding how much effort you have expanded, particularly against various high level opponents. It is more advantageous for a child to learn that success always occurs from working hard, while winning does not always bring with it the pride that it should; particularly if a win has been gained with little effort against a mediocre opponent.

COGNITIVE BEHAVIORAL THERAPY, USING SELF-TALK: PROBLEMS AND ADVANTAGES WHEN WORKING WITH YOUTH

In several of the previous chapters, reference has been made to the use of cognitive adjustments in the form of "self-talk," in efforts to modify anxiety, concentration, and aggression. It is likely that similar principles may be applied to more youthful competitors in efforts to positively change both their skills and emotions. Indeed the younger competitor may be more amenable to change in so far as they are often not as cynical and more flexible emotionally than their more mature brothers and sisters in sport.

When using this approach with youngsters the following principles should be kept in mind.

(a) When using "self-talk" to correct irrational thoughts relative to the need of being perfect, and of pleasing all other people, the statements extended to the child include general observations such as: "I must always do my best, but I should not let myself get upset when I am not perfect."

Care should be taken that the relatively naive child does not "over correct," and interpret such pressure relieving statements as defeatist in nature. Thus, the child may interpret the statements in the previous paragraph, as "if I don't have to be perfect, I don't think I will try very hard."

(b) Statements meant to place aggression in focus, when the child has evidenced the apparent desire or tendencies to hurt others, may be useful. Thus, when a child has aggressed too vigorously in a game or practice, he/she might be taken aside and encouraged to "talk inwardly" with such statements as "I really shouldn't think about hurting someone else, but should try harder when I feel myself getting mad at someone." Again, however, the child may over-react, and perhaps "lighten up" too much, displaying too little overall effort.

(c) Self-talk statements which are meant to heighten a child's concentration may be highly important. Children and younger performers often have more problems with concentration than do the more experienced athlete. Additionally, children are often at a loss as to how to make themselves focus in on important components of their competition for prolonged periods of time. Thus, self-talk which either excludes distractions, and/or focuses in upon central components of the athletic experience should prove helpful (Chapter 7).

Again, however, some modifications of this type of concentration strategy may be needed when working with younger children. Too much emphasis upon the imagery of exclusion, "Imagine yourself in an empty room, looking at only your target on the other wall," might encourage a child to believe himself really within such a compartment. Thinking about a creative strategy of this nature may become too intense, thus distracting from the pain point of the exercise, i.e., concentrating upon important qualities in the athletic environment.

(d) Various kinds of imagery, and self-talk may also heighten skill acquisition in children. However, individual differences may be encountered relative to the vividness of the imagery each child may "turn on" when asked to do so. Some might view such practice "silly" and thus it should be carefully explained to the child, both its reasons, and its techniques. It is likely also that an instructor in this kind of skill learning (Chapter 3), needs to remain with the child or youth for periods of time, longer than may be necessary with the more experienced athlete. The adolescent may become more quickly independent of the person explaining the processes and operations involved; whereas the child may lack the self-discipline, and intellectual maturity to continue the activity, without prompting help. Indeed a number of studies in which "self-talk" has been used indicates that a reasonable level of intellectual maturity is necessary for it to work. It is therefore important when using it as a skill enhancer, or in the other ways recommended (for fear, concentration, and aggression), to make sure that (a) the child is mature enough to perceive the intent, and operations involved, or (b) to make certain that some kind of pre-cognitive therapy sessions be held to instruct the child about the purposes the coach psychologist or instructors had in mind when asking the child to "think out loud."

This type of "pre-instruction" should start with the child attempting to arrive at answers to very basic questions: (a) "What do you think about . . . your sport, . . . your coach . . . (b) "Do you ever think scarey things; tell me what they are?" . . . (c) "Do you ever talk to yourself about your sport? . . . What do you say to yourself?" In this way the child may be encouraged to first (a) vocalize his/her thoughts, and then (b) later the child should be brought gradually to other realizations, including the fact that his/her behaviors change. "Have you gotten better at broadjumping this year?", then (c) that thoughts may be changed . . . "Have you ever changed your mind about something, or someone?" . . . "What did you change your mind about?" The child may then be encouraged to (d) pair actions with thoughts. For example, the youth may be asked to "show me a trick, and now tell me what you thought about just before you performed the skill." Later the child may be asked to do a skill quickly without thinking and then to reflect backward in time . . . eg. "tell me what you are thinking about at the completion of the movement." (e) The child may also be asked to "expose" some of their inner thoughts or feelings by voicing these out loud through "self-talk" that can be heard. The child may be asked for example, to "tell me what you are thinking just before you do a skill" . . . or perhaps to "tell me how you feel about your sport, and show me that feeling in your face . . ." (f) Changes in apparent feelings may be thought about by the child. These fluctuations may be reflected by responding to such requests as, "Tell me how you felt before, during, and after your last competition." Very precise statements may be requested by the psychologist, coach, or parent, for example, "I know you were worried before the last game, but worried about what, or who?" might be directed toward the young competitor.

Following such carefully given direction as these, modified to suit the child and sport, the youthful competitor may be led toward the acceptance of the following ideas.

(a) My thoughts underlie my feelings, and thus my performance qualities.

(b) Much of what I think, I say to myself.

(c) Thoughts may be learned, and changed in positive directions just as I learn physical skills and change them.

(d) I may change my moods and emotions in positive directions by changing the thoughts which underlie those moods.

(e) A useful way to modify how I feel, and perform, is to change what I am thinking by voicing (first to others and then to myself) phrases and words which reflect positive changes.

OVERVIEW

Many of the strategies and interventions recommended in other parts of the book, are useful and appropriate for children in sport. For example, relaxation training is equally useful for older and for younger athletes in certain situations. Various cognitive adjustments using "self-talk" techniques may also be employed with children, with modifications. However, children may need special help in the acceptance of more rational thought patterns underlying sound emotional and physical performance.

Care should be taken, for example, when using "self-talk" techniques with children to avoid simply having them echo "useful" statements without finally really adjusting how they internally think about what they are saying.

Cognitively immature children, for example, may simply echo "useful" self-talk statements for a prolonged period of time without really accepting conceptual changes internally, as might occur in more mature athletes. The young child may, for example, simply be engaging in conforming behavior intended to make the adult "adjusters" happy.

The emotional health of children in sport could be carefully monitored both when they enter competition for the first time, and as they participate in continuing seasons and contests. Among the changes in their behaviors and habits which might be cause for concern include: marked mood changes, modifications in eating patterns, their sleep schedules, or social withdrawal from family or friends.

Cognitive behavioral strategies using self-talk techniques have been shown to be useful in helping children in classroom situations. Among the changes which have been elicited are heightening attention span, reducing hyperactivity, and the adoption of useful reflective (thinking) strategies. These same useful techniques, if carefully and intelligently applied, may be used to help the younger athlete control destructive emotions, optimizing performance, and otherwise make their competitive experiences more positive ones.

REFERENCES

Alderman, R.B. and N.L. Wood, "An analysis of incentive motivation in young Canadian athletes," *Canadian Journal of Applied Sport Sciences,* 1976, 1, pp. 169-176.

Cratty, B.J., *Physical Expressions Of Intelligence,* Prentice-Hall, Englewood Cliffs, N.J., 1973.

Cratty, B.J., "Children in sport" *Psychology in Contemporary Sport,* 2nd. Edition, Prentice-Hall, Englewood Cliffs, N.J., 1983, pp. 195-212.

Dice, E.L., "Intrinsic motivation," *Theory and Application in Psychology of Motor Behavior and Sport,* Human Kinetics, Champaign, IL., 1977, pp. 388-396.

Kendall, P.C. and S.D. Hollon, (eds.), *Cognitive-Behavioral Interventions, Theory, Research, and Procedures,* New York Academic Press, 1979.

Mayer, S.A., et al., "Cognitive contributions to the development of gymnastic skills," *Cognitive Therapy and Research,* 1979, 3, pp. 75-85.

Rogers, J. and C. Stanley, "The effects of self-talk procedures upon modifications of childrens' thinking strategies," unpublished study, Perceptual-Motor Learning Laboratory, UCLA, 1983.

Setterland, S. and G. Patriksson, "Teaching children to relax," *Mental Training for Coaches and Athletes,* Coaching Association of Canada, Ottawa, Canada, 1982, pp. 35-36.

Sherif, M., *Experiments in Group Conflicts,* Scientific American, New York, 1956.

CHAPTER 10

THE ATHLETE INTERACTS WITH TEAMMATES

A significant part of the athlete's mental life revolves around his or her interactions with teammates. These thoughts may contain feelings about the relative contributions of teammates to the total effort, and feelings and communications that are present among team members. At times these feelings and communications, and the accompanying thoughts, remain hidden. However, at other times, often during stressful contests, these powerful social forces emerge and often disrupt performance.

Further, the performer may also think about how others on the team perceive him or her. Part of this important feedback the athlete may receive are attitudes transmitted by others on the team. The emotions others on the team project toward the athlete may thus exert important influences upon both the feelings and the performance of the competitor.

Most of these powerful social forces within small groups interacting with the performance and feelings of an individual have been explored by social psychologists. Virtually all the information collected by this "breed" of social scientist (part sociologist and part psychologist) are applicable to the athlete on a team. Since the 1960s several books have appeared which have contained direct applications of social psychology to athletes and athletics (Cratty 1968, Cratty 1981, Carron 1980). The sports science community within the Soviet Union contains about fifty social psychologists whose jobs are to analyze and help the interactions on sports teams. Thus, both in this country and abroad, there is concern about the social forces on athletic teams, and how these forces mold athletic performance and the moods of teams and of individuals.

During the interview conducted in our laboratory, we obtained numerous responses which indicated the athlete's concern about others on the team. Team members are often mentioned when an athlete is asked who is in their most frequent "athletic dream." Again, teammates are referred to when an athlete is asked what phrases are continually brought to mind in efforts to engage in self-motivation, or to reduce negative thoughts during competition.

A number of topics dealing with the social forces within athletic teams have been written about, within the research literature. Within the following section only the most important and pertinent subjects will be covered. But among the questions such research has attempted to answer include:

1. What are the influences of being a "closely knit" team upon group performance? How might one positively influence group cohesion?

2. What kind of communication between teammates occurs, and what are the meanings of this communication relative to team success?

3. What kind of roles do various individuals play within a team's status hierarchy? What roles are potentially disruptive of maximum group effort, what kinds of

roles heighten a team's potential?

4. What influence does a "glory seeker" have upon a team's morale?

5. Do a team's motives and reactions to failure and success differ from those same feelings and reactions of individual athletes?

6. What kinds of qualities and behaviors are useful to a team captain, and how might these qualities be enhanced by teammates and coach?

7. What differences, if any, may be seen when analyzing the motives and feelings of athletes on larger versus smaller teams; does team size make a difference?

The following section will not contain clear-cut answers to all of these questions. The analysis of the forces within a group under the stress typical in sport is an extremely complex undertaking. Even more fraught with peril is attempting to determine just how such inter-personal qualities and forces influence winning and losing.

WHAT THE RESEARCH SAYS

Group Cohesion, "We" Feelings

The togetherness on a sports team is traditionally felt to be important in promoting team success. The words teamwork, "getting together with each other," and "learning cooperation," frequently are voiced by coaches to denote positive team attributes, qualities which purportedly help chances to win. However, it is often difficult to find useful and direct relationships between degrees of team togetherness (cohesion) and performance.

For example, one must first determine what "togetherness" means to each player on the team, and then also to find out just what each sport may demand relative to the closeness of athlete's interactions. Some players, for example, may value their membership on a team because it gives them the opportunity to be among, and to make friends. Other athletes may view friendships and warm personal feelings on a team as incidental to their main motive for team membership, to be a part of a well performing and highly recognizable unit.

Additionally, some sports require close inter-personal cooperation constantly during competition; basketball, ice-hockey, and team handball are only some of the obvious examples. Other teams require rather intermittent interactions together, as when a track and field team or a swimming team enters a relay, and members must anticipate the movements of others; while in other events within the same sports rather independent functioning occurs. Finally some sports, namely golf, archery, and rifle shooting require relatively little, if any direct interpersonal interactions. The participants may reside within their own worlds as they compete, despite the fact that their scores contribute to some group success measure.

In general, the literature despite some periodic controversies, confirm the common sense expectation. That is, in athletic situations in which close inter-personal cooperation is important, high levels of team cohesion are desirable. In other situations which do not require close inter-personal timing and contact; team "togetherness" is less important.

It should be emphasized, however, that one's definition of cohesion or togetherness is important to consider. Athletes often give vastly different answers as to why they wish to be members of a team, and why one team "feels" close, and another seems composed of separate isolated members.

At the highest levels of competition the need to belong to a team, for "belonging's sake" is not very high on an athlete's list of motives. Rather, athletes and their coaches tend to be extremely performance oriented, and the worth of one's teammates, and of team membership itself is almost entirely based upon the degree to which an athlete perceives the team and team membership as a vehicle which will insure him/her optimum performance opportunities.

Thus, selfish and apparently hostile behaviors and emotions often surface on highly successful, performance-oriented teams. Some of these behaviors with which a coach or athlete must often confront, ignore, or otherwise deal with include (a) Superior performers may be intolerant of the mistakes of those less able to perform on the team. (b) Better performers may also view those who perform poorly as not valuable, in general ways, as people. (c) Cliques may form on teams composed of the better performers. Cliques which also may appear outside the performance context. (d) Some of the less favored, or less able athletes may decrease in performance, withdraw socially from the others on the team, and contribute less and less to the team's performance, and to the team's practices.

At times, apparent hostilities between teammates are positive signs that the performers really care about winning, and about achieving success. These performance-oriented athletes are thus showing that they are not particularly interested in either being well liked, or in engendering warm feelings between members, but in doing well in the competition.

If carried to extremes, however, these signs of inter-personal stress may have negative effects upon performance. This stress, in the form of inter-personal problems may show up when a substitute does not perform up to capabilities when called upon to do so, or perhaps when fights (physical or verbal) break out during games or practices.

Thus, the concept of balance or equilibrium is a useful one to consider. The team should project an atmosphere of useful tension between members as they practice and perform. Athletes should both care about performance, and also care about the emotional mix of the team. There should be a balance of behaviors present, reflecting both the need to be together as valuable people and human beings, as well as behaviors which signal the fact that all present need to perform well. This scale of performance versus inter-personal feelings is tipped usefully in one direction when a team sport is being participated in; that is, more inter-group caring is needed when close physical cooperation is also required. On the other hand, more selfish kinds of behaviors may be tolerated in many individual sports, with less disruption of performance apparent.

Often these balances and needs in inter-group cooperation and forces, may be assessed by a social psychologist attached to a team for a prolonged period of time. These social scientists have both formal and informal assessment instruments at their disposal with which to carry out useful evaluations of this kind, assessments that are often invaluable to the coach and athletes alike.

IMPROVING INTRAGROUP FEELINGS

A few studies, both in this country, as well as abroad have attempted to determine what kinds of behaviors and strategies may be used with a team, in efforts to obtain greater inter-personal cooperation. These pilot investigations have, for example, produced findings which suggest that: If first team members are simply "armed" with ways to behave in cooperative ways toward teammates, (thanking them for a "set-up" in basketball), they will later begin to achieve closer feelings towards others on the team. That is behavior may be inserted which will subsequently change emotional feelings of togetherness. Often, however, a behavioral scientist will have to first assess and then introduce various interpersonal interventions, together with individual conferences, before producing radical observable changes in group cohesion and "good feelings."

At times, the high performance oriented athlete may need to submerge his/her impatience when a less able teammate committs an error, an error which may reduce the effectiveness of the team, and of the star athlete. This submergence of feelings, may result in overall increases in team performance in subsequent competitions. Social psychologists of sport in the Soviet Union have identified what they term "victims" and "oppressors" on teams (Cratty and Hanin 1980). Often, rectifying the behaviors of an oppressor has been found to be helpful in improving the whole "tone" of the team, and thus the team's performance. The two ways in which this may be accomplished include: (a) direct ways, by counseling the "oppressor" to engage in non-oppressive, friendly behaviors toward teammates, and (b) indirect ways, in which a satire may be carried out by a "victim," reflecting the obnoxious behavior of the "oppressor," an act which when "picked up on" by the oppressor will often elicit the desired changes.

Inter-athlete communication has also been carefully collected by social psychologists in sport within the Eastern European countries. Both verbal as well as non-verbal (gestures) behaviors have been categorized, often over extended periods of time. Among the most important findings from these investigations, has been the relationship between success in a competition and the incidence of positive versus negative remarks passing between teammates. As a team starts to lose, more and more negative comments are likely to pass between athletes; in contrast, when winning the remarks are likely to be positive and instructive.

And while it cannot be said that the negative remarks cause a decrease in performance, it is probably true that negativisms in communication often accelerate and are part of a down-hill spiral being experienced by a team, as they begin to lose ground in competition. Special attention may be needed in order to correct negative language which may pass between teammates as a team starts to lose. Both the athletes, as well as the coach, when modifying this kind of negative communication may also help to reverse a losing trend, rather than exaggerate it.

OTHER "ROLES" ON A TEAM

In addition to the simple roles of oppressor and victim, there are other roles which appear on teams, roles reflecting performance aspirations, as well as the solidarity of an individual's group membership. All team athletes should be aware of both the negative and positive values of various roles, and the manner in which group performance may be improved if team members "treat" those evidencing these roles in positive ways. For example, each team has one or more performance "stars," people who contribute most to team success. These members are vitally needed, and should be supported by others on the team. However, the research suggests that teams on which all are stars, do not perform as well as those on which there are those who wish to be seen excelling, and those who work as "backup" players, supporting those who are more visible. Thus, those who work in subordinate roles should realize that both types are needed on many successful interacting teams, and not be jealous of the visibility of their peers. Likewise, the "star(s)" should be appreciative of those who support them, and in every way give credit to those who work in subordinate roles. Every good interacting team needs both for success.

Teams, like individuals, set group goals. Like successful individuals, the more striving teams set intermediate goals, not too high or too low, prior to competition. Thus, a swimming team might decide just how many points it should score prior to an important competition. Often leaders on the team must aid in this group goal setting, a group "project" which is extremely important to later group morale, as well as to later group estimates of whether or not "success" was achieved.

Unlike individual athletes, teams are less likely to over-react to failures or successes. Thus, teams (groups) seem more stable after success or failure, and do not fluctuate widely when setting future goals. That is, a team is not as likely to suddenly and drastically shift goals downward after failure as much as might an individual athlete; nor conversely will a team suddenly shift estimates of future success as high as might an individual when both have met with success. Thus, the individual athlete should be sensitive to this kind of stabilizing effect which he/she might encounter within a team of interactors (basketball etc.). This effect might not be as pronounced when an individual athlete competes in such sports as swimming, track-and-field, or in gymnastics.

Estimates of group success, as is true among individuals, are dependent not always upon absolute scores, or number of points, or goals scored in a given contest, or even upon winning. More likely, success will be judged both by groups and individuals according to how close some performance was to a prior estimate of what might be accomplished. An unsuccessful competition might be a winning effort against a weak team, by a close margin; whereas a competition judged successful might be in a close loss to an opponent who had been judged, prior to the competition, to be much stronger. Thus, the individual athlete may at times, play an important part in the establishment of future estimates, as well as in forming judgements about success or failure following a competition. It is likely, moreover, that some group members play more important roles in group assessment and in goal setting than do others.

Group size is another important group quality that is influential of an individual's feelings about success and failure, and the personal responsibility for the outcomes of competition. In teams whose members are more numerous it is often difficult for an individual to feel important following a win, due to the proportionally small part he/she has played in the success. In contrast, on a smaller team (basketball) each member starting the game is likely to feel more elated or depressed following a success or failure. Athletes must be made to feel personally responsible for successes or losses on larger teams; groups whose size often precludes, or suppresses, personal feelings of elation or depression due to their large numbers.

Highly competitive teams are work groups under stress; stress due to their high visibility, and to the constant and easily evaluated signs of success or failure which eminate from their efforts. Like any group under stress, whether soldiers or workers in under-sea laboratories, feelings of group oneness on teams may fluctuate in predictable ways as stress is heightened or lessened. That is, moderate stress is likely to result in more group cohesion, in higher feelings of solidarity; however, if stress levels are heightened further, the team may tend to "come apart."

This alternate coming together and breaking apart may be apparent as a team progresses through a season; from early season games in which success is achieved, through middle season stresses, to late season contests which may be critical to the formation of a "successful season." More and more, competitive stress with accompanying demands by the group and fans to produce wins, can make a previously cohesive unit tend to disintegrate, if efforts are not made to maintain cohesion and feelings of togetherness. Both athletes and coaches should be sensitive to the appearance of signs which signal poor group cohesion, and of group stress. Among these psychological "disturbances" are increases in a number of interpersonal comments during losing endeavors, as well as, negative non-verbal communication between coaches and athletes which reflect lack of mutual respect.

LEADERS AND SUBSTITUTES

Several types of people are important to consider when studying the social dynamics of teams. One of these is a rather central figure, a team captain, while another is more peripherel, a substitute. Still a third may be a recent entrant to the scene, a new team member.

The team leader, often designated a captain, may have an important influence upon the behavior of others. For the most part, on highly successful performance oriented team, the captain is selected not because of personal or social popularity, but the selection is based upon the criterion that he/she is the one best able to assist the team to achieve success. Thus, popularity in a social context is often not a prerequisite for becoming a team captain; the quality of leadership coupled usually with at least a moderate performance capability are sometimes the most important criteria. Captains and leaders are those most likely to know well the status hierarchy in a group, to be able to communicate best with everyone according to their needs, and to get the best out of the team, as well as individuals. The team captain is often found to be the one who best knows what seems to motivate others on the team toward success.

Team captains, just as is true of coaches, need to somehow judge the degree of authoritarian versus democratic behaviors they may project toward others on the team. For the most part, teams who seem to tolerate best a more authoritarian approach are those who: (a) are under some stress, (b) whose members are numerous in contrast to a smaller team, and (c) whose social structure is reasonably well formed, and whose objectives are the most clear. Teams and work groups who seemingly are least tolerant of authoritarian leadership, and who seek a more democratic, benevolent leadership behavior are those: (a) who have been in existence a long time and whose group status and hierarchy are well known to all, (b) whose members are not numerous, and who are reasonably sophisticated, (c) whose members are more mature and who can seemingly handle the stresses of competition easily as individuals.

Newcomers to teams often are more quickly accepted superficially and even socially than they are as well integrated functioning team members. That is, a new and good performer may be lauded by all concerned as he/she enters the team social and performance structure; however, depending upon the sport and the capabilities of others, the integration of the performer's specific skills with those of others on the team may take a considerably longer period of time. A year or more is sometimes needed in highly intricate sports such as soccer-football. Sports within which highly integrated physical skills are required, (doubles tennis, basketball, ice-hockey, and the like) require not only high levels of skills by each player, but also a less obvious

149

"group quality" in physical skills. That is, each player on a good team, must not only evidence high levels of individual skill (making difficult shots), but must display also the ability to integrate their movements with others, judge the speeds of others on the team with responses of their own, or to pass well to teammates, whose movements and characteristics may be very different from their own. Thus, the best functioning teams are those in which all players are able to demonstrate both individual skills, and to integrate these skills with each other in useful ways. The newcomer to the team, despite displaying high levels of individual skill, must also possess the ability to quickly learn to adapt to the movements of his/her new teammates. Special help must often be given to the newcomer in order to acquire these skills.

The new team member commonly engages in behavior similar to that reported in studies of the hen-houses, or of groups of primates; he or she must establish their order within the status hierarchy of the team. Thus, just as is true within the animal kingdom, while superficial friendliness is at first displayed, the new player must undergo subtle "tests" (both social and physical) as they enter a new team situation, trials which the group imposes in order to determine just where within the status hierarchy of the team the newcomer belongs.

While it may be difficult to motivate an individual on a large team because of his/her perceptions of their role as insignificant, an even more difficult task is involved when helping the substitute to remain motivated, and to perceive the role they may play in achieving team success. Successful coaches are aware of this, and often engage in various contrivances, i.e., giving the substitute unit a special name, in order to maintain morale of the "benchwarmers." Substitutes note with interest the amount of attention the coach pays to them, as well as the amount of interest and effort the more able players-leaders on the team may contribute to those less well endowed with physical skills. Overall team morale, as well as, future team success may rest, however, on how successful both teammates and coaches are at these endeavors. Substitutes often become starters, and if a malcontented substitute becomes a starter, suddenly the results may be disastrous.

The new team member must also search for group norms, and become acquainted with them. The degree to which the newcomer is permitted to deviate from these norms (to become a team "flake," or comedienne) etc., without undue pressure or censure from others, depends upon his/her ability to contribute to the group in concrete ways, as well as the length of time he/she has conformed to the group norms for behavior and performance. Thus, someone who contributes a great deal to the team, whether a newcomer or not, builds up "idiosyncratic" credits to draw upon later. It is like an interpersonal bank. Old teammates first give a newcomer positive "credits" for useful contributions to the team. The new player may then subtly draw upon these credits, if he or she engages in behavior later which is not as approved by the team. A player who has thus contributed greatly to the team's success can "get away" with more than one who has not.

The new team member usually passes through several "stages" when entering, and attempting to integrate with the team. First there may be a self-examination of the basic needs which prompted them to join the group; second is the search for group norms, for group structure, including attempts to sort out the pecking order, and leadership-followership roles; next the new player must attempt to place himself/herself somewhere in the social hierarchy, and to assign a followership or leadership role to himself/herself. Finally, the new player begins to search outward for group goals, and for their role in achieving those goals.

150

STAGES IN THE FORMATION AND LIFE OF A TEAM

Investigations both in the United States and abroad have studied the psychological and social changes which a group undergoes as it is first formed (or the players come together), how the group reacts during its "mid-life" and how towards the end of the "life of the group" it may respond in a social and psychological context. As social groups go, athletic teams are reasonably stable, and remain together for periods of time longer than many social groups. However, their "stages of life" resemble those of other work, play, and social groups.

Initially, as a group comes together, its formation reflects the inclusion of members, and a searching for goals and expectations. During this formative stage a more authoritarian leadership quality may be tolerated or even sought by members. Status hierarchies are worked out. Leaders, both formal and informal (not appointed) are found, and leadership may be eagerly sought by some members.

Next, a rather stormy period may be encountered wherein the group members compete and test each other, while competing and finding out information about the total group from outside sources, eg., other teams. Initial conflicts may arise and group tensions may begin at times to influence performance. Often the leader (a player) or the coach, may usefully relax their authoritarian hold on the members to some degree to permit them to assume responsibilities for the setting of personal and group goals, and even to aid them in the formation of strategies and workout programs.

Social psychologists have identified a final period, a "norming" period. Group expectations and goals are firmly set. Affection may replace excessive intra-group competition, and leadership patterns may become well set and accepted by others. This final stage, if it is near the end of a season, often brings with it higher and higher performance demands, and the accompanying stress.

Thus, toward the terminal end of a season or when a team seems to begin to disband, its cohesion may improve to a point and then inter-group feelings of togetherness may be strained, and bonds between players may even break even. Again during this final stage, an authoritarian leadership pattern may be more acceptable as the stress to succeed may heighten, and as intergroup conflicts may be perceived as able to be resolved through strong team leaders or by a forceful coach or team captain.

WHAT ATHLETES SAY

Many of our interviews with athletes did not contain questions which directly dealt with how they felt, and what they thought about others with whom they came in contact. This type of information, when interviewed by those who may not be well known and perhaps not completely trusted, is among the most difficult information to obtain. Feelings about coaches were usually paramount in the minds of many athletes, particularly when they were asked to supply a question(s) which had not been asked them, and then answer it. However, these feelings were often submerged if the interviewer appeared to resemble their coach in age, and/or if they were uncertain as to the absolute confidentiality of their reports.

The responses we did obtain from athletes, however, revolved around several feelings and interactions. For the most part the kinds of feelings and even their depth varied from team to team, and differed between team sport and individual sport athletes. Overall, it was our feeling that an athlete is far more likely to impart information on short acquaintance about himself/herself and their thoughts and feelings within themselves, rather than about how they feel about others.

MODELS

Athletes spend some time observing and modeling after others on a team. Gymnasts would respond, for example, that they attempted to attack their apparatus-routines as aggressively as "Tom" at times; and "when doing so I am successful." When asked in one case, why he did not attempt to emulate this type of successful model all the time, the athlete responded that he simply did not know. The question seemed to puzzle him and to make him reflect upon its answer, and the reason he did not always emulate a successful model.

Other modeling that athletes do, even at high competitive levels revolves around well known performers. Professional athletes are cited by university athletes, while university athletes are mentioned by high school athletes. Usually the athlete will benefit most from models which closely resemble him/her in performance styles, capacities, and even facial and bodily conformations. The ability to sustain some kind of modeling behavior seemingly is related to just how close the model is to the one modeling. Usually such modeling has beneficial results. Galloway, for example, in his "inner" books recommends this type of athlete imagery, as it is not likely to result in over-analysis as the athlete tries to emulate in general ways the performance and behavioral characteristics of another.

THOUGHTS ABOUT FANS, FRIENDS

The clinical literature in sport psychology (results of long-term interviews) has consistently found that when an in-depth analysis is made of the feelings of athletes, it is generally found that athletes either dislike or have a marked disdain for their fans. Probing deeper into these feelings in a prolonged therapy session will usually reveal that the athlete dislikes the fan for two primary reasons: (a) the fans are certain to be fickle, to switch from one mode of social interaction to the other, and (b) fans are not seen by athletes to share equally the responsibilities that lead to excellence. The fans are not at practice every day, nor do they hurt, work, and otherwise apply themselves to the underpinnings of success. They always seem to be around when success is achieved, and depart quickly if success is not acquired.

This is not to say that athletes do not feel their fans are important to their performance (and financial) success. They *want* fans around them, even friends are asked to meets to help them do better. However, both impersonal fans and close friends should "watch" their behaviors if their "favorite" athlete does not do well. Athletes have reported to us feeling negative even toward family members when they negatively react to less than successful performance, even though athletes may have invited their family and friends to a competition to bolster their own efforts. A family member-fan should be extremely aware of how sensitive their athlete-family member may be just after a loss!

More than one athlete reported to us that they use fans, consisting of close friends, to set up a reward system for their efforts. Typical of their comments was one athlete who said, "My girl friend said she would reward me for my run, it was really motivating . . ." Among a number of student interviews in a recent class I taught in sport psychology, were those in which the student interviewed a close athlete friend, in order to ascertain components of the competitor's "mental life." Reports of these interviews reflected how important was "a special other" in the mental life of the athlete, particularly as stressful competition occurs. However, the special others were sometimes reduced in "rank" within the athlete's life, if their reactions were negative after a less successful effort. Just as true on the part of a parent of a child athlete, the "special other" in an athlete's life should be certain to let the athlete know they are an important and valuable individual to them, independent of their prowess in sport.

STATUS, MY PLACE IN THE HIERARCHY

Athletes reported to us in several ways, the ways in which their performances often relfected how they were treated by others on the team, and by their coach in particular. Most important in this context were shifts in importance, felt by the athlete, as reflected in changes of behaviors of coaches and of others on the team. Within this same context were reports by those just entering a team, who seemed intent, even content, in remaining at lower levels in the status and performance rankings in order not to: (a) incur social censure by others on the team, and (b) to keep pressures to perform well at a minimum. Some seemed content to remain "good and popular freshmen" on their teams . . . or sophomores who were not about to "rock the boat" by attempting to "beat out" more senior members.

One beginning player, however, on a highly competitive and aggressive team, informed us of how he would quickly become first string his first year; and how he was going to let others know that what he was about. His first year socially and in terms of performance was a disaster. He possessed superior skills, and indeed could probably have made the first group, or at least been able to play well and long in the games. However, his over aggressiveness in practice, his continual fights with others more senior on the team whom he affronted and offended, relegated him to a subordinate role. In contrast, another first year player with less skill rose to the top because he did so with less offensive behaviors. In more subtle ways he quickly performed well, instead of flaunting his skills.

Newly forming teams, on which there is not a great deal of talent, will generally better tolerate new, younger, and outspoken high-performing newcomers. However, well established teams containing established members with relatively high levels of skill require newcomers to proceed with caution, gradually building up "idiosyncratic credits," before bursting loose with too much noise and aggression. A case could be made for the fact that a newcomer with higher levels of skills should proceed with more diplomacy than might a less talented newcomer, one who is less threatening to the more senior members of a team.

More than one athlete informed us of the crushing effects of shifts in a coach's reliance upon him/her, from season to season. That is, an athlete may be initially elated, if upon entering a team they are given a high position in the performance hierarchy. The coach first lets them know how important their contribution is the success of the team. But later the coach may act as do the fickle fans, as younger and more talented performers enter a team. The coach may emit behaviors which reflect an obvious shift in his/her feelings about the possible performance contribution of an "older" athlete, whose performance was once highly valued. This type of shift-in-confidence may have a devastating effect upon the emotions and thus the performance of the former "star" athlete. Several women athletes whom we interviewed reported this type of "status shift" and of the negative effects upon their feelings and performances as they remained on a team for several years. All reported that rather than improving, their present efforts were inferior to their successes during the first years on the team; years during which they enjoyed high performance status, and during which they were obviously depended upon to do well.

COALITIONS OR IN-GROUPS

Numerous athletes reported to us about the negative and positive effects of in-groups of athletes within larger teams; collections of individuals who seemed to band together either to socialize during practice or afterward, and/or to help each other perform better during competition. Usually the athlete who reported these conditions, refered to the oppressive effect such in-groups had upon their personal feelings and performance.

The athletes seemed to ignore the probability that all reasonably large groups of 3 or more, will contain coalitions. The research indicates that coalitions form for two reasons: (a) to form blocks of power, as two or more strong figures combine together, and (b) the forming together of two or more people to counter-act another powerful block. Thus, in small groups the same ebb and flow of alliances and power-blocks, come and go, as occurs within the world of nations! Most athletes we interviewed did not perceive the inevitability of these forces forming and breaking up in their team setting, and most of the time were both surprised and annoyed when groups collected together to exert power or counter-act power. Much of the time, however, when questioned further, the athlete admitted that he/she was also in an in-group or quickly sought the protection and support of one, when confronted with the power of others.

ME, OR OTHERS: WHAT'S IMPORTANT HERE?

Many athletes whom we talked to were attempting to deal with conflicting feelings of group affiliation versus their own personal feelings and needs to stand out, to be stars. Some were relatively content in subordinate roles, supporting others; but even these were attempting to: (a) perform in excellent ways so that they would stand out in subordinate roles, and (b) to make their subordination somehow exaggerate the "starring roles" of others, and thus place the stars in a less than a favorable light!

Many athletes were unaware that most well functioning teams contain a favorable mix of personalities and goal-striving. Usually, teams with "all stars," if the teams require close interaction continually, are less than successful than those with a balance. At times "stars" were uncomfortable in their highly visible roles, and seemed to yearn for subordinate roles. While the reverse was true among some of those who habitually support the stars! The later liked their support roles.

In individual sports, both the stars and subordinates were seemingly more comfortable with their roles and places. Perhaps because on such teams "starring" results in success for all. The reverse may be true in closely interacting team sports. That is a "star" with overly expansive scoring attempts may likely detract from the overall efforts of the group. The higher the score a gymnast may achieve, or the faster a swimmer swims, the runner runs, the better the overall team effort. However, even on these individual sport teams, the standouts reported that they took special pains not to engage in behaviors which might appear bragging, or oppressive to those less gifted on the team.

Some athletes interviewed indicated that their personal and often selfish strivings, even on interdependent team sports, resulted in increased team success. And they were often correct. However, other athletes were seemingly guilty, when carefully exposing their personal goals, goals which were individualistic rather than team oriented.

Thus, overall it appeared that many of the athletes we interviewed had only a vague grasp of the social psychological forces which may be impinging upon them while participating on a team. Some seemed only to "work" at the emotional level, and could *not* rise above the confusion and look down on the group dynamics and their role and place within such forces. Many athletes were unforgiving of overly aggressive teammates, or of teammates who competed with them too hard during practices. One runner, a girl, said that the girl she practiced with upset her greatly because she "is always so aggressive during our runs . . ." Most athletes interviewed apparently were without the knowledge that "pure cooperative" behavior is seldom found in sport; the vast majority of the time, athletes both compete with teammates while attempting to cooperate with them in at least minimal ways. Finally, marked differences were found relative to feelings about "standouts" on individual (gymnastics, running etc.) teams, in contrast to teams which required close physical interactions (basketball etc.). On the latter teams a "star" may have both negative and positive effects while on an individual-sport team, standouts often contribute to the success of all, without detracting from others' performance.

IMPLICATIONS: COACHES AND ATHLETES

In consulting the literature, and after reflecting about the often superficial information regarding social interaction and "feelings of others" extended to us by athletes in our research, I came to the following conclusions relative to strategies and implications. I believe that these principles should govern programs of improvement intended to change the athlete's perceptions of what goes on around him/her socially, and to subsequently improve their emotions and the resultant performance.

Find Out

First and most important, the athlete should be exposed to classic findings regarding small-group forces and interactions provided by social psychologists (in general and in sport). The forces acting upon then in sport are similar to those which will act upon them in work, play, and educational groups which they will likely confront later in their lives. Understanding some of the principles and ways which govern how people treat people in group performance situations will help to reduce the "personal impact" of pressures, insults, and even of overly effusive praise the athlete may receive from teammates, coaches, and fans (including family).

The athletes who discovers the manner in which intra-group coalitions form, and the reasons for their formation, will less likely become upset when confronting these in groups on his/her team, and will view them more dispassionately and more impersonally. The athlete who is resigned to the fickle nature of fans and friends who change in their social rewards as the winds of success change, is less likely to become disconcerted when fans use the personal pronoun "you" in sentences, following losing contests i.e., "you guys really blew it," in contrast to a different pronoun after winning efforts. "Boy, *we* really did well last Saturday, didn't *we?*"

Block Off

After finding out about what is likely to happen socially after winning and losing efforts, the athlete may have to learn to block off some of the incoming and distracting "social noise" to which they may be subjected. While calmly and outwardly agreeing with those analyzing their poor performance, or those heaping effusive praise on his/her head, the athlete may learn to keep their own counsel to an increasing degree as he/she matures and excells more an more in the sport.

Indeed some studies of personality change in athletes over a period of time, indicate that many superior athletes really are seen to pull into themselves, to become more introverted and less communicative with others as they near an apex in their careers. They have learned to block off, and not to over-react to the praise and blame wished upon them by others. This does not mean that the athlete should become increasingly social, for this is invariably looked upon as arrogance, and as conceit by those less gifted on a team. Rather the athlete should quietly get about his/her business, rather than reacting quickly and often percipitously to the criticism of others. Some of the concentration techniques outlined in Chapter 7 should help in this undertaking.

Paying heed to one of Albert Ellis' irrational thoughts should serve well here. The thought that everyone should react as you wish them to react, that everyone should do what you expect, and should be nice to you, is irrational. Thinking that these accolades are your due, will lead toward continued disappointment(s). Rather the athlete should think various self-talk statements which will enable him/her to "handle" the stress of social situations fostered upon them in sport, e.g., "My coach is likely to be as changeable as are the fans, expect it, don't get upset when it happens after a loss. Others on the team are not likely to be as happy as I am about success and high performance scores by me, indeed they may be hostile after I win; expect it, don't let it upset you." Or maybe, "It is always difficult to earn the respect of new team, I must proceed slowly, threaten as few as possible with my personality, and yet refuse to be intimidated, as I try hard to excel."

Adapt and Change

Finally, the athlete should learn to "go-with-the-flow," and at times, attempt to change (manipulate is a negative term!) the social conditions he/she sees swirling around them. Team social norms, if not too absurd should be adhered to. Oppressive coalitions on a team, should be confronted, and at times, met with another coalition perhaps formed by the athlete himself/herself.

The athlete should attempt to enchance his/her performances by inviting not only those whose opinion is important to them to important contests, but also those whose judgements afterward are likely to reflect concern and sensitivity. Hostile feelings toward the athlete's own fans, or toward hostile fans of the visiting team should be re-directed toward the skills and efforts needed to excel, instead of being wasted in needless emotional energy directed toward the offending audiences.

Inter-team competition which is inevitable, should be welcomed by the athlete. He/she might even suggest drills which heighten these competitions in positive ways, and participate vigorously, realizing that strong teammates prepare one for the stress of inter-team competition. At the same time this intra-team competition should be held within reasonable bounds, and winning and losing should not be exploited in obvious ways either during practices or subsequent competitions.

It is inevitable that an athlete will be given some kind of role by a group (team) and the assignment of this role (or the athlete's tacit assumption of it) may impede performance and striving. For example, a newly arriving younger athlete may be given the role, and accept; and indeed play because he/she wants to be socially accepted by the team initially. The acceptance of such a role, however, is a subordinate performance assignment; one which the younger athlete may be more comfortable in but at the same time one which inhibits his/her striving and success. Thus, often an athlete must learn to "shrug" off roles assigned to them, roles which will relegate them to performance capabilities which may be less than his/her potential.

Finally, the athlete might give some thought to the type of coalition in which he/she may be drawn. It is probable that the new athlete may be subtly or obviously invited to join some sub-group of the team. When joining such a sub-group, however, the athlete should take care not to make their possible social affiliation too obvious to other team members. That is, joining a sub-group of the team for parties is inevitable; but bringing social affiliations onto the practice or playing field should be avoided.

OVERVIEW

Virtually no information arising from research by social psychologists is without value for those attempting to understand how groups and people in groups interact within athletic teams. Most pertinent, are studies which have explored various group forces and how they mold individual's behavior, studies of group motivation and stress, as well as investigations of inter-group hostilities and coalitions.

A rather large "army" of sport social psychologists, in many countries of the world, have focused specifically on the interpersonal forces within and between athletic teams and their members.

REFERENCES

Carron, A.V., *Social Psychology of Sport,* Mouvement Publications, Ithaca, N.Y., 1980.

Cratty, B.J., *Social Dimensions of Physical Activity,* Prentice-Hall, Englewood Cliffs, N.J., 1968.

Cratty, B.J., *Social Psychology of Athletics,* Prentice-Hall, Englewood Cliffs, N.J., 1981.

Cratty, B.J., and V. Hanin, *The Athlete in the Sport Team,* Love Publications, Denver, Colo., 1980.

CHAPTER 11

THE COACH AND THE ATHLETE

Coaches and athletes have close and often volatile relationships with each other. The coach may be the athlete's parent, antagonist, irritant, confidant, often psychiatrist, and hopefully teacher. Coaches form early role models for youth in their formative years. They often provide the child's first experience of authority outside the home. It is no wonder that when we began to poll athletes concerning their thoughts related to their sport, the young competitors often provided us with both additional questions as well as answers revolving around their relationships with, and feelings about their coach.

The coach is the ultimate in authority figures within the team, and within our society; for he or she has the final reward or punishment to mete out to athletes, the privilege of playing or the shame of sitting on the bench. For this and other reasons the coach and athlete may have difficult times communicating fully, for one does not usually reveal their inner-most thoughts to an individual who has the ability to reward or punish in so devastating a manner.

For young athletes, the coach may function as a substitute mother or father. In a previous book I have written, I suggested that the style of child rearing that the young athlete was accustomed to, at least partially, dictates the manner in which the athlete and coach would "hit if off." Moreover, it is likely that whether the child was reared permissively, strictly, or laisse faire, will influence just what type of "coaching style" will best meet their needs as they enter the athletic arena (Cratty, 1981).

Many times the athletes we interviewed said that their thoughts about their coach and coaching entered their heads in a rather continuous manner. These thoughts were sometimes negative, as they reflected upon harsh and authoritarian coaching personalities, while at other times the respect they held for their coach prompted them to be more anxious for fear that they would let down their favorite mentor. Many athletes thus hold rather mixed feelings about their coach, a kind of love-hate relationship; a relationship in which negative feelings about personal style, mannerisms, and/or sarcasm contrast with their feelings about gaining respect and acceptance from a highly potent authority figure.

Sport psychologists conducting research in many countries have explored coach-athlete relationships. At times these efforts have been cursory and superficial; but at other times the relationship has been examined in depth, and with sophisticated hypotheses and evaluation tools. A researcher from the Soviet Union, with whom I have co-authored a book, for example interviews athletes concerning the manner in which they perceive not only their present coach, but all coaches in their past. After rating them on a three-part scale, this same researcher-psychologist attempts to contrast the athlete's perceptions of an "ideal" coach with their ratings of both present and past mentors. In this way the athlete is matched with coaches, when possible, who personify his or her ideal. At other times long-term coach-athlete pairings are separated, and the athlete re-matched with a coach who might better meet their needs, both personally and technically.

One of the more penetrating and wide-spread problems between coach and athlete, which is just being identified by sport psychologists, concerns the changes in such a relationship over time. That is, the coach who confronts a young relatively inexperienced and unsophisticated athlete, begins a relationship which is likely to change when the latter gains experience, emotional maturity, and technical expertise five and ten years in the future. Not too long ago I counseled a world class field performer who was feeling guilty regarding his long-standing relationship with his coach. The athlete realized that his own technical expertise in his event surpassed that of his long-time teacher. The athlete was struggling with the unpleasant possibility that he would need to "fire" his old friend by leaving, in favor of another more qualified teacher-coach. This problem often arises in sports whose events require individual technical knowledge, such as are found in archery, shooting, gymnastics, and the field events in track and field (athletics).

As in the previous chapters, this section will be organized so that first we will discuss the most pertinent and important research which has been carried out in this topic. Next, we will relate what athletes have been telling us in our current program of scientific work. Finally, the chapter will conclude with suggestions and implications helpful to both the athlete and coach.

WHAT THE RESEARCH SAYS

The research dealing with the coach has been of several types. Studies have been carried out depicting the "typical" or "atypical" coaching personality. In these an effort has been made to ascertain just what so-called stable personality traits seem to accompany coaching and coaching behaviors. One of the more important findings was that the more flexible, sensitive coach is more likely to quickly adopt new and successful coaching practices and strategies. The more recent work on the so-called "coaching personality" indicates that the accepted stereotype of the authoritarian coach may be at odds with the "true" types of traits and behaviors that contemporary coaches possess. While many coaches may feel that they must act in authoritarian and dogmatic ways, in truth they are flexible and sensitive as individuals.

Other research has depicted just how closely the coach is emotionally and even physically involved with the competition. His or her feelings of responsibility are reflected in marked changes in heart rates during critical portions of the contests. The coach's heart rate reflecting emotional states, often parallel the same levels of activation which might be measured in their younger and often fitter athletes. This kind of information suggests that: (a) the coach must be wary lest his or her emotional states during competition influence judgements in less-than-useful ways, and (b) coaches should attempt to maintain high levels of fitness, so that when undue strain is placed on their cardio-respiratory systems during the emotional "heat" of contests, critical organs are able to maintain their integrity under stress.

Most important, however, for the purposes and directions of this book, are research studies which are beginning to illuminate the manner in which the coach and athlete "get along," and just how the athlete feels about coaches and coaching behaviors. These investigations range from the picturesque and interesting, to those which recently have begun to delineate important principles and information, pointed

159

to more effective working relationships which are possible between coach and athlete.

Among the more pertinent findings is the indication that athletes in individual sports, track-and-field, gymnastics, and the like, feel more intensely about their coach, both negatively and positively, than do athletes in the so-called team sports. Somehow the athlete in the team sport, when not functioning well with his or her coach, can somehow relate to other team members, perhaps discuss problems with them, or otherwise feel sympathy from teammates. The athlete in the individual sport, on the other hand, seems to be more closely "locked-into" a relationship with the coach, a relationship which seems more critical to the success of both.

When athletes are asked about the qualities they most like, and least like about their coach, a pattern of positive and negative behaviors and feelings emerge. For the most part, for example, athletes like a coach who is competent, without being overly scientific in his or her language with them, a coach who relates equally well to the more able and the less able athletes on the team[1], and most of all a coach who is free of sarcasm.

Athletes like enthusiasm from their coach, behavior denoting that he or she really cares. However, the athlete does not like a coach who "loses his or her cool," who yells and becomes excited excessively during the course of the contest, or practices. The athlete likes a motivator, but not an immature child, in the person of their coach. The athlete wants a coach who leads through controlled mature example, not through emotion and pressure.

Finally, athletes like a coach who does not constantly take credit for performances which are often the result of superior effort and/or ability of the athlete. The athlete likes a modest coach, when recanting his or her part in victories. The athlete wants organized practices and technical help of the highest caliber, from a coach who is emotionally mature and relatively modest when successes are achieved by the combined efforts of athlete and coach.

More sophisticated research conducted recently indicates that athletes perceive the roles of coaches as having several somewhat independent dimensions. That is, an athlete might feel that a coach is good at one or more of the following types of behaviors and abilities, but not necessarily in others. These separate and independent dimensions of coaching behaviors identified by Danielson (1975) and his colleagues consist of the following:

1. "A Motivator:" some coaches are seen as evidencing behaviors which highly motivate athletes to do their best; some are not seen in this way.

2. "Problem Solvers:" Some coaches are believed by their athletes to be good at cooly solving problems, at emphasizing new methods in practices and competition, and in getting better performance as a result; some do not possess this characteristic, according to athletes.

3. "Aids Teammate Relationships:" Coaches are seen by some athletes as good at helping athletes get along with each other, at aiding in the reduction of tensions that may arise between players and athletes; not all coaches are seen as equally good

---

[1]One writer has designated this type of behavior in a coach, as one who "travels" up and down the status hierarchy of the team, relating equally well to the "stars" of the team and to the substitutes.

at this type of interpersonal problem solving.

4. "Social Representative:" Some coaches are believed good at the social relationships outside the team, relating to reporters, alumni, and fans. Other coaches have difficulty with this type of role, according to athletes who observe them.

5. "Communicators:" Fifth dimension of coaching behavior, independent of the previous four, involves the organization of communication efforts both within the team, and between the team and outsiders.

6. "Democratic Behaviors:" Some coaches aid players to participate in team decisions affecting them, and in communicating to the team how their democratic efforts may aid them to perform better; other coaches do not function well in this respect, and make all decisions themselves.

7. "Motivator with Excitement:" This final dimension of coaching behavior is reflected in efforts to generally excite and motivate the team; a quality not possessed by all coaches to the same degree.

The point of this investigation and others, which will be discussed shortly, is that coaching behavior is in truth composed of many sub-behaviors which collectively make an impression on an athlete. Moreover, the athlete may believe the coach to be "good" or "bad" depending upon just how the total collection of behaviors, or any given group of them interact with his or her needs, expectations, as well as with the demands of the sport placed upon the athlete. Much of the time the athlete is engaged in a "trade-off" of feelings; that is, he or she feels good about some coaching behaviors and not good about others. Often technical expertise will override negative feelings engendered by various emotional dimensions of the coach's behaviors. This type of trade-off is particularly prevalent at higher levels of competition, in which the athlete wants good technical help, and may be less concerned with the emotional dimensions of what is occurring, particularly if the relationship is relatively transitory as would be true on a national team in the United States.

For example, just before the 1976 Olympics, I spoke for a day to the International Organization of Diving Coaches in Montreal, Canada. As the day progressed, one of the coaches took his feet and stated that, "I don't know why athletes come to me. I am abrasive; I don't get along with many of them, and I know they do not like me very much." The answer, I believe, hinges on the "trade-off" concept discussed previously. The athletes who came to him did not do so because of his tranquil personality or emotional empathy, but to gain (often on a short-term basis) his expertise in the area of competitive diving. He satisfied their needs for technical help, which probably in turn satisfied their long-term emotional needs for success and optimum performance.

Another example of this type of matching up of needs to coaching competencies was brought to my attention as I wrote a book in an apartment in Leningrad.[2] My co-author had formulated a questionnaire in which he asked athletes to rate coaches on a 1-10 scale, within three dimensions of their expertise and behavior. These three parts consisted of: (a) a *thinking dimension,* behaviors reflecting predicting of an athlete's performance and general competitive readiness, (b) an *emotional interaction* dimension, reflecting how the coach feels about people, and about the athlete

---

[2]Y. Hanin, *The Athlete in the Sports Team,* Love Publishing Co., Denver, Colorado, 1980.

emotionally, and (c) a *technique* dimension reflecting how the coach managed practices, knew techniques, and how well he or she conditioned the athlete.

Athletes were asked to formulate several ratings, one reflecting how important they felt each dimension to be in what they perceived as an "ideal" coach, and finally to rate both present and past coaches on this three part scale. In this way it could be seen how a coach presently in the life of the athlete contrasted to the athlete's perceptions of an ideal coach, and also to the feelings of the athlete about the qualities in past coaches. On the basis of the data, present coach-athlete pairs were sometimes left alone, and at other times broken up, in favor of new athlete-coach pairings.

This same concept of pairing athlete's needs, to the abilities and needs of coaches is reflected in the newest, most useful studies of coaches and athletes.[3] These studies are based upon the premise that when two or more people get together, their tendency to remain together and to interact productively reflects the presence of three types of needs; these include: (a) the need to control, or to reject control and be free, (b) the need to accept, or reject the social overtures of the other, a socialization dimension, and (c) the need to either receive, or reject affection, to receive or give love and caring.

Researchers extending these ideas into the area of sport, and focusing upon coach-athlete relationships concluded that compatable coach-athlete duos, based upon success in the competition itself, were those whose needs seemed to be congruent, to fit together along the three dimensions of needs outlined above: control, affection, and socialization. Some examples of both compatable and incompatable coach-athlete duos might be described in the following ways.

1. The coach is a sociable sort, he gives a team party twice a season at his home to start and end the season. He is a bit of a controller, however, makes his athletes mark the line, get in on time, and obey instructions at practice without hesitation and comment. He adopts a fatherly air toward his players, encourages them to confide in him concerning personal problems, frequently puts his arm around a player when talking to him after practice. Thus, the coach apparently needs to extend himself socially, and also to give affection, moreover he likes to control his players. According to the reseach he will do best with an athlete who needs to receive signs of affection and socialization. The athlete who is conforming will also do best with this type of controlling coach.

2. The second coach is cold, seemingly without emotion during practices and games. He is a technician, whom the players respect. He confers with players concerning how they feel about strategies, practice content, and individual differences in their techniques. He tends to leave the players alone and is not aware of problems in their personal life, nor does he encourage his players to confide in him. This type of coach will do best with an athlete who does not need to receive, or experience signs of affection from the coach. Similarly, athletes who may not tend to need control extended from another, but rather like to make some of the decisions concerning their practices and skills themselves, will do best within the coaching situation described.

Obviously, numerous other combinations of coaches and athletes could be de-

---

[3]The original model is from Schutz (1966), and studies in sport psychology relating to coach-athlete include that by Carron and Bennett (1977).

scribed. It should be remembered that coaching qualities are highly subjective in nature, and difficult to measure. Additionally, within a single coach-athlete pair these needs may change, either gradually or suddenly over time. A typical example is of an athlete during his or her formative years who desires to be instructed carefully within a controlled situation; while later in his career this same athlete may prefer to be more independent of a controlling coach. The coach who fails to perceive these changes in the needs of the athlete with whom he or she is dealing is likely to create a situation which is less than productive.

Also within the real world, this reciprocal interaction of needs takes place in a subtle fashion. There are innumerable trade-offs possible for both coach and athlete. For example, the athlete who may value independence, may "put up" with a controlling coach because of the valuable technical advice which may be forthcoming, or because no other better coach is available. Likewise, an athlete may prefer to be left alone and not receive either signs of affection or socialization may again compromise, and endulge a coach, because of the lack of a better one relative to the technical help and/or environment-facilities available.

When consulting with teams both in the United States and abroad, I have frequently pointed out this type of "model," relative to effective athlete-coach interactions. Often, a pairing of athlete and coach is possible in optimum ways, on teams having more than one coach. For example, with numerous coaches, often numbering from 8-12 on an American football team, it is possible to informally pair compatable athlete-coach duos with personal needs in mind. Sometimes the coaches paired in this manner with athletes are not necessarily the coach each athlete uses for technical help. Thus, a coach may have an athlete, or more than one, whom he or she counsels, and between whom confidences are exchanged, who is different from the athlete toward whom technical help is rendered. Sometimes this pairing happens informally, but often this type of formal pairing is helpful because of the information described in the previous paragraphs.

Numerous research studies, both within the pages of journals dealing with industrial psychology and leadership, as well as those dealing with "pure social psychology" have for decades striven to find out just what kind of leadership is best, and the traits that make a leader. The coach who hopes best to lead a team, and earn the respect of athletes is one who carefully analyzes the forces present in the situation and in the group relative to their needs to be dependent or independent. Also helpful, is for the coach to analyze his or her own need for control, and the capacity to give or receive affection and socialization. Following this type of analysis the coach should then formulate a plan of action, taking into account these forces. Further complicating the problem for devising a behavioral plan of action are the changes which have been refered to; changes in the needs of athletes, and most complicated of all, changes in the social and group forces found within a team from month to month and from year to year. In a previous book on this subject, a chapter was devoted to discussion of the changes in a team, to its "mid-life" and finally to its "later life" and ending.[4] The perceptive coach tries to analyze these complicated forces as best he or she can, and act accordingly. The less sensitive leader does not,

---

[4]Hanin, Y. and B.J. Cratty, *The Athlete in the Sports Team,* Love Publishing Co., Denver, Colo., 1980.

163

and proceeds with great risk to exert authority in ways which may not be useful or productive to the team and to the athletes involved.

WHAT ATHLETES SAY

Often as we concluded initial interviews with athletes concerning their mental life and sport, we would ask what other questions we might have asked them. When they supplied us with one or more, we then would ask them to answer their own queries. Invariably, if our interview contained no reference to the coach, the athlete would suggest a question concerning thoughts about their coach, and what he or she might have said. Thus, in subsequent interviews we formally posed such questions as:

(1) Have any sentences, words, or phrases spoken to you by a coach aided you in athletic competition; are there some that you think about as you perform?

(2) Are there any words or phrases which seem to inhibit or hurt your performance, which have been uttered to you by your coach?

If the athlete answered to the affirmative to either of these qustions, we pursued the subject, asking them what the words or phrases were and how they seemed to help or impede their performance.

The responses to these questions as would be expected varied greatly. In at least one investigation, differences in the responses of athletes depended upon the age of the interviewer involved. An older interviewer who had been introduced to the team by the coach as "a long time friend, who goes back so many years I can't remember" . . . received no negativisms in athletes who were subsequently spoken to. A second interviewer in the same investigation, a much younger man near to the age of the university athletes queried, received an almost constant stream of complaints concerning the coach.

Both in our investigations and in previous research on the subject, it has been dramatically demonstrated that athletes spend a great deal of time and energy thinking about, and otherwise relating to their coach. Indeed most psychologists attached to athlete teams for any prolonged duration, often find themselves spending more time with the important central figure in the scenario, the coach, than with the team as a whole!

In our interview surveys of athletes, it was also found that the coach occupied a central portion of their "dream about the sport" and was the figure most present in this type of dream. Likewise, about one-half of the athletes mentioned that something the coach had said to them influenced their performance in positive ways. For the most part these phrases were those usually heard within an athletic context . . . "to concentrate" . . . "to think aggressively" . . . and even "to kick ass" . . . generally popped up in conversations with the various athletes. Occasionally a philosophical phrase stuck in the athlete's mind, such as "waterpolo is like life speeded up!"

Less often, but often more vividly in the athlete's were words and phrases which inflicted both short-term and sustained psychological injuries upon the psyche of the athletes. A large and aggressive football lineman, for example, had been dubbed a "candy" by a coach during his high school competition, a phrase which still raged within his mind at critical times in competition.

One of the most striking findings, however, concerned probable sex differences in the sensitivity displayed by athletes, in both individual and team sports regarding exactly what had been said to them during practice and competition by both male and female coaches. The women athletes in our investigations seemed to record exactly the negative words and phrases which had been beamed their way. They "played" these over and over in their mind with negative consequences. The bombastic verbal behaviors of coaches were more often forgiven by the male athletes interviewed. "Coaches get mad and then cool down" they would respond, and thus I don't take personally what they say to me when they are upset." To the contrary, the girls and women athletes we interviewed took what was said to them personally, and seemed reluctant to ever forgive the coach who emitted insulting and/or negative remarks.

Among the more prevalent types of verbage to which females particularly objected, were phrases which the coach had undoubtedly intended to relieve the pressures of competition, to make the game or meet somehow easier on an apparently nervous female competitor. Often the girl appeared at a competition, usually in an individual sport (gymnastics or track and field) prepared to do her best, to win if at all possible. Confrontations with the coach often elicited such phrases as "don't worry about winning, just place." Or perhaps, "We don't count much on you today . . . relax and do the best you can."

In contrast to the positive effects such "low-pressure" phrases were apparently intended to have upon feminine competitors, the reverse occurred. These types of "we don't count on you much" phrases indicated to the girls and women that the coach had little confidence in them; all reported that they needed his or her "vote" as a performer to do well. They needed to feel that the coach was totally behind them as they entered competition, and when they heard the words described, what confidence they had vanished and they did extremely poorly.

One track and field coach was quoted as saying to a girl during a distance race in which she was doing poorly, that she must lack "self respect." The words haunted, and scalded her. She recalled with vividness the insults extended to her. *What did he mean, I had no self respect;* she grated at our interview with her, several years later!

IMPLICATIONS FOR THE COACH AND ATHLETE

A survey of the available research, plus a perusal of the information we obtained when interviewing athletic teams, prompted the formulation of several principles, intended to aid athletes with regard to thoughts about their coach.

1. Whenever possible, daily if practical, the coach should endeavor to somehow communicate to the athlete that the latter has worth in the eyes of the former, independent of their athletic skills. If the athlete perceives that the coach is considering them as an individual, independent of what the athlete can do for the status of the mentor, the air should be cleared for more effective communication of a number of problems.

2. The coach should be technically competent, displaying excellent knowledge of a variety of scientific and practical principles relative to the sport. At the same time the athlete should not be unduly overloaded with the coach's scientific expertise, but should instead be extended useful information as is called for and needed by the performer. There is no substitute for the coach's technical excellence. The coach should also be honest when it is necessary to consult others, or the literature for technical advice. The majority of so-called psychological problems on teams could be eliminated or greatly reduced if this criterion was met by coaches.

analyses that are currently being used by each athlete. A special instrument used to accomplish this may be found in the final chapter. In this way the coach may ascertain just how he or she may aid the athlete, and which athletes may need special help in adjusting their mental life to more realistically meet the demands of the performance and practice situations.

7. The coach should seek professional help in order to ascertain just what behavioral signs should be looked for when an athlete is in need of professional help in dealing with the stresses of life and athletic competition. The athlete should not be expected at all times to simply think away their fears, nor should the coach, who is not trained as an emotional health professional, take it upon himself or herself to "play at psychiatry" when it may be dangerous to do so.

8. The athlete also should be aware of the difficult role the coach must play as he/she must both interact with various diverse personalities on a team, as well as somehow function and teach skills, within highly visible performance situations, in which the coach obviously bears a great deal of responsibility for both success and failure. Just as the coach should try to say something positive to each athlete each day, the athlete should also attempt to relate to the coach in ways which are not directly related to their joint performance venture.

9. The athlete should be aware that the coach can not serve all his/her emotional and performance needs. Harking back to our discussion of "rational emotive therapy" the mature athlete should not expect all people, including the coach, to act just as he/she wishes them to. The coach should be expected, much of the time, to act in ways which are not perfect in the eyes of the athlete. With this kind of expectation, the athlete is less likely to be stressed with "unexpected" behaviors given off by the coach.

10. The coach should also be aware that an athlete's hostility directed toward his or her mentor, may not always be a personal affront. The coach should carefully weigh signs of anger emitted toward him or her by an athlete. Often such behavior is a sign of excess anxiety experienced by the performer. At other times the athlete may feel hostility towards others within the athletic environment, and be able only to express this hostility toward the available coach.

OVERVIEW

The coach-athlete relationship is the most critical one in the sporting environment. Both are under stress in highly visible circumstances. The manner in which they handle that stress to a large degree, may be reflected in the ways in which they can deal with each other's emotions, needs and personal characteristics.

It has been found in our studies that athletes spend a great deal of time thinking about their coach, carefully weighing the phrases he/she has uttered relative to sport, and becoming either upset or elated depending upon the nature of verbal and gestural communication sent their way.

In our work, and in the work of others, it is found that athletes expect a coach to be technically competent, without being overly scientific, to be friendly without extending too much warmth, and to be democratic and fair in their treatment of all players, rather than relating only to the stars of the team. Additional competencies seen in good coaches by athletes include good organizational skills, effectively motivating athletes, and possessing calm exteriors conductive to good planning, and the formulation of effective strategies during hotly contested games.

3. The coach should attempt to "travel up and down" the social hierarchy and skill ladder within the team. He or she should relate socially, personally, and equally to those who are contributing a great deal to the team's performance, the stars, as well as to those whose roles are subordinate. If this is not carried out, the team's "stars" may perceive that the coach may value them only for the performance contribution they make, rather than because of their general worth as people. Further, the "stars" are likely to perceive that when they fall from grace, by not performing well, they are likely not to be as well liked as people. The subordinates on the team should likewise feel slighted, when the coach does not, or cannot relate to them. Thus the subordinates are less likely to perform to their optimum when they are called upon to make more substantial contributions to the team. They may simply let the team and the coach down. My staff and I have become convinced as we interview numerous athletes at all levels, that if athletes do not like the coach as a person they are likely to lose and thus lower the status of their disliked mentor. Often these negative feelings are well masked, or even present in the athletes' psyche unconsciously. These negative feelings will often surface at the completion of a season, when a close contest is at stake. A team or individual, who is "supposed" to win, suddenly loses. The coach is dismayed, and sometimes the athlete(s) are also. However, the cause is simply a strong aversion that the athlete, or team has for the coach and his or her success needs.

4. At all times, channels of communication should be kept open between athlete and coach. Adherence to principle 1, helps in this respect. A university athlete has a number of stresses in their lives, including school and the team's expectations, as well as personal expectations. If, in addition, personal problems arise, and the mentor is unaware of a presence of this new stress, the athlete will engage in behaviors which are a "mystery" to the coach. On the other hand, if free and frequent communications has passed between the coach and athlete during the majority of the season, when a new problem arises in the life of the athlete, the coach is likely to be made aware of the discord, and make steps to help reduce the problem.

5. Our interviews with athletes about pre-game strategies intended to reduce or control anxiety, indicate that the coach should be particularly sensitive to individual differences among athletes in his or her charge. The coach should directly confront players with questions as to what each would prefer to do, prior to games. The players who prefer to be alone, to think and contemplate about various aspects of the games should be permitted time, and if needed, a place in which this kind of pre-game "trance state" may take place. Players who seem to need companionship should be queried as to the type of social associations they wish to engage in. Others who may wish to engage in various equipment, or "field" rituals should also be allowed to do so . . . i.e., to touch, walk around, or otherwise "relate" to the facilities in which they are to be performing. Nothing an athlete does, within reason, and which is apparently calming or results in the adjustment of arousal to optimum levels, should be overlooked, or refused by the coach. It is apparent that athletes engage in a wide diversity of behaviors and mental strategies prior to games, in order to deal with pre-competition anxiety. The coach should respect those strategies, and should survey the team to ascertain what each athlete prefers, prior to imposing his or her own "special pre-game" noise or panacea; (or permits a sport psychologist to introduce his or her special ointment for the psyche).

6. The coach should provide special ways in which he or she may assess just what the mental strategies, imagery, and ways of dealing with anxiety and post-game

Effective coach-athlete combinations are those who need to give or receive affection, to socialize or not to socialize, and to give or receive control. The competent coach is seen by the athletes as being able to relate to them well as people, not just as athletes. The coach who is able to do this effectively, together with possessing the necessary technical skills, is likely to be the successful coach.

REFERENCES

Carron, A.V. and B.B. Bennett, "Compatability in the coach-athlete dyad," *Research Quarterly,* 1977, 48, pp. 671-679.

Cratty, B.J., "The coach," *Psychology in Contemporary Sport,* Prentice-Hall, Englewood Cliffs, N.J. 1983.

Cratty, B.J., *Social Psychology of Sport,* Prentice-Hall, Englewood Cliffs, N.J., 1981.

Danielson, R.R., P.F. Zelhart and C.J. Drake, "Multidimensional scaling and factor analysis of coaching behavior as perceived by high school hockey players," *Research Quarterly,* 1975, 46, pp. 323-334.

Percival L., (ed.), "The coach from the athlete's viewpoint," *Proceedings Art and Science of Coaching Symposium,* sponsored by the Mutual Assurance Company of Canada and the Fitness Institute, Toronto, 1971.

Schutz, W.C., *The Interpersonal Underground* (5th Edition), Science and Behavior Books, New York, 1966.

CHAPTER 12

SELF-PREPARATION, GUIDELINES FOR ATHLETES

This final chapter is directed toward an audience which I most hope will review this book, and consider the material, the athlete. Athletes were the most help in the preparation of this book, and thus I hope to in some way repay those whom we interviewed, as well as other athletes by writing a book that they may feel is useful. I hope that the previous material reflects respect for the athlete and for his/her efforts to physically perform and to prevail psychologically over fickle and noisy fans, overbearing families, cantankerous coaches, and the pressures inherent in sport itself.

The more we interviewed athletes, most performing at high levels of competition and at optimum levels of mental health, the more respect I gained for not only their physical performances, but for the creative and useful ways they had learned to cope with the psychological stresses accompanying their sport. At the same time we learned that athletes were sometimes as conceptually egocentric as are some psychologists, they would often report that "Yes, that's how I do it, (or think about it), everyone else does too!!" That is, the athlete felt that what went on inside his/her head reflected what all his/her teammates did (thought) also! I hope that at this point, however, the reader has gained an awareness of the vast individual differences in how various athletes tend to deal with the problems inherent in sport. Each athlete we interviewed was likely to introduce us to a unique way of thinking about their sport, and of managing their emotions while performing.

Additionally, we began to find out that the more experienced athletes did things somewhat differently than did less experienced ones. For the most part the former had made some decisions about: (a) how much thinking to do about their mental life and to what degree they might structure it, or might "let thoughts come," and secondly, (b) if they had decided to structure their coping strategies and thoughts about skill, the more advanced athlete was often more sophisticated about selecting useful ways of thinking, and managing skills and emotions. Thus, it is hoped that useful ways of thinking have been brought out in the previous chapters. It is hoped that you will select some to try out and that you have learned to identify moderate, or mild problems which you have decided to deal with, and finally, that the problems you have selected to deal with will soon become less annoying.

I have decided in this final chapter to help bring into clear focus how you might approach the various problems, mental strategies, attention focusing techniques, and the like which appear on the previous pages of this volume. To expedite this selection process, I have divided this final chapter into several parts. These sections are introduced to aid you to engage in operations which help you to identify problem areas, to select strategies to use (including seeking professional help from others), and to find ways of knowing (or guessing) whether what you are doing now is probably best left unchanged.

The topic we have been dealing with in the previous chapters are complex. As you compete, both in practices and in contests with others, you are beseiged with all kinds of pressures and a vast amount of information. This information stems from your own thoughts and feelings as well as from others, and from fluctuating performance. This book is not meant to add to this vast "information load," but rather to provide some reassurance that (a) you are probably doing well psychologically most of the time, or you could not have been able to perform as well as you have, and that (b) you may benefit from a kind of "sorting out," process, at least some kind of minimal "self analysis," of "stock taking" which may benefit you personally while in sport, and even thereafter as you confront other challenges in life, work, play, and pleasure seeking. We are not trying to make the complex more complex, but in some ways trying to help you classify and to simplify what is going on inside your head, and in your relationships with others who "impact" upon you as you perform.

AREAS OF CONCERN

The previous chapters dealt with several possible areas which may concern you. While, by necessity, the information contained in these chapters were neatly separated, and discussed, it is not unusual for problem areas to be interrelated, and over-lapping. However, let's first consider two types of issues; one type is more operational, and involves skill, concentration, and the like. Another group of problems is more emotional in nature, and includes aggression, anxiety, together with depression or at least concern.

PERSONAL INVENTORIES

One useful way which psychologists have traditionally used to aid people to look at themselves, is through the use of self-applied personal inventories. These inventories, usually simple check-lists, are often used by the person filling them out, to see how they "stack-up," or how they compare with others (if norms are available). At times, the responses are used by the athlete's therapist in order to initiate conversations and to get a "handle" on what is going on.

The first of these personal inventories we are providing here involve the assessment of the more operational and straight-forward parts of your athletic experiences; including the learning of skills, physical conditioning, aiding concentration, and general activation. Later, the inventories will deal with more subtle emotional areas, including aggression control, coping with fear, how you deal with others, and dream-trance states. The results of these inventories are meant only for your eyes and consideration; however you may wish to share some of the information with coaches or emotional health professionals, if you wish. At the completion of each inventory are suggestions for their interpretation, and what you might do about problems identified.

SKILL LEARNING

Magnitude of the problem:
1. I am having a great deal of trouble acquiring skills in my sport.
   _____ (yes-no)

2. I am encountering moderate difficulties learning the skills.
_____ (yes-no)
3. I am learning the skills to my sport more easily than most.

Sources, Difficulty, Causes

If you checked 2 or 3 above, continue with the following to identify areas of difficulty. Rate each problem area on a 1-5 scale, from 1 a minor cause of difficulty, to 5 the major cause of difficulty.

1. My coach doesnot teach me properly._____
2. I have not had as good a background as my teammates._____
3. I am simply not well skilled, inherently able._____
4. I do not put forth sufficient effort._____
5. I do not spend the time I need to practice._____
6. I cannot put forth the time and effort due to other work responsibilities, school etc._____
7. I do not concentrate well upon the skills when they are required. _____
8. My fears (of failure or injury) prevent me from performing well. _____
9. The skills of others on the team do not properly mesh with mine. _____
10. (Another reason?) _____

PROBLEM REDUCTION METHODS AND APPROACHES

If you have had problems learning skills, you may correct these kinds of problems in a variety of ways, depending upon the "sources of difficulty" you checked, for example:

(a) If numbers 1 and 9 are checked, they indicate you may have problems relating to others, including your coach. His/her coaching skills may be deficit, in which case you can seek help elsewhere, or from teammates. I know of several Olympic caliber gymnasts, in this country, who shopped from coach to coach to obtain the needed skills, moving from gymnasium to gymnasium, on consecutive nights, over a period of years. You may review Chapter 11 (you and your coach), as well as chapter 10, in which interactions with teammates are described. Your problems with teammates, however, should be brought to the coach's attention; you may need your position and/or role changed so that your skills match those of your teammates.

(b) Numbers 2, and 5, may be aided with reference to mental practice; review Chapter 3, and also the Chapter 2; you may be working too intensely either mentally or physically.

(c) If number 8 seems to be your problem, you may look again at Chapter 6, on fear management, and possibly combine some of the positive "self-talk" found there with relaxation training and skill imagery.

(d) Reason 3, inherently unable, may be a cop out, are you really not able or do you simply not know how to apply yourself, or are yo not putting forward enough effort?

(e) Reason 7 involves concentration; you might work on the concentration activities suggested in Chapter 7, as well as spending some time in mental imagery. Reason 6 might also be reduced in magnitude (other things), if special time in mental imagery was alloted just before retiring each night.

CONDITIONING

Magnitude of the problem

1. I am having no problems conditioning, I am fit for my sport.
   _____ (yes-no)
2. I am having problems getting in condition, it is hard for me.
   _____ (yes-no)
3. I am having extreme difficulties conditioning for the sport.
   _____ (yes-no)

Sources of your problems

If you checked 2 or 3 above, delve further into your problem with reference to possible sources listed below. Check each problem on a 1-5 basis as before (one a slight problem, 5 an extremely important problem).

1. I seem to lack energy to work hard at practices._____
2. I cannot work under the direction of my coach._____
3. I cannot endure well, the pain of strength-endurance conditioning. _____
4. I don't concentrate when I work on conditioning._____
5. Conditioning bores me. I am undermotivated._____
6. Other reasons. _____

REDUCTION OF PROBLEMS

If you have problems conditioning, psychological causes might be reduced, with reference to the problems checked in the following manner.

(a) If you checked 1, you may have to work on activation techniques prior to practice, and/or check your diet with the help of a nutritionist physician. The energy problem may not be in your head!

(b) Motivation is discussed in various chapters in the book, relative to reason 5. You may need to call upon all your resources, tell yourself that conditioning is an underlying reason to and end, not an end in itself. Motivation to do well can come most from you, from the satisfaction you will get out of performing well; performance is often based upon the drudgery of conditioning.

(c) Your coach may or may not know how to condition you, but if you don't wish to work under him/her, you might determine why. It is due to some inherent dislike (see Chapter 11) or because the coach lacks good motivational and conditioning skills. In this latter case you must take charge of yourself, and work hard despite your coach, (if changing coaches is out of the question).

(d) Pain reduction may be accomplished (reason 3) with positive mental imagery. You might imagine that you are rising above pain, that you are working outside your painful body, or that you are in another time/or place as you try to endure. Enduring pain is a requisite for many sports. Indeed experiencing pain in practice or competition indicates that you are improving; withdrawing from pain as you reach your threshold in a competition (in endurance sport) will lower your performance; while knowing that you will again experience pain, and must triumph over it will enable you to better previous efforts. Often a record set in endurance running will be followed by an inferior performance, as the athlete consciously withdraws from the pain he/she experienced in the preceding competition. If you back off in this manner from pain you will never overcome endurance barriers.

172

(e) Concentration problems, reason 4, are dealt with in Chapter 7. While Chapter 4 (activation) might also help you to overcome being "down" or lacking concentration.

CONCENTRATION

Magnitude of the problem
1. I have few problems concentrating, both in practice and in competition.
   _____ (yes-no)
2. Concentration problems come and go, as does my concentration.
   _____ (yes-no)
3. I have problems concentrating often, and it hurts my performance.
   _____ (yes-no)

Possible reasons
Check on a 1-5 basis, how important each of the following possible reasons might be (if you indicated yes to 2 or 3 above). A 1 indicates a relatively unimportant reason, while a 5 is an important reason.
1. I have problems sustaining my concentration for the entire competition. __
2. I have problems concentrating in practices, but in games I do better. _____
3. I seem just to "trance" out, and go into "flights of fantasy"_____ at various points in the competition._____
4. Crowd noise, unexpected events often break my concentration. _____
5. At times anger at myself, an opponent, the coach, or an official breaks my concentration._____
6. I have problems sustaining my attention and concentration during important competitions_____, during less important contests._____
7. When I am fearful my concentration is poor._____

REDUCTION OF THE PROBLEM

If you checked one or more of the above, with a 4 or 5, you should review the concentration chapter. However, specifically you might . . .

(a) Work on various "time out" procedures, and then "time-in" imagery, if your attention comes and goes as indicated in reason 2 above.

(b) You might block out distractions mentally, or "zero-in" on central parts of your sport (i.e., aiming places), in order to overcome problems indicated by your check of reason 4.

(c) "Trancing out" (reason 3) seems common in endurance events (see Chapter 8) you may have to work out means of reducing this (see this same chapter). You will usually do better if you remain in contact with the event, and with your body while in competition!

(d) Anger control is dealt with in Chapter 5, you may have to combine this with relaxation work (Chapter 4), together with exercises to focus your attention on the task, rather than on anger-stimulating people and the situations they may trigger.

(e) Situational differences in concentration, as indicated by your responses to questions 2 and 6, may be dealt with by applying different concentration techniques in different situations, i.e., in games and practices. The ability you may show to concentrate when it counts, however, may be a plus. variations in concentration when the pressure is not on may not be a serious problem. Game anxiety may also interfere (refer to Chapter 7 for suggestions).

(f) Anxiety often conflicts with good attention. Attention to techniques to reduce anxiety, Chapter 6, may have to come before good concentration is acquired (via suggestions in Chapter 7). The reverse may also work for you, you may become anxious because you can't or don't concentrate. You may have to attempt some concentration exercises first, indeed engaging in them may give you something to think about instead of the fearful outcome of competition.

THE UPS AND DOWNS OF ACTIVATION

Magnitude of the problem
(indicate yes-no answers to the following)
1. "I am always 'up'" for important contests, and yet relaxed enough to perform well._____
2. I am usually too "high" to do well in important competitions. _____
3. I am often not excited enough to really do my best._____
4. I have my "ups-and-downs," sometimes I am ready, other times I may be too relaxed, these unwanted shifts come often._____

Possible Causes

The possible causes may be numerous for this type of problem. Some of them are listed below, score a 0 if the cause is not valid for you, or a 1 to 5 from of little importance to maximum importance.
1. I just can't seem to get excited, to become motivated to perform well all the time._____
2. I am too excited, for reasons I don't know._____
3. I get too much sleep and come to competitions "dopey."_____
4. Sometimes I am over, or undertrained for the contest._____
5. Other reasons _____

REDUCTION OF THE PROBLEM

Problems with activation are usually caused by other underlying problems, fear, wishing to avoid a contest, not liking the sport any more, or the coach. Sometimes nutrition, poor training habits, or even sleeping too much (an escape?) before a contest can cause this kind of problem.

(a) For cause 1, reference to the chapter on "getting up" (4), might help, as might the chapter on attention. For the most part, however, you might attempt to seek formal counseling to determine why levels of activation are not proper, e.g., what thoughts seem to prompt the up or down condition you experience. When these are discovered, then they may be worked on first (i.e., anxiety Chapter 6).

(b) It is common for athletes to use sleep as an adjustor of activation, reason 3, prior to a game, and to reduce the time prior to a contest during which they may become too fearful or excited. Often getting up earlier prior to a contest and then filling that time with relaxing or useful experiences. Music, a movie, skill rehearsal, review of tactics and the like are helpful.

(c) Under-motivation may be dealt with in several ways (reason 1). Later on in this chapter the formulation of reasons why you might want to do well in athletics are discussed. A most important reason is to display excellence in physical skill, during that time of life when you are able to display the most vigor, your youth!

EMOTIONS AND FEELINGS

The next section contains ways which you might wish to deal with specific kinds of emotional states which are not useful to you as a competitor. These states are often more difficult to deal with by yourself, and you may wish or need the supportive help of a psychologist, or another trusted counselor (your father, mother, or a friend?). The feelings to be dealt with include aggression, fear, dreams and "special states."

AGGRESSION

1. Most of the time my aggressions are well under control, I am able to channel them into constructive play and performance.
   _____ (yes-no)
2. I just don't seem to be able to get mad enough.
   _____ (yes-no)
3. I am constantly angry at myself, for my poor play, and my play becomes worse, as a result.
   _____ (yes-no)
4. My anger at my opponents frequently causes me to commit fouls and try to hurt my play and the team's effots.
   _____ (yes-no)
5. My anger "flares" periodically and unexpectedly.
   _____ (yes-no)
6. Other problems?_____ (yes-no)

Possible cause for anger
The possible causes, if you checked one or more from 2-5 above, may include the following. Indicate on a 0-5 point scale the presence of one of the following possible causes.
1. I came from a family which contained a lot of hostility, kids frequently fought with each other, and with parents._____
2. I may be frightened, and this I turn into anger._____
3. My feelings are too easily hurt, and when I am hurt I fight. _____
4. When others on my team are fouled, it really makes me mad. _____
5. My performance standards for myself are high, and it angers me when I cannot deliver._____
6. I am so excited before, and during a game, that anything "sets me off." _____

REDUCTION OF THE PROBLEM(S)

Locating the sources of over aggression is difficult. The various kinds of actual aggression and aggression imagery are numerous (see Chapter 5). However, you might consider some of the strategies and sources below for help with this kind of problem.

175

(a) If you checked (a) above, you might realize that a family background of this type inevitably leads toward aggression in life, and often in sport. You may now need to seek professional counseling to reduce this tendency.

(b) Fear and anger are closely aligned, often, fearful people turn this feeling, by way of re-interpretation, into anger, that it is more courageous to be angry, than to admit fear (reason (b) above). You might seek help with reference to fear management (Chapter 6) in order to help your anger problem.

(c) Answer (c) might indicate a problem with concentration during the contest, concentration upon the performance, not upon others. Help may come from Chapter 7, as well as counseling which may help you to determine why you are so easily hurt (feelings). You may be setting performance standards which are too high also (answer e), and thus you should consider one of Ellis' irrational statements we make to ourselves . . . "If I don't perform to perfection, I am worthless." Less than perfect performance is often the result. Feelings of worthlessness stem from personal standards which are set too high (see reason (e) above also).

(d) Activation and anger often accompany each other. If you gave answer (f) (a high score 3-5) you might try engaging in pre-competition relaxation training, or calming visual imagery, (Chapter 4) as well as considering the possibility that you are also fearful prior to a contest, and make need to reduce this fear (Chapter 6).

FEAR AND ANXIETY

Fear reduction may require more than simply "thinking your way out of it." Thus, often professional help is needed, however, you may reduce, or at least adjust moderate amounts of fear yourself, or with the help of others who are sympathetic.

Magnitude of the Problem
(indicate yes-no answers)
1. I am virtually always self-confident, fear does not inhibit me.
   _____ (yes-no)
2. I am periodically fearful, when some important competitions arise.
   _____ (yes-no)
3. My fears are constant, and often they disrupt my performance.
   _____ (yes-no)
4. Fear at high levels plagues me during my practices, mental life away from sport, and during and before competitions, usually my performance suffers.
   _____ (yes-no)

Possible Sources of Anxiety
You should look for more than one reason, if appropriate, and check each possibility from a 0 to a 5, indicating the degree of importance for each cause, from not important (0), to highly important (5).
1. I am fearful of letting my friends and teammates down._____
2. I am afraid of how I will feel when I do poorly, relative to my own feelings about myself (self-esteem)._____
3. I am afraid of getting hurt physically._____
4. I am afraid that I will not meet high goals I set for myself._____
5. I am often afraid of the power of my opponents._____
6. I am afraid of what the coach will do (say) when I do not do well. _____

7. I am afraid of audience, fan reactions when I perform._____
8. I am afraid of not being up or down enough when I perform. _____
9. I am often afraid of being unprepared._____

REDUCTION OF THE PROBLEM(S)

(a) Several statements above, if you checked them with high scores (3-5) indicate that you may be overly concerned about the opinions of others. (statements 1, 6, and 7). If this is the case you might look at the use of rational "self-talk" to overcome irrational thoughts regarding achievement and performance (that if I do not please everyone I am worthless). (Chapter 6). Combining this with relaxation work (Chapter 4) together with some positive imagery in which you picture yourself successfully winning, should be of help. Trining hard and learning a skill well can also project you into personal standards with which you are faced, rather than being overly concerned about the performance standards and criticisms of others.

(b) One's personal standards, and often shakey self-esteem can cause anxiety, as reflected in sources 2 and 4. In order to rectify fear, because of this "personal" problem, one should examine: (1) Whether or not standards set for oneself are too high, or based upon the irrationality of personal perfection. (2) One may need to acquire more success experiences and couple them with "success imagery," as discussed in Chapter 8. Association with family, friends, or coaches "put you down" frequently may lead to this kind of anxiety problem. Eliminate the source of this seems to be the case; associate with different people, or "cut out" communications from those who propose standards which are too high for you, and which seem primarily designed to make them happy!

(c) Fears of getting hurt physically, although not as frequent as fears of social failure, may be well founded. Obtaining accurate medical advice, may help to place these into perspective, as might information concerning whether real injuries are likely to occur in you in your situation (reason 3). Moreover, well conditioned and well-taught athletes are usually subject to fewer injuries! Ask yourself also if your *fear* of injuries is actually a *wish for an injury,* thus providing for you a useful and respectable way to avoid competition, a way which others will not condemn. A injury may make you a hero!

(d) Fear of being unprepared physically (or in skill) may be a logical, well-founded one (reason 9). Often the best fear reducer, we have found is self-talk reflecting high skill and conditioning levels, rational self-talk based upon the fact that you really are conditioned well, and prepared to fully help. Prepare yourself fully, or seek a coach who is able to do this. Lack of preparation is an important, but modifiable source of fear. Prepare well!

(e) Being afraid of one's opponents has both negative and positive possibilities. Powerful opponents often offer a source of pride, for even if you lose, by exerting good effort, you will be proud of the outcome! Powerful opponents (reason 5) should not be a source of embarrassment, but a source of pride. You must be good in order to even confront them, and to have the possibility of overcoming (or even looking good) against the powerful! Concentrate upon your own performance, not your opponent's,

(f) Problems with fear of one's coach should be dealt with in several ways (reason 6) including finding a less pressuring coach! You may need an intermediary to help you and the coach understand each other, and the performance. You might also engage in rational "self-talk" regarding your inordinate necessity to please everyone (your father-coach-mother-etc.), rather than doing your "own thing" and pleasing yourself: Say to yourself "I can do well for myself and need not please everyone else all the time," (see Chapter 6).

(g) Finally, fear of fan reactions, may also be dealt with (reason 7) via positive self-talk regarding the possible irrational need to please everyone. Likewise, hostile fans' reactions may be used by you, to focus your anger into high levels of effort and skill. Additionally, some of the attention focusing activities may be of help to you here (Chapter 7). There are ways for you to exclude mentally the fan-audience reactions which plague you.

DREAMS AND SPECIAL STATES

Magnitude of the problem(s)
1. I seldom dream, nor do I trance-out in ways which impede my performance. _____ (yes-no)
2. My dreams at times contain disturbing "athletic-content." _____ (yes-no)
3. Often I am out of contact with myself during important parts of the performance, impeding me. _____ (yes-no)
4. Some special states have disturbed me, as I have performed. _____ (yes-no)

Sources of the problem
(indicate on a 0-5 scale, which problems you have and their magnitude, 1 = slight, 5 = marked)
1. I seem to "buzz out" when I am really activated or scared. _____
2. I seem unable to remain "in contact" during the main parts of my endurance race._____
3. I dream in often disturbing ways, just before critical contests._____
4. Often my concentration is disrupted when I "trance-out," before a contest _____, during a contest_____, and this hurts my performance.

REDUCTION OF THE PROBLEM

(a) One overall way to deal with possibly disturbing dreams, is to understand that (reason 3) most of the research indicates that even a disturbing dream probably has therapeutic effects. It is a safety valve to release tension, a kind of unconscious therapy your mind is engaging in. If the disturbance in your dream continues a skill fault, practice through that fault the next day. This kind of content is an extension of your conscious mental life. You were worried about the skill that day, weren't you?!

(b) Going out-of-contact states has been dealt with in Chapter 8, and is probably caused by high levels of activation, and/or the need to avoid pain. You should be aware of both useful and less than useful ways in which these special trance-states "work" for you, when you perform. Getting into and out of them, may not be as hard as you think, particularly if you don't think too much when trying to get into a useful one (a flowing feeling, relaxed, and performing well feeling). (source 2, 1). If high levels of activation trigger disrupting trance-states, consult the chapter dealing with activation reduction (4).

(c) If concentration is a problem when you trance-out, you may also be helped by referring to Chapter 7. Often it may be necessary to deal with both concentration, and activation and to exert effort attempting to stay in contact.

YOUR "STATE OF MIND" OVER TIME: AN ATHLETIC DIARY

During the previous pages and paragraphs, it has been attempted to help you personally assess your emotional states, as well as various operations (learning skill) which may be dependent upon how you think and feel about your sport. However, this kind of assessment is confined to relatively brief periods of time, this month, last week, just before the last important contest. It may also be useful, however, to explore and trace fluctuating psychological states, over a period of time. Many athletes keep athletic diaries. Yours might include references to various ways you feel about impending competitions and how you felt after competition.

A diary is fun to keep. It is interesting, for example, to look up just what you were doing a year ago. I had this experience during the past years keeping a running diary, of times and distances I ran. Also on the pages were contained where I was (I did a considerable amount of traveling) whom I was meeting, and what I was doing. Some of my runs were in the Peruvian Alps, while others were on the Copacabana Beach in Rio de Janiero, and in the Himalayas!

An athletic diary can contain two important kinds of information; performance data (and thus overtime fluctuations in performance) as well as feelings and mood states which also may then be plotted over time. Critical people in your athletic life, may also be documented and contrasted to events in your athletic and personal life. A relatively small percent of athletes keep such a document. For the most part it is kept by individual-sport athletes, runners, and swimmers. Less frequently do team sport athletes attend to this function. Keeping a diary need not be a time consuming effort. Regularity is the main requisite. If not attended to each day, time lags will blur memories of feelings and events, just a few days previously. This type of document, however, is likely to afford you important insights about yourself; insights obtained as you contrast your mood — feeling with actual performance.

The page for such a diary might look like this.

Date and day:

_____, location_____

performance_____, workout_____, (check one), off-season_____, early season, mid-season_____, late season_____.
Performance data: (times distances, scores of a team sport)

_____

_____

Your scores: (in a team sport) _____

Workout information: (distances, intensity, duration, times) _____

_____

Energy Level	Low		Moderate		High
(circle one)	1	2	3	4	6

Happy-sad	Sad		Neutral		Happy
(circle one)	1	2	3	4	5

Anxiety	Anxious		Neutral		Relaxed
(circle one)	1	2	3	4	5

Self-Confidence	Low		Moderate		High Self-confidence
(circle one)	1	2	3	4	5

Other feelings: _____

Special problems with teammates, coaches: _____

Athletic dream(s)?_____

Special circumstances in your personal life? _____

_____

Other comments, conditions worthy of mention: _____

_____

This document may be used by you to survey your recent and even distant past; or may also be used to enhance communications and provide data (with your permission) for a counselor, should you need to talk to another (parent, special friend, or psychologist).

You might wish to copy this page as it stands, and place it in a folder, or you may wish to construct your own scales, or special types of comments. For example, your scale may reflect some special problem, or strategy you may have or will engage in. Special places might be used to mentally practice, or overcome special skill problems encountered. You may also wish to indicate the degree to which you are confronting and dealing with a special problem, i.e., aggression reduction. Thus your diary might contain an aggression scale as indicated below:

	Low Levels		Moderate Control	and Under	High Levels Impeding Performance
Aggression Felt	1	2	3	4	5

Whatever format you decide upon, I believe that keeping such a longitudinal document, for even a year, will prove useful to you; it may help you get to know yourself better. If kept for several years, you will often be able to plot significant changes in your pschological make-up as well as in peformance capacities as you mature in your sport.

WHAT ABOUT YOU?

There were several purposes in writing this book, with regard to readers who are presently participating in competitive athletics. One of the foremost of these was to inform you. It was believed that by helping you to understand the psychological forces within you, the thoughts and emotions that impel you, as well as those outside you (people, events), you will become better prepared as an athlete and as a person. Expecting the unexpected, makes the unexpected more easy to deal with. Being able to evaluate these forces, and the impact your thoughts and mental approaches may have upon others, upon your feelings, and upon your performance may help you to take satisfaction that your present mental life is productive. Your thinking about your sport may be realistic and satisfactory! However, it is possible that you may wish to make moderate changes in your approach to athletics, modifications in how you "talk to yourself" when trying to give yourself reasons for performing, and when trying to adjust fear and aggression and concentration.

It was hoped, that as you reviewed the sections dealing with "what research tells us" you were able to formulate, or re-formulate, how you deal with your sport. The sections titled "what athletes tell us," may have given you the opportunity to contrast the things you think and feel about sport, to the mental activity reported by a rather large group of successful and well functioning athletes.

It is hoped that reviewing some of the strategies which we have collected from other athletes will be of interest to you. Despite the diversity of these reports, many useful ways seem to be employed by athletes in order to achieve performance success and at the same time promote psychological harmony. It is hoped that some of the successful and creative ways athletes reported helping themselves psychologically, will be considered by you. Perhaps some of these strategies may be adopted, and at least tried out.

Finally, the last sections of the chapters, containing guidelines and "implications" often urged you to keep your own counsel, to at times not only understand, but to "cut off" social-psychological "noise" which may deter you from doing your best. You were urged to formulate your own methods of dealing with such problems as improving concentration, adjusting fear, or improving your interactions with others. For even a book this size, or many times larger, cannot predict the multitude of situations all the athletes in all the sports of the world will confront and with which they must often cope. This last section, therefore, asks you to apply principles, to transfer ideas and operations to your own unique situation. You, as an athlete, may be able to adopt some of the more obvious and useful principles yourself. Others you may need assistance with in the form of a trusted friend or of a sensitive coach. Still further, you should not be hesitant to enlist the aid of a mental health professional if your problems and the stresses you feel are too great.

RIGHTS AND OPTIONS

Much of the material contained in the previous chapters, and in this one, was intended to inform. However, information of the type contained in this book cannot be written about, in my opinion, without advancing philosophical viewpoints, and thus biases . . . One continuous thoughtful thread through the past pages was the implication that at times, the athlete must keep his/her own counsel. Often athletes must pull back, go inside themselves psychologically, and think their way through the often difficult mazes of stresses, people, and competitions that arise in athletics. This "coming inside ones' own head" has been noted before as psychologists have observed and studied high level athletes. They are often judged as increasingly introverted (within themselves) as they reach higher and higher levels of competition.

The athlete functioning with increased success, may encounter fewer and fewer real friends from among fellow competitors. Successful competitors must more and more rely upon their own instincts, with perhaps a helping hand from a counselor (professional or friend) who is not overly interested in reflected glory, but in really helping the athlete through what are often difficult times.

As success is achieved, pressures from family and fans usually increase. Again the athlete may have to admit to himself/herself that often the fans do not only not count, but cannot be "depended on" for support.

The athlete may have to devise clever ways to psychologically "cut off" crowd influences during contests, as well as fan overtures and reactions following contests, without really offending in obvious ways those who are offering their support.

With increased payments (if professional) or increased accolades from others which may include trophies and jackets, the athlete may have to consider the "real" and important motives which impel him/her to continue in and excel in sport. Reports about motivation from high level professional athletes, often parallel those which we have collected from well functioning amateurs. Both kinds of competitors usually try to perform well in order to experience excellence, to master a difficult sport. They say that they are motivated to perform the sport for its own sake, rather than to receive perks from others. Often they seem to know that the more they rely upon social approval, the less likely they are to strive for the intrinsic satisfactions that sport may give to them.

One of the best philosophers to write about sport, Paul Weiss (1969) has suggested that sport is one of the primary ways in which youth can exhibit excellence. Further, he states that satisfaction in mastering sport is one of society's achievement arenas in which youth may be expected to do well, since it is youth who possess the necessary physical "equipment" to meet the rigorous demands of competitive athletics. Philosophers and historians can exhibit excellence only with time, as they obtain and sift informaiton; athletics, on the other hand can only be mastered by youth, and therefore youth should make the most of opportunities afforded them, and of the abilities with which the young are uniquely endowed. I agree with Professor Weiss. Those studying the motives of athletes, and of others in achievement situations often concur that one of the most prevalent drives inherent in the make-up of the human animal is the desire to achieve mastery and excellence for its own sake. I also believe that the coach or athlete who consults this book need look no farther for the strongest motive possible, when participating in various aspects of athletics.

Your options are thus several. You should attempt to understand the psychological forces both inside you and those which impinge upon you from outside yourself. Often you must keep your own counsel, and must make up your own mind about how to deal with distractions and stresses which beset you. You should build upon your understandings and try to: (1) block off distracting people, thoughts and social forces which may plague you as you try to perform well, (2) formulate your own base of motivation, (3) set realistic, achievable goals, (4) define your own criteria for success.

Additionally you should learn to tolerate things you cannot change, including people with realistic expectations for you, coaches who may be abrasive, as well as competitive situations which may be less than ideal. But you should set limits. I have often been struck by how some athletes, both young and old, are placed into or find themselves in situations which I personally would find impossible. There are intolerable situations and you should be aware of these. You should not sacrifice your self-respect for the privilege of participating, despite the possible high social rewards for doing so. You should carefully decide what you want out of sport, when encountering highly abrasive people (coaches) and situations (teammates who may be intolerable). Immediate social discomfort and pressures as you leave a team, to join another one, are usually offset by positive feelings about yourself which you will reflect upon in later years; "I stood for something, my own self-respect," you will later tell yourself, self-esteem that would not be sacrificed upon the altar of someone else's needs to gain satisfaction from your athleticism.

When encountering a problem in sport participation, a coach, or team setting, which you find difficult, you should stand back and carefully define what you want out of sport, and from those who guide athletes. Research in the Soviet Union, for example, has asked athletes to reflect upon what they want in an ideal coach, relative to balance between expert knowledge, emotional warmth, and the operations necessary to practice well (Cratty and Hanin 1980). These same athletes are then asked to rate their past coaches as well as their present coaches, as to how close each has come and is coming to their ideal. Discrepancies between what an athlete wants and apparently needs, and the type of coaching they are encountering are often enough to prompt a change of athlete-coach combination.

You should "take stock" of the situation, and your coaching in the same manner. You should ask yourself what do you want out of your sport: An opportunity to develop and to excel to your optimum? To what degree does the present situation prevent you from doing so? What would be the outcome of a change? At times a change will produce less positive benefits than remaining and attempting to exert change where you are. You should also be wary that you are not blaming situations and coaches for your own psyche and/or physical problems. At the same time it is reasonable that you should not put up with people, events, situations, and conditions which not only prevent you from doing your best, but may be exacting their price upon your emotional health.

A final important option should again be emphasized here. Despite the apparent glibness with which various "self-help" psychological solutions to all problems may have been presented in these chapters, it is often true that one cannot always bail himself/herself out of psychological dead ends. Simply "self-talking" your way out of an emotional corner is not always practical or possible. You may need the help of others. These others may include the coach, but it is usually difficult to be totally open and honest with a person who is in a position to reward (play you), or punish you (bench you), as is true with your mentor. Thus you need often to seek counsel elsewhere.

The youthful, vigorous years during which athletic prowess is at its apex are also the years during which high levels of life's stresses impose themselves. The youth, while seeking to make a coach and himself happy in sport, is also obliged to start a career, achieve success in school, meet the needs of an often demanding family while searching for the beginnings of personal happiness with a special other person. These forces often combine to exact a tremendous toll upon the young and apparently able competitor. Middle aged coaches and parents viewing the strong muscles of an athlete cannot understand why they are not the happiest people alive. But often this external physical vigor is not matched by internal peace.

If the forces within you, triggered by events in your life cannot be understood and reduced to manageable terms, you should seek the advice of others. Psychological or psychiatric counseling is not a stigma. Your refusal or reluctance to participate in them, however, may be a serious mistake. Talking to another person, particularly one whose profession is the improvement of the emotional health of others, may be a useful way for you to gain self-understanding, and insight into your problems as an athlete or coach. Reading and understanding the simple psychology found in books such as this is not necessarily as easy as applying the techniques suggested in your own life. Your feelings and solutions often have to be weighed by knowledgeable others, in order to enable you to construct helpful strategies for meeting the stresses of life, love, and your sport.

REFERENCES

Cratty, B.J., V. Hanin, *The Athlete and the Sport Team,* Love Publishing, Co., Denver, Co., 1980.

Weiss, P., *Sport: A Philosophical Inquiry,* University Press, Carbondale, Il., 1963.

About The Author

Bryant J. Cratty has been a Professor of Kinesiology at UCLA for the past twenty-five years. In the 1960s he was a founder of and the second President of the North American Society for Psychology in Sport and Physical Activity. He has written over 50 books and monographs, currently translated into fifteen languages. These books have dealt with the psychology and social psychology of sport, motor learning, as well as, motor characteristics of special children and youth. Dr. Cratty is the author of the sensory-motor learning section of the Encyclopaedia Britannica.

He has given workshops and courses on five continents, appearing in thirty foreign countries and most states of the Union, since the 1950s. While an undergraduate at UCLA, he lettered in gymnastics and waterpolo. Following graduation he coached at the junior high school and high school levels, as well as at colleges and universities; the sports included gymnastics, waterpolo, swimming, basketball, and football.

Dr. Cratty has consulted with the American Figure Skating Coaches Association, the Alpine Skiing Coaches Association, as well as the National Swimming Coaches Association, at both Squaw Valley and Colorado Springs Olympic Training Sites. Abroad he has consulted with professional athletic-sports medicine groups in Brazil, Nigeria, U.S.S.R., Brazil, Canada, South Africa, as well as, Czechoslovakia, Finland, Holland, Italy, and Spain.